# ULTIMATE
# SPITFIRES

# ULTIMATE
# SPITFIRES

Peter Caygill

Pen & Sword
**AVIATION**

First published in Great Britain in 2006
and reprinted in this format in 2020 and 2021 by
Pen & Sword Aviation
an imprint of
Pen & Sword Books Ltd
47 Church Street
Barnsley
South Yorkshire
S70 2AS

ISBN 978 1 52678 229 8

Typeset in Palatino by
Phoenix Typesetting, Auldgirth, Dumfriesshire

Printed and bound in the UK by TJ Books Limited, Padstow, Cornwall

Pen & Sword Books Ltd incorporates the imprints of Pen & Sword Aviation,
Pen & Sword Maritime, Pen & Sword Military, Wharncliffe Local History,
Pen & Sword Select, Pen & Sword Military Classics and Leo Cooper.

For a complete list of Pen & Sword titles please contact
PEN & SWORD BOOKS LIMITED
47 Church Street, Barnsley, South Yorkshire, S70 2AS, England
E-mail: enquiries@pen-and-sword.co.uk
Website: www.pen-and-sword.co.uk

# Contents

# Introduction

When Supermarine Chief Test Pilot J. 'Mutt' Summers took K5054, the prototype Spitfire, on its first flight on 5 March 1936, few who witnessed the event could have envisaged that R.J. Mitchell's creation would still be in widespread service ten years later and would continue to perform a useful role until its twenty-first year. At the time the very existence of the Spitfire was uncertain and it was only when it showed speed superiority over the rival Hawker Hurricane (at first there was little to choose between the two) that its future was assured. The fact that Supermarine were able to 'tweak' the propeller to obtain a few more miles per hour was to be of paramount importance not only for Britain, but for the whole of the western world as a Battle of Britain fought without Spitfires may well have resulted in a different outcome.

The decision to persevere with the Spitfire (its early life was also beset by producton difficulties) proved to be inspired as it was recognised at an early stage that the aircraft was capable of considerable development. In contrast, the Hurricane was the culmination of a design stream going back to the classic biplane fighters of the inter-war years and employed tried and tested construction techniques, comprising a tubular metal fuselage and two-spar wing with fabric covering. The Spitfire, on the other hand, featured stressed skin construction throughout and had a very advanced wing which was elliptical in plan and of extremely low thickness/chord ratio. Such an airframe was able to take advantage of the increased power levels offered by developed versions of the Rolls-Royce Merlin engine and the later Griffon with relative ease. This was just as well as the second-generation Hawker Typhoon was to suffer serious engine problems and was to be a complete failure in its intended role as a high altitude fighter.

Although the Spitfire IX with it two-speed, two-stage supercharged Merlin was to be one of the classic fighters of the Second World War, it was felt that an engine of larger capacity was needed if the Spitfire was to continue to compete with advanced versions of the Focke-Wulf Fw 190 and Messerschmitt Bf 109. Use of the Rolls-Royce Griffon, which was developed from the 'R' engine used on the Supermarine S.6B that won the Schneider Trophy for Britain in 1931, gave the Spitfire the increase in power that was needed for it to remain at the forefront of piston-engined fighter technology.

This book looks at the development and flight testing of the Griffon-powered Spitfires and Seafires, together with an operational history both during and after the Second World War. Consideration is also given to the Spiteful and Seafang which were the ultimate developments of the basic Spitfire line and capable of performance levels in excess of the early jet-powered fighters. The last in line was the Seafire F.47 which was capable of a top speed of 453 mph (or around 100 mph faster than K5054) and was cleared for gentle flying at an overloaded weight of 12,900 lbs, or nearly two and a half times the normal take off weight of the first Spitfire. Not surprisingly, with such a prodigious rise in all-up weight, the handling characteristics of some of the later Spitfires/Seafires began to deteriorate, causing adverse comment from the RAF's testing establishments which resulted in a considerable amount of controversy. The problems that were experienced and the solutions that Supermarine came up with are fully explained.

By the end of 1945 jet engines were being developed that were capable of producing around 5,000 lbs thrust and it was clear that the days of the piston-engined fighter were drawing to a close. Had this not been the case, the descendents of the Spitfire, the Spiteful and Seafang may well have played a significant role in the post war RAF and Fleet Air Arm, as performance testing showed that they had extended the boundaries close to the ultimate in terms of what could be achieved by a propeller-driven aircraft. In the event the Spiteful design was to be quietly forgotten but the Griffon-Spitfire lived on and flew its last operational sortie with the RAF on 1 April 1954 in Malaya. The Spitfire's last official sortie in RAF colours was conducted by the THUM Flight at Woodvale on 10 June 1957.

# PART ONE

# Development and Flight Testing

CHAPTER ONE

# A Better Spitfire

The Supermarine Spitfire has gone down in history as one of the finest fighter interceptors of all time, its performance and fine handling characteristics, in particular its superb rate of turn, making it a firm favourite with pilots. It also possessed a grace of line that added an aura of glamour and the Spitfire's reputation was already well established in the public's perception before it had even entered service. Due to the tireless work of Rolls-Royce in its quest to derive more power from the Merlin engine and the development of better fuels, the Spitfire was able to maintain its pre-eminent position throughout the war and even by 1945 the Spitfire IX/XVI was still the most numerous variant in service.

Despite the undoubted qualities of the Merlin-engined Spitfire, especially the altitude performance of aircraft powered by the two-speed, two-stage supercharged Merlin 61 series, it was obvious quite early in the war that if it was to surpass the likely performance of the new generation of fighters, as typified by the Hawker Typhoon and Focke Wulf Fw 190A, the Spitfire needed to be powered by an engine of much greater capacity. Of all the principal engines of the Second World War, the Merlin, at 27-litres, was one of the smallest. In contrast the Daimler-Benz DB601N which powered the Messerschmitt Bf 109F-1 had a capacity of 33.9 litres, while the BMW 801 fourteen-cylinder radial of the Fw 190A was even larger at 41.8 litres. Whereas other manufacturers tended to favour the use of large, moderately supercharged engines to develop the necessary power, Rolls-Royce chose to utilise their expertise in the field of supercharging to a much higher degree. Even so, there was a limit to the amount of development that the Merlin could withstand and Supermarine and Rolls-Royce began to consider the options for a re-engined Spitfire shortly after the outbreak of war.

Fortuitously, a suitable engine already existed in the 36.7 litre Griffon which could trace its ancestry back to the Buzzard and the 'R' racing engine that powered the Supermarine S.6 and S.6B Schneider racers. The Buzzard, rated at 825 hp, was a larger development of the Kestrel and proved to be a particularly popular powerplant for flying-boats, including the Blackburn Iris V and the Short Sarafand. It served as the basis for the development of the 'R' racing engine which employed an identical layout, a liquid-cooled 60-degree V-12, and many of its moving parts. With a bore and stroke of 6 in by 6.6 in and a compression ratio of 6:1, the 'R' engine ran at a higher speed than the Buzzard but its significantly greater power was due to the use of extremely efficient supercharging.

Throughout the 1920s Rolls-Royce had made greater strides in the supercharging of aero engines than any other manufacturer. This was mainly due to the work of one man, James Ellor, who had joined the company in 1921 from the Royal Aircraft Establishment at Farnborough. At the time supercharging was very much in its infancy but one of Ellor's innovations was the use of a forward-facing air intake to convert air energy into pressure energy to boost power levels. He was to go on to develop the huge double-sided supercharger that was largely responsible for the high power of the 'R' engine which, by July 1929, had been made to run for the requisite 100 minutes at an output of 1,850 hp using a fuel mix of 78 per cent benzole, 22 per cent aviation spirit with 3 cc of tetra-ethyl lead per gallon to suppress any tendency towards detonation. The engine was used in the Supermarine S.6 which went on to win the 1929 Schneider contest at an average speed of 328.63 mph. Over the next two years the 'R' engine was further developed and more exotic fuel cocktails were devised by F.R. 'Rod' Banks of the Ethyl Export Corporation which included 10 per cent alcohol. Power was raised yet again to the unprecedented figure of 2,350 hp and in the S.6B, Flt Lt J.N. Boothman flew to victory at Calshot on 13 September 1931 to claim the Schneider Trophy outright for Great Britain. To further reinforce Britain's dominance, Flt Lt G.H. Stainforth flew S.6B S1595 later in the month to a new world speed record of 407.5 mph using a 'sprint' version of the 'R' engine and special fuel.

The first use of the name Griffon can be traced back to 1932 when Rolls-Royce began bench tests with an 'R' engine de-tuned to give 1,000 hp. One of the design problems of the time was that aerodynamic drag created by conventional radiators tended to be a major factor in reducing performance in fighter aircraft. Evaporative cooling, as fitted to the Goshawk engine of the Supermarine Type 224, did away with such excrescencies and was also contemplated for the Griffon, however, continuing development difficulties led to this form of engine cooling being abandoned. Although it was the most powerful engine around in the early 1930s, the Griffon was somewhat ahead of its time which left the way open for development of the smaller PV-12 (Merlin) to power the Hawker Hurricane and the early Spitfire variants.

The Griffon was largely forgotten about until 1938 when the Royal Navy made a tentative approach to Rolls-Royce, but in contrast the Air

Ministry showed little interest as the Merlin appeared to be capable of supplying its needs for the foreseeable future. Shortly after the outbreak of war in September 1939, however, there was a change of heart and three months later Supermarine was asked to produce a specification for a Griffon-engined Spitfire. Thanks to its racing pedigree, the Griffon had a relatively low frontal area of only 7.9 sq.ft., which was only 5 per cent greater than that of the Merlin, and although it weighed around 600 lb more, it was only 3 in longer. As its dimensions were not significantly greater than the Merlin, it could be accommodated by the Spitfire with the minimum of alteration, although the strengthening that was required did cause a number of design headaches. A stronger engine mounting was required, together with re-designed fuselage longerons which had to be made out of steel instead of dural to cater for the engine's increased weight.

Initial performance estimates of a Griffon-engined Spitfire were promising with a top speed of around 420 mph, a climb rate of 3,500 ft/min and a service ceiling of 36,000 ft, figures that were significantly better than the Spitfire I (Merlin II) which had a quoted maximum speed of 362 mph, a climb rate of 2,500 ft/min and a service ceiling of around 32,000 ft. Although the Air Staff had put its faith in the Hawker Tornado (Rolls-Royce Vulture) or its close relation the Typhoon (Napier Sabre) as the next generation of interceptor fighters for the RAF, it also recognised that if the Spitfire was to be developed, the Griffon was the ultimate way to go even though, at first, it did not offer that much more in the way of power than the latest versions of the Merlin. Initially Griffon development was relatively relaxed but with both the Vulture and Sabre engines running into severe technical difficulties, the pressure was gradually increased on Rolls-Royce and Supermarine to come up with solutions to an impending crisis for Fighter Command. In the event, the Tornado was abandoned when the Vulture programme was cancelled and the Typhoon proved to be a disappointing failure in its intended role as an interceptor, although it went on to achieve fame later in the war as a fighter-bomber.

The Rolls-Royce Griffon was first flown in a Hawker Henley test bed (L3414) in 1940 which prompted Sydney Camm, Hawker's Chief Designer, to produce a rather optimistic performance estimate for a Griffon-powered Hurricane which showed it to be slightly faster than a similarly engined Spitfire. Even in time of war the rivalry that existed between Hawker and Supermarine was still apparent, but most viewed Camm's proposal as nothing more than a rather desperate attempt to extend the Hurricane's development potential. If the Griffon was to be fitted to an RAF fighter it was always going to be utilised in the Spitfire, and its development for such a use had a champion in Air Marshal Sir Wilfrid Freeman who before the war held the position of Air Member for Research and Development. Freeman had expressed doubts as early as 1939 as to whether the Rolls-Royce Vulture was a viable proposition due to unreliability and excessive weight. He had a somewhat surprising ally in Ernest Hives (later Lord Hives) of Rolls-Royce who was also less than enthusiastic about the Vulture and had offered the Griffon to the Air Ministry in January 1939. In the event the Vulture staggered on until its eventual demise in late 1941; had the Griffon-Spitfire been given full priority it may well have been in service by 1942 providing Fighter Command with a welcome boost at a time when it was firmly on the back foot thanks to the arrival of the Focke-Wulf Fw 190A.

Supermarine carried out a considerable amount of work on the new Spitfire in 1940 as the result of a verbal request from Freeman and it was not until early 1941 that a more formal authorisation was received. This was in the form of Specification F.4/41 which was issued in February 1941 and was formulated around Supermarine's design proposal. It called for a top speed of not less than 410 mph and a service ceiling of at least 39,000 ft. Various combinations of armament were requested, including six 20 mm cannon, two 20 mm cannon and eight 0.303 in machine-guns or twelve 0.303in machine-guns. The Griffon-Spitfire was initially referred to as the Mark IV and continued to be developed throughout 1941, the official view being that it should begin to replace all Merlin-powered Spitfires (excluding the pressurised Marks VI and VII) from 1942, by which time a top speed of at least 400 mph would be needed to maintain parity with the fighter opposition likely to be encountered over northern Europe. This timescale proved to be rather optimistic and it was to be a full two years before Griffon-engined Spitfires were able to make their operational debut. In the meantime, the Spitfire IX (Merlin 61) not only filled in as a temporary stop-gap but proved to have exceptional high altitude performance, so much so that it was to see widespread service until the end of the war.

The armament that the Spitfire IV should carry was discussed at length and initial suggestions that it should be armed with up to twelve 0.303 in machine-guns were soon discarded due to a need to increase the amount of fuel carried. The Griffon consumed about 25 per cent more fuel than the Merlin at equivalent power settings and it was proposed that two small fuel tanks be incorporated, one in each wing leading edge, in addition to the normal tanks mounted in the front fuselage between engine firewall and cockpit. The use of wing tanks naturally reduced the amount of space available for wing-mounted guns. At this stage an armament of six 20 mm cannon was still considered an option, the Spitfire IV eventually appearing with a mock up of this configuration, however, it quickly reverted to a more normal

Spitfire weapons fit of two 20 mm Hispano cannon and four 0.303 in Browning machine-guns.

The prototype Spitfire IV (DP845) was flown for the first time on 27 November 1941 by Jeffrey Quill, Supermarine's Chief Test Pilot. The extra power of the Griffon was immediately apparent on take off, as was the opposite direction of propeller rotation when compared to the Merlin, a distinct swing to the right being experienced instead of the one to the left. Although the basic handling characteristics of the Mark IV were similar to previous aircraft, it felt rather different from earlier variants in some respects, particularly with regard to the amount of directional and longitudinal trimming that was required with each change of power setting. This was the first hint that stability had been affected by use of the new engine, a problem that was to become more serious with later developments of the Griffon-Spitfire.

In its original form the Griffon featured a single-stage supercharger which tended to limit its effectiveness to operations at low to medium levels. At this stage of the war, however, the requirement was for increased performance at altitude, a task that was about to be fulfilled by the Merlin 61 which was already being tested in N3297, an aircraft that had begun its life as the Spitfire III, a variant that was subsequently abandoned. It was recognised at an early stage that the supercharger technology that had been developed for the Merlin could also be applied to its bigger brother, but this would invariably lengthen the development period still further. Even so, the promise shown by the Griffon-powered Spitfire at low altitudes augured well for the future, despite the fact that its operational use would have to be limited in the short term.

By the beginning of 1942 the Spitfire IV was being referred to as the Mark XX to avoid confusion with the PR.IV, one of the photo-reconnaissance conversions of the basic Spitfire airframe. A few weeks later it had been re-designated yet again as the Spitfire XII and it continued to be flown by Supermarine and various service test establishments for the remainder of the year. DP845 was to achieve a degree of notoriety on 20 July 1942 when it was entered for a low level speed race against a Hawker Typhoon and a captured Fw 190A at Farnborough. Various high-ranking RAF officers were to view the outcome of the contest including Air Marshal Sir W. Sholto Douglas, the AOC of Fighter Command. As a result of the air battles that had been fought over northern France in the early part of 1942, the Fw 190 had developed a fearsome reputation, to the extent that the alarm engendered bordered on paranoia. Such was its apparent aura at the time it was expected to win the race with ease, although this did not allow for a little skulduggery on the part of Jeffrey Quill.

As Supermarine had just been asked by the Air Ministry to supply a

Spitfire, Quill immediately chose DP845 as he knew how fast it was at low level. The other contenders in the race were Wing Commander H.J. 'Willie' Wilson, O.C. of the Aerodynamics Flight at RAE, in the Fw 190 and Ken Seth-Smith of Hawkers in the Typhoon. The three aircraft were flown in line abreast formation to a point to the west of Farnborough where, on Wilson's command, full power was selected. Although he trailed slightly at first, Quill was gaining on the other two when the BMW engine of the 190 expired in an ominous cloud of black smoke, requiring Wilson to snatch the throttle back and leave the race. With the 190 out of the way, Quill passed the Typhoon with ease and continued to pull away, eventually crossing the finishing line at Farnborough well ahead. The result caused considerable consternation among the assembled luminaries on the ground as it was exactly the reverse of what had been expected. What it did show was that there was still plenty of life left in the Spitfire and with the Griffon at an early stage of development there was the prospect of much more to come. Such an impressive showing certainly smoothed the way for the Griffon Spitfire to be accepted by the RAF.

During its initial testing at Supermarine DP845 had created a considerable impression and Jeffrey Quill rated it as one of the highlights of his career as he recalled in his book *Spitfire – A Test Pilot's Story* (Crecy, 1998)

> 'DP845 felt like the airborne equivalent of a very powerful sports car and was great fun to fly. Compared with a standard Spitfire, changes of trim with changes of power were much more in evidence, both directionally and longitudinally, and the aeroplane sheared about a bit during tight manoeuvres and simulated dogfights. It was immediately evident that we should have to improve its directional characteristics and also its longitudinal stability, both of which in due time we achieved. Indeed, DP845 eventually went through many phases of development, remaining in our flight development unit throughout. I and others flew it a great deal and it became one of our favourite aeroplanes.'

Clive Gosling was another to get an early taste of the Griffon Spitfire during a spell at Supermarine as a production test pilot

> 'I flew the Spitfire XII prototype DP845 on one occasion against Jeffrey Quill who was flying a Spitfire LF.VB with the cropped blower and at full power we reached 15,000 ft together. Due to the greater power of the Griffon, however, I was able to gain on JKQ in a turn and when he rolled under and dived away I was able to catch him easily in the dive.'

Over the next few months the Spitfire XII was flown by a number of service test pilots at the RAF's testing establishments at Boscombe Down and Duxford to assess its qualities and their findings are the subject of the next chapter.

CHAPTER TWO

# Spitfire XII

Following its impressive showing at Farnborough the immediate future of the Griffon-Spitfire seemed to be assured and Supermarine began work on an order for 100 production examples of the Spitfire XII. The airframe was a modified version of the Mark VC strengthened to accommodate the Griffon engine. The lengthening of the nose, the adoption of an elongated spinner and fitment of a pointed broad-chord rudder of increased area to maintain directional stability, resulted in length being increased by 1 ft 11 in to 31 ft 10 in. As the longer nose led to a worsening of the view forwards, the engine was enclosed in a close fitting cowling to reduce this disadvantage to a minimum and a distinctive feature of the Mark XII were the elongated blisters covering each cylinder bank. As befitting its low level role, all production aircraft emerged with clipped wings to increase rate of roll, the resultant wing span being 32 ft 7 in. Early production aircraft appeared with a fixed tailwheel, however, the majority were fitted with a retractable installation. The Spitfire XII retained the smaller, circular oil cooler of the Mark V under the port wing but the repositioning of the oil tank from underneath the engine (as on all Merlin-engined variants) to the forward bulkhead resulted in a smaller top fuselage fuel tank which had a capacity of 36 gallons. Armament was standard Spitfire 'C' wing type, comprising two 20 mm Hispano cannon and four 0.303 in Browning machine-guns and power was provided by a 1,750 hp Griffon III/IV driving a four-blade Rotol constant-speed propeller.

The Spitfire XII prototype (DP845) was delivered to the Aeroplane and Armament Experimental Establishment (A&AEE) at Boscombe Down on 3 September 1942 to begin a comprehensive series of trials to include a handling assessment, oil cooling and radiator suitability, carbon monoxide contamination tests and measurements of climb and level speed performance. On arrival it was noted that considerable attention had been given to the surface finish of the aircraft as all external surfaces were flush riveted and filling had been applied at joints and edges of overlapping panels (on the standard Spitfire V flush riveting was limited to the wings and the forward part of the fuselage).

The whole surface, including fabric work, was polished to give the smoothest finish possible.

The trials carried out at A&AEE were flown at an all-up weight of 7,415 lbs which represented a typical service load. DP845 was fitted with revised brakes which appeared to offer more braking action than previous Spitfires, they were smooth and progressive in action and their application produced no feeling that the aircraft was about to nose over. Despite the longer nose to accommodate the Griffon engine, it was felt that the view from the cockpit when on the ground was not appreciably different from Merlin-engined Spitfires. The Mark XII's tendency to swing to the right instead of to the left as on previous Spitfires was not in itself a problem, however, the swing produced was considerably more powerful, particularly if the engine was opened up rapidly. This occurred in the early part of the take off run and the rudder was not powerful enough to check the swing even though it was of increased area. Some direction was inevitably lost in such a situation, the amount depending upon the speed with which the engine was opened up. It was therefore necessary to take off with full left rudder trim applied. In an effort to reduce the severity of the swing on take off the aircraft was operated with reduced boost but this did little to alleviate it. In this condition full rpm could not be obtained and the run was noticeably longer. Although a large amount of left rudder was needed on the initial climb, there was just sufficient rudder trim to climb continuously with zero foot load.

The general flying characteristics of the Spitfire XII were very similar to the Mark V although the rudder control was heavier and the directional trim changes caused by alterations in power and speed could not be comfortably held by rudder pedal pressure alone and frequent adjustment of the rudder trimmer was necessary. Aileron control was normal, although a little on the heavy side. It was, however, conceded that the aileron forces noted on other Spitfires did tend to vary with individual aircraft. The elevator forces were normal and satisfactory. Stability about all three axes was acceptable, the only real difference from previous Spitfires was that longitudinal stability proved to be rather more positive than on the Mark V due largely to the more forward position of the centre of gravity. This increase in longitudinal stability did not result in any notable reduction in manoeuvrability, however, the elevator movements and forces were a little greater. During tight turns the aircraft showed no tendency to tighten up. Under most engine conditions there was a notable vibration from the Griffon which had not been apparent on Merlin Spitfires and with the throttle lever as fitted to DP845, there was a tendency for it to creep shut which meant that the friction damper to prevent this had to be at its tightest setting.

A number of dives were made up to 450 mph IAS, the only difficulty being the heavy rudder which was incapable of countering the Spitfire's normal tendency of yawing to the left when trimmed for all-out level flight. To maintain balanced flight it was necessary to utilise the rudder trimmer. Recovery from these dives was normal and the Spitfire XII did not shown any sign of tightening on the pull out or of producing excessive accelerations. At the opposite end of the speed range, the stalling characteristics were very similar to other Spitfires and at the weight tested the stalling speed flaps and undercarriage up was 75 mph IAS, with 65 mph IAS being noted with flaps and undercarriage down. From the pilot's point of view aerobatics were as delightful as ever, the only variation being that a little more speed was needed for manoeuvres in the vertical plane because of the Mark XII's increased all-up weight. The approach and landing was normal and straightforward and there was adequate elevator control to produce a touchdown on all three points.

Although in conclusion A&AEE found the flying characteristics of the Spitfire XII to be very similar to previous marks, it did call for improvements in the aircraft's rudder control, particularly as regards its general heaviness, its inability to control the swing on take off and the need to constantly retrim after each change of power and speed. Pending an improved rudder (one that was lightened first rather than increased in area) it was recommended that care be taken not to open up the engine too rapidly on take off, particularly when using a runway or taking off in formation.

Performance testing was commenced shortly after the arrival of DP845 at Boscombe Down. The recommended engine limitations of the Griffon IIB at the time of test were 2,750 rpm and +12 lbs/sq.in boost for take off and for all-out level flight and combat climbs (5 minutes limit). The normal maximum figures for continuous climbing were 2,600 rpm and +9 lbs/sq.in boost (60 minutes limit). For the purposes of the test, however, this service restriction was conveniently disregarded and the full combat rating was used to determine the aircraft's maximum performance in the climb. These were then compared with the measurements taken when using the normal rating. The best climbing speed was found to be 190 mph IAS up to 16,000 ft, this speed then decreasing by 3½ mph per 1,000 ft. When using full combat power the rate of climb of the Spitfire XII was as follows

| Height | 2,000 ft | 4,000 ft | 6,000 ft | 8,000 ft | 10,000 ft |
|---|---|---|---|---|---|
| Rate of climb – ft/min | 3,760 | 3,600 | 3,370 | 3,130 | 2,900 |
| Time from start – mins | 0.55 | 1.05 | 1.65 | 2.25 | 2.95 |

| Height | 14,000 ft | 18,000 ft | 22,000 ft | 26,000 ft | 30,000 ft |
|---|---|---|---|---|---|
| Rate of climb – ft/min | 2,760 | 2,460 | 2,000 | 1,560 | 1,110 |
| Time from start – mins | 4.35 | 5.85 | 7.65 | 9.90 | 12.95 |

Not surprisingly, there was a significant reduction in climb performance when the aircraft was operated at the normal rating, the equivalent figures being as follows

| Height | 2,000 ft | 4,000 ft | 6,000 ft | 8,000 ft | 10,000 ft |
|---|---|---|---|---|---|
| Rate of climb – ft/min | 3,040 | 3,040 | 2,800 | 2,570 | 2,340 |
| Time from start – mins | 0.65 | 1.30 | 2.00 | 2.75 | 3.55 |

| Height | 14,000 ft | 18,000 ft | 22,000 ft | 26,000 ft | 30,000 ft |
|---|---|---|---|---|---|
| Rate of climb – ft/min | 2,240 | 2,110 | 1,720 | 1,320 | 920 |
| Time from start – mins | 5.35 | 7.15 | 9.25 | 11.90 | 15.50 |

When using combat rating, the maximum rate of climb in MS (Moderately Supercharged) gear was 3,760 ft/min at 2,600 ft and in FS (Fully Supercharged) gear it was 2,760 ft/min at 15,300 ft. The same figures when climbing at the normal rating showed a maximum rate of climb in MS gear of 3,040 ft/min at 4,000 ft and 2,240 ft/min at 16,700 ft in FS gear. Service ceiling was considered to be 39,000 ft with an absolute ceiling of 40,000 ft. At the same time as DP845 was being evaluated, Spitfire IX 'BF274' (actually BS274) was being put through its paces and this aircraft, powered by a Merlin 61, was slightly superior in the climb, showing a maximum rate of climb at combat power in MS gear of 3,860 ft/min. Although its time to height at lower altitudes was only marginally better, the two-stage supercharger of the Spitfire IX meant that it became much superior above 25,000 ft, taking just 20.2 minutes to reach 40,000 ft (climb rate on the Spitfire XII fell away rapidly above 30,000 ft and it took a full 35 minutes to reach its service ceiling at combat power).

Maximum level speed performance was assessed at the full combat rating of +12 lbs/sq.in boost with mixture rich and the radiator shutter in the minimum drag position. The speeds obtained were as follows

| Height | Sea level | 2,000 ft | 4,000 ft | 8,000 ft | 10,000 ft |
|---|---|---|---|---|---|
| TAS – mph | 346 | 355 | 364.5 | 372 | 370.5 |
| IAS – mph | 355 | 355 | 354 | 340.5 | 329 |

| Height | 12,000 ft | 14,000 ft | 16,000 ft | 20,000 ft | 24,000 ft |
|---|---|---|---|---|---|
| TAS – mph | 368 | 364 | 388.5 | 397 | 392 |
| IAS – mph | 316.5 | 317 | 314.5 | 301.5 | 278 |

The highest speed attained in MS gear was 372 mph TAS at 5,700 ft (full throttle height) and in FS gear, 397 mph TAS at a full throttle height of 17,800 ft. In comparison, the Spitfire IX was slightly slower achieving 366 mph TAS at 15,400 ft in MS gear and 389 mph TAS at 27,400 ft in FS gear.

Following the initial handling and performance trials carried out at Boscombe Down, the third production Spitfire XII (EN223) was delivered to the Air Fighting Development Unit (AFDU) at Duxford on 21 December 1942 for a tactical assessment to be made. As an early production aircraft EN223 was fitted with a dural propeller (subsequent machines had wooden propellers) and its Griffon III was fitted with .45 reduction gear which resulted in a slightly reduced rate of climb when compared with later aircraft which had .51 reduction gearing. Fuel capacity remained at 85 gallons so that endurance was less than an equivalent Merlin-powered Spitfire and, as befitting its low level role, the wing tips were clipped. Engine starting was by means of a Coffman cartridge. The trial was carried out with a full load of ammunition which resulted in a loaded weight of 7,400 lbs.

The findings of the service test pilots at Duxford as regards the Spitfire XII were broadly similar to those of their counterparts at Boscombe Down. Although the Mark XII had the normal Spitfire feel when in the air, the swing on take off was much more pronounced and if not anticipated, it could not be corrected, even with full rudder. This tendency was later eased by reducing the propeller fine pitch stop which allowed greater rpm to be used at a lower boost setting. Handling was generally rated as superior to both the Spitfire V and IX, lateral control in particular being crisp and light due to the removal of the wing tips. Longitudinal stability also showed an improvement over earlier Spitfires and the aircraft could be eased out of dives without inducing excessive 'g' forces. Due to the increased power of the Griffon, however, pilots did have to spend much more time using the rudder trimmer when changing power settings. It was also noticed that the Griffon engine felt quite harsh at all times and was not as smooth as the Merlin.

Low level speed performance was impressive, the Spitfire XII easily outpacing a Mark V, and it also proved to be superior to the low altitude version of the Spitfire IX (Merlin 66), being 14 mph faster at sea level. Top speed was a shade below 400 mph at 18,000 ft, an almost identical figure to that achieved by DP845 during the speed trials carried out at Boscombe Down. Climb performance was not as impressive, however, and during sustained climbs the Mark XII took around thirty seconds longer to reach 10,000 ft than the LF.IX, a further forty-five seconds being lost if the climb was maintained to 20,000 ft. Comparative trials were also carried out with a Spitfire V fitted with the low altitude cropped supercharger Merlin 45M which showed the two aircraft to be very evenly matched during climbs up to 10,000 ft. Service ceiling, assuming this to be the height at which climb rate had fallen to 1,000 ft/min, was 28,500 ft. Dive performance of the Spitfire XII was very similar to that of the Mark IX, although the XII had a slight edge at anything other than full throttle.

The Mark XII performed well at low levels during simulated dogfights with a Spitfire LF.IX, although as the latter was fitted with standard wings, any comparison with the clipped-wing XII was, perhaps, a little unfair. The advantage enjoyed by the Mark XII had run out by the time that 20,000 ft was reached and above that height the Spitfire IX not only had better all-round performance, but could out-manoeuvre its opponent with relative ease. From these trials it was considered that at heights below 20,000 ft the Spitfire XII would be more than a match for the Fw 190 as it was faster, could roll as well and was superior in the turn. However, it did lose out in one important respect as its Claude Hobson carburettor could not operate with even the slightest amount of negative-g and this led to the engine cutting out, a characteristic that was not shared by the fuel-injected BMW 801 radial of the Focke-Wulf.

For the pilot, the view forwards from the Spitfire XII was actually considered to be an improvement as the Griffon engine was set lower in the airframe. This, together with the clipped wings, was beneficial during low flying as it provided much better lookout and made for increased pilot confidence during low level manoeuvring. In general the aircraft handled well at low level, although pilots had to concentrate when making throttle alterations during turns as this upset the directional trim. This was particularly important when turning to the right as the direction of yaw was towards the ground. In its con-clusion, AFDU reported favourably on the handling of the Spitfire XII, in particular its longitudinal stability, which was much improved, and its rate of roll. Directional control was rather less satisfactory as the rudder control was relatively heavy and the constant need to re-trim when making throttle alterations was, at best, an annoying distraction. When in combat it was felt that the resultant increase in cockpit work-load would most likely lead to a situation in which lookout and general combat effectiveness would be compromised.

Back at Boscombe Down the first production Spitfire XII (EN221) was delivered on 5 November 1942 for intensive flying trials and it was joined a month later by EN222. This involved flying both aircraft as frequently as possible until a total of 150 hours had been attained, the intention being to bring to light any defects or difficulties of main-tenance that were likely to occur in service, particularly in connection with the engine installation. In addition the opportunity was also taken to perform various tests, the most important of which were investiga-tions into the aircraft's rolling manoeuvrability with and without wing tips, and various tests to reduce the amount of swing on take off. All flying and maintenance work during the trial was carried out by pilots and ground crews seconded from operational units.

On arrival, EN221 was fitted with normal 'universal' wings but

EN222 had its wing tips removed and fairings in their place. During the course of the flying, wing tips were put on EN222 and removed from EN221 for comparative tests. EN222 also arrived with elevators with a modified horn balance, but the tailplane and elevators were changed back to normal at the same time as the wing tip change. Both aircraft were powered by a Griffon III engine which was virtually the same as the earlier II except for the engine-mounting brackets and some items of auxiliary equipment. EN221 was initially fitted with a Rotol four-bladed metal propeller of 10 ft 5 in diameter which was subsequently replaced by propellers of the same type and diameter with hydulignum blades. EN222 had a similar propeller with metal blades which had been cropped to remove damage to the tips as a result of ground contact during a previous landing. This was also later replaced by one with hydulignum blades.

During the trial period EN222 was flown with two types of experimental exhaust stubs made up by Rolls-Royce of stainless and mild steel. When it arrived at Boscombe Down, EN221 was fitted with inertia weights to the elevator controls, but this was apparently an error by the manufacturers and these were later removed. In the course of the test schedule which was commenced on 6 November, EN221 was flown for a total of 151 hours 35 minutes during which it made 167 landings. EN222 joined the trial on 8 December and completed 152 hours and 154 landings. Speeds of over 400 mph IAS and up to the limiting speed of 470 mph IAS were regularly obtained in dives. The maximum accelerations recorded were up to +7½ g (and frequently over +6g) and up to -2g with -4g being recorded on one occasion.

From a maintenance point of view the use of a semi-cantilever engine mounting, instead of a tubular mounting as on Merlin-engined Spitfires, allowed somewhat better access to the engine auxiliaries. The Griffon engines gave very little trouble during the trial and starting, which was by a Coffman cartridge, was usually achieved on the first firing with no priming, assuming that the engine had already been warmed up. Even if the aircraft had been left overnight, however, it could still be started up on the first or second cartridge with little or no priming. The normal type of fuel used was 100-octane although on one occasion EN222 had to land away from base due to fuel shortage and was unable to obtain supplies of 100-octane to fill up for the return journey. Permission was eventually given to use DTD230 (87-octane) provided that power was limited to +6 lbs/sq.in boost. When the aircraft returned to Boscombe Down it was discovered that, due to lack of proper supervision, it had been refuelled with an even lower grade of fuel (DTD224 or 77-octane) but no problems resulted from the use of the wrong type of fuel.

The minimal ground clearance of the propeller was a constant hazard and there were several instances of the propeller tips being damaged when landing on grass. A considerable number of complaints were made by pilots that they were unable to obtain maximum rpm. On many occasions no more than 2,650 rpm could be achieved with corresponding losses in obtainable boost. It was eventually found that this was due to the existence of lumps of coagulated oil in the propeller hub cylinders on both aircraft and about 1 lb of this greasy substance was removed from EN221 after 44 hours flying time. It was suspected that the small bleed hole in the piston was responsible for this coagulation and the bleed hole was therefore stopped up by the Rotol representative. After this modification no more trouble was experienced with loss of maximum rpm and no more solidified oil was found in the hub cylinders. As the function of the bleed hole was to prevent freezing of the oil by maintaining a constant circulation, it was feared that the deletion of the bleed would lead to trouble at very low outside air temperatures, but this proved not to be the case.

The fuel system of the Spitfire XII was the same as that on the Mark V. At the beginning of the trial pilots commented that the Griffon engine tended to cut under even very slight negative accelerations. To get round this problem a Griffon type fuel restrictor valve was fitted to EN221 and no more complaints of engine cutting were received. A Merlin 61 type restrictor was fitted to EN222 but this was not as successful as there were occasions when the engine cut during tight turns. As a result a Griffon type valve was also fitted. Over time, the excellent surface finish of the aircraft tended to deteriorate, in particular the ailerons where the top surface either peeled off or cracked.

The intensive flying trials report also contained comments by the pilots. As the cockpit of the Spitfire XII was virtually the same as that of the Mark V they were well acquainted with the layout of all the main flying controls and instruments, the only criticisms referring to one or two points of detail. The jettisonable fuel tank cock was inconveniently placed and difficult to operate and the compass was difficult to read when flying at night, ideally requiring an additional light. The lack of an indicator showing the number of rounds fired by the 20 mm Hispano cannons was also remarked upon. Despite the larger engine cowling and the elongated bumps covering each cylinder bank, the view appeared to be equally good as on the Spitfire V or IX.

In the air the Spitfire XII was pleasant to fly and was generally preferred to the Mark IXs that the pilots had been flying operationally. Although the Griffon engines ran relatively smoothly, they were not as sweet as the Merlin and it was found that the instruments were difficult to read because of the levels of vibration. Before the negative-g fuel restrictor was fitted to EN221 the engine would cut on the slightest application of negative acceleration, such as when momentarily levelling the aircraft after take off. This cutting was not experienced after the restrictors were fitted. The exhaust emissions were found to be a little rich when operating at low rpm and if the aircraft was taxied at too low an engine speed, there was a danger of the windscreen becoming obscured by deposits from the exhaust. With the high levels of torque generated by the Griffon on take off, which quite often led to a dipping of the starboard wing as well as a strong swing to the right, it was felt that the disadvantage of the Spitfire's narrow track undercarriage was emphasised rather more on the Mark XII than on the Merlin powered variants.

In early 1943 DP845 was returned to Supermarine to have the fine pitch stop of the propeller reduced from 40 degrees to 31 degrees 15 minutes to enable higher rpm to be used with reduced boost. This was an attempt to reduce the Spitfire XII's violent swing to starboard on take off. After returning to Boscombe Down in March it was concluded that the swing was less severe than it had been, but as the Griffon-engined Spitfire was being considered as a naval fighter it was considered that a further reduction was needed for safe carrier operation.

The following month DP845 was used to ascertain the Spitfire XII's spinning characteristics during two turn spins to the right and left from 15,000 ft. With the engine throttled right back, speed was reduced until the aircraft was just at the stall (80–85 mph IAS) and the spin was then commenced by applying rudder in the desired direction. Just before entering the spin the aircraft adopted a nose high attitude and around one quarter of rudder travel was needed to get it to depart. The Spitfire did not give the appearance of being properly stalled during the first turn but when the spin was established there was marked fore-and-aft pitching, accompanied by rolling. In addition there was strong snatching of the control column and considerable buffeting developed. The height lost with each turn was approximately 700 ft and the time taken varied from about 7 seconds for the first turn, to 3½–5 seconds for the second turn. Recovery was effected by applying opposite rudder and easing the control column forward a little. The aircraft tended to speed up for ¾ turn but stopped turning after another ¼–½ turn. The buffeting did not disappear until 150–160 mph IAS was reached in the pull out dive. Spins to the right and left exhibited similar characteristics, although right-hand spins proved to be rather more violent with the recovery taking slightly longer. In general, however, the spin character-istics of the Spitfire XII were similar to previous marks of Spitfire and the pitching and buffeting that occurred was not considered to be serious.

In addition to its normal duties of evaluating new aircraft types, A&AEE were occasionally asked to report on so-called 'rogue' aircraft which exhibited characteristics far removed from what was normally expected. One such example occurred in August 1943 when Spitfire XII EN624 of No.91 Squadron arrived for an investigation of extremely heavy aileron control, coupled with excessive aileron up-float. This aircraft had been delivered to 91 Squadron at Westhampnett on 13 May but had quickly been declared as being 'un-manoeuvrable' at high speed owing to excessively heavy ailerons. With the original starboard aileron as fitted by the manufacturers it was necessary to reflex the aileron in excess of 4 ft to prevent it rising over ½ in at 400 mph. A replacement aileron was fitted but this showed identical flying characteristics to the previous one. Subsequently both ailerons were replaced and a complete check of the aileron control system was carried out but without improvement. The troubles experienced with this aircraft rendered it unsuitable for operational flying and a restriction was imposed in which it was only allowed to fly locally at reduced airspeeds.

On arrival at Boscombe Down the aircraft was flown in the condition in which it was received and when flying at over 200 mph IAS it was noted that it flew left wing low, this tendency increasing so that at 300 mph IAS the control force needed to fly straight and level was very large, so much so that it was virtually impossible to bank to the right. In all conditions of flight the ailerons were excessively heavy. It had already been noted, however, that the aileron shrouds were distorted, the edge of the shroud drooping in places by as much as 0.20 in, reducing the gap between the aileron and the shroud. To try to eradicate the aircraft's lateral characteristics the aileron shrouds were straightened out, the aileron cables on the starboard side were tensioned to the maximum permissible, all reflexing was removed from the ailerons and 12 in of upward reflexing was restored to the starboard aileron. A check flight was made after each operation and it was found that the large change in lateral trim with speed was largely eliminated by straightening the aileron shrouds. In its final condition the aircraft was practically normal, being slightly right wing low at low speed, in trim at cruising speeds and almost in trim at 450 mph IAS. The ailerons were still rather heavy, but not abnormally so, the total up-float of the ailerons in this condition being just within limits. EN624 was returned to squadron service, but was eventually written off in a flying accident on 23 January 1944.

By the end of 1943, with the prospect of the second front opening up the following year, thought was given to converting many RAF fighters to become fighter-bombers to provide tactical support to the invasion. A Spitfire XII (MB878) was tested at Boscombe Down in September 1943 to determine the performance reduction when carrying a 500 lb bomb under the fuselage centreline. Without the bomb and its associated rack, MB878 attained a maximum speed of 394 mph IAS at its full throttle height of 18,100 ft in FS gear when using full combat power, or just 3 mph less than had been achieved with DP845 a year before. With the bomb and rack in place, top speed was reduced to 371 mph IAS at 17,900 ft, this result being broadly similar to the performance penalty noted with the Spitfire IX when carrying a bomb. In the event the Spitfire XII was never used in the dive-bombing role and was to remain as a low altitude fighter throughout its service life.

The testing carried out at Boscombe Down and Duxford had shown that the Griffon-Spitfire had great potential. The Mark XII was one of the fastest fighters of its day at low level and if this level of performance could be extended to higher altitudes, as was likely if a more advanced version of the Griffon was to be used, the Spitfire was assured of matching anything that Germany could produce. The first Griffon engine to employ a two-speed, two-stage supercharger was first tested in a modified Spitfire VIII and the following chapter looks at the development and flight testing of the Spitfire XIV, the last fighter variant to see widespread operational use during the Second World War.

CHAPTER THREE

# Spitfire XIV

Although the Spitfire XII had shown a great deal of promise, the operational limitations imposed by its single-stage Griffon were a severe handicap as its performance fell away rapidly above 20,000 ft. If it was to become a really effective fighter it needed an engine that could continue to deliver high power levels to much greater altitudes. The expertise that Rolls-Royce had built up with the Merlin was also applied to the Griffon and by early 1943 the first examples of a two-speed, two-stage supercharged Griffon were being tested, an engine that held the tantalising prospect of significant performance advances equal to those achieved with the Merlin 61 of the Spitfire IX.

At this stage development of the Spitfire airframe was tending to lag behind the advances made by Rolls-Royce and this resulted in another interim variant, the Spitfire XIV (a major re-design of the Spitfire would fly later as the Mark XVIII which is discussed in the following chapter). The Mark XIV was powered by a two-speed, two-stage Griffon 65 driving a five-blade Rotol propeller with Jablo or Hydulignum blades. It was based on the Spitfire VIII and six such aircraft (JF316-JF321) were fitted with Griffon engines to act as prototypes. For the first time in the Spitfire's development it was necessary to increase fin area to keep the aircraft in balance directionally. Initially a straight-edged fin was tried on the prototypes but all production aircraft featured a curved profile which blended into the fuselage spine. A further difference from the Mark XII was the use of rectangular radiator ducts under both wings of slightly deeper section. A coolant radiator was located in each duct, together with the intercooler radiator for the supercharger under the starboard wing and oil cooler under the port wing. The first Spitfire XIVs emerged with the 'C' Type or 'universal' wing but this was soon changed to the 'E' wing with two 20 mm Hispano cannon and two 0.5 in Browning machine-guns.

Like the Merlin-engined Spitfire VII and VIII, the Mark XIV had fuel capacity in the wings and 13 gallons could be carried in each leading edge. This was augmented in the later FR.XIV by a rear-mounted fuel tank of 33 gallons which was pressurised and had its own individual contents gauge. This variant also featured an F.24 camera for oblique photography and clipped wings. Late production examples of the Spitfire XIV were delivered with a cut-back rear fuselage and teardrop canopies. Use of the two-stage Griffon meant that length increased yet again to 32 ft 8 in and a fully loaded Mark XIV weighed in at around 8,400 lbs producing a wing loading of 34.7 lbs/sq.ft.

One of the batch of six converted Spitfire VIIIs (JF317) was delivered to A&AEE in July 1943 for handling tests and to ascertain its lateral and directional behaviour. It featured the straight-edged fin extension, a rather inelegant feature which was in marked contrast to the finely sculpted contours of the rest of the aircraft. The areas for the vertical tail surfaces were as follows (equivalent figures for the Spitfire XII in brackets) – area of fin and rudder, 18.22 sq.ft (12.84 sq.ft); gross area of rudder, 10.80 sq.ft (8.23 sq.ft); area of rudder trimmer 0.70 sq.ft (0.91 sq.ft). Throughout the trials, which lasted for four weeks commencing on 13 July, the aircraft was flown at a take off weight of 8,375 lbs.

During ground handling with the hood open it was noted that a considerable amount of exhaust fumes and heat tended to enter the cockpit, making it impossible for the pilot to put his head over the side. As the long nose obscured more of the view directly forwards than on other marks of Spitfire it was thus more important than ever to weave the aircraft from side to side with the rudder to ensure that the way ahead during taxying was clear. Fast taxying was not particularly pleasant due to the shock absorbing qualities of the undercarriage being rather poor. Although the aircraft still swung strongly to the right on take off, this tendency was not as pronounced as with the standard fin and it could be comfortably controlled with the rudder, provided that full left trim had been applied. After leaving the ground following a relatively short run, pilots noted that the elevator tended to 'hunt', particularly when flying in rough air. JF317 was fitted with an elevator of enlarged horn balance and although this hunting had been reported on other Spitfires fitted with the same elevator, the effect on this aircraft was much more noticeable. This type of elevator was an attempt to improve the aircraft's longitudinal stability by aerodynamic means and although relatively successful in this respect, it did produce some unwanted side-effects in other areas of flight.

When JF317 was delivered to Boscombe Down it was badly out of trim laterally. This was remedied by reflexing the trailing edges of the ailerons before the general handling tests were made. After this work had been carried out the aileron characteristics were similar to those of an average Spitfire although it was noted that the ailerons were a little heavier and the response, whilst still good, was slightly inferior. There was a negligible change of lateral trim with speed, and only a slight change between engine on and engine off. The right wing tended to become slightly low with the engine off.

The effectiveness of the rudder and the response obtained was generally considered to be satisfactory. The amount of force needed to move the rudder over normal deflections was moderate but became heavy if a larger movement was required. As already noted with the Spitfire XII, there was a large change in directional trim with alterations in speed and power. These changes could be held on the rudder over the normal speed range if sufficiently large foot forces were used, but it was conceded that in practice most pilots would probably prefer to use the trimmer which would then be in constant use during manoeuvres. Because of this it was again recommended that the rudder be made lighter. At low speeds the application of yaw also produced a pitching couple, but this feature tended to decrease with speed and had almost disappeared at diving speeds.

The characteristics of the elevator control on JF317 were broadly similar to those of a Spitfire IX when fitted with the enlarged horn balance elevator. If displaced very slightly the control column oscillated five or six times before settling down, suggesting that the amount of horn balance on this aircraft was slightly too large. If the elevator was displaced through a larger amount, it moved quickly and firmly back to its trimmed position giving a large corrective tendency to the aircraft. It was for this reason that the elevator was considered to be a little on the heavy side for manoeuvring.

At the stall JF317 behaved like most other Spitfires and the stall speeds at the loading tested were 88 mph IAS with flaps and undercarriage up and 75 mph IAS with flaps and undercarriage down. The approach to land with the engine off was best made at 110 mph IAS as at lower speeds the rate of sink tended to become excessive. At this speed, however, there was rather a long float after flaring the aircraft prior to touchdown. With the engine on, the approach was normal although the nose was rather high. In this configuration the aircraft could be brought in at speeds down to 85 mph IAS although care had to be taken when landing on rough ground as the tail tended to bounce with considerable force.

Following its initial assessment at Boscombe Down, JF317 was flown to Wittering to be evaluated by AFDU, the main objective being to carry out a comparison with a Spitfire VIII (JF664) powered by a Merlin 63. Pilots at AFDU were somewhat more critical of the elevator control of JF317 describing it as 'unpleasantly heavy', but in spite of this it was found to be more manoeuvrable than the Spitfire VIII at all heights, even though the latter was much lighter on the elevators and was easier for the average pilot to fly. Spins were attempted in JF317 from 25,000 ft, the aircraft showing a marked reluctance to perform this manoeuvre and requiring positive action on the part of the pilot before it would depart. On releasing pro-spin controls the aircraft recovered immediately. As previously noted on spins with a Spitfire XII, the nose position tended to vary considerably from almost vertically downwards, to a position well above the horizon. During the spin most of the time was spent in this flat attitude but at no time did it give the impression of becoming uncontrollable. Both aircraft carried the same amount of fuel (96 gallons in the main tank and 27 gallons in two wing tanks), a comparative test showing that the Griffon-powered machine used approximately 10–15 gallons more fuel per hour than the Merlin. Performance testing showed that the Spitfire VIII held a slight advantage up to 25,000 ft but that the Griffon-Spitfire became much the better aircraft above this height [at the time JF317 was fitted with a Griffon 61 which had a lower MS supercharger gear ratio than the Griffon 65 of production aircraft].

In early September 1943 JF319, another Griffon-powered Spitfire VIII, was delivered to Boscombe Down for climb and level speed performance trials. Partial climbs at combat rating were carried out at mean heights of 9,000 ft in MS supercharger gear and 21,000 ft and 36,500 ft in FS gear to determine the best climbing speed. This was found to be 175 mph IAS up to 22,000 ft (approximately full throttle height in FS gear), decreasing by 3 mph per 1,000 ft thereafter. To obtain the climb performance of the Spitfire XIV a total of six climbs were made at combat rating, two using MS gear throughout, two using FS gear throughout and two combining both (once again the five minute limitation for the use of combat power was ignored for test purposes). The results are given below and show a significant improvement over the figures obtained with the Spitfire XII

| Height | 4,000 ft | 8,000 ft | 12,000 ft | 16,000 ft | 20,000 ft |
|---|---|---|---|---|---|
| Rate of climb – ft/min | 4,640 | 3,830 | 3,600 | 3,600 | 3,600 |
| Time from start – mins | 0.80 | 1.75 | 2.85 | 3.95 | 5.10 |

| Height | 24,000 ft | 28,000 ft | 32,000 ft | 36,000 ft | 40,000 ft |
|---|---|---|---|---|---|
| Rate of climb – ft/min | 3,290 | 2,690 | 2,100 | 1,500 | 810 |
| Time from start – mins | 6.20 | 7.55 | 9.25 | 11.47 | 15.05 |

The maximum rate of climb at combat power in MS gear was 5,110 ft/min at 1,700 ft, that for FS gear being 3,600 ft/min at 21,800 ft. The rate of climb only fell below 1,000 ft/min at 38,900 ft and the absolute ceiling was estimated to be 44,600 ft. As it was not permitted to run the engine up to +18 lbs/sq.in on the ground, difficulty was experienced in setting the boost control accurately. Consequently the controlled boost obtained during the climbing trials was slightly higher than the nominal value (+18.3 lbs/sq.in on the climb). When corrected for +18 lbs/sq.in, the results were marginally lower than the figures given above. This also affected level speed performance as it was found that +18.5 lbs/sq.in was being obtained which had the effect of increasing top speed by approximately 3 mph TAS over that which could be expected when using the correct boost. The uncorrected results from the level speed trials were as follows

| Height | Sea level | 4,000 ft | 8,000 ft | 12,000 ft | 16,000 ft |
|---|---|---|---|---|---|
| TAS – mph | 363 | 385 | 389 | 386 | 382 |
| IAS – mph | 373 | 374 | 357 | 334 | 311 |

| Height | 20,000 ft | 24,000 ft | 28,000 ft | 32,000 ft | 36,000 ft |
|---|---|---|---|---|---|
| TAS – mph | 423 | 440 | 444 | 440 | 430 |
| IAS – mph | 323 | 315 | 297 | 273 | 247 |

The maximum speed in MS gear was 391 mph TAS at the full throttle height of 5,000 ft and in FS gear it was 446 mph TAS at 25,400 ft. The normal take off weight of JF319 during these trials was 8,400 lbs, however, the above figures were corrected to 95 per cent of this weight, i.e. 7,980 lbs.

At the same time as JF319 was being tested to ascertain its performance, further handling trials were carried out as it featured a combined trimmer and balance tab on the rudder which was intended to improve the aircraft's directional trimming characteristics. Other than this modification it was virtually identical to JF317, the only difference in the cockpit being a larger type of fuel gauge reading from 0–85 gallons. Unfortunately this proved to be extremely erratic in operation and gave no reliable indication whatever of the fuel contents. Taxying gave the impression that the load on the tail wheel was rather light which resulted in 'bucketing' if the tail was kicked up by a bump in the ground. The engine also did not open up smoothly at low throttle settings and so taxying tended to be carried out using spasmodic bursts of engine rather than a steady low power.

The take off was carried out at 2,750 rpm and +12 lbs/sq.in boost, starting with full left rudder bias. In addition to the expected swing to the right, there was a marked tendency for the starboard wing to go well down which felt rather uncomfortable and accentuated the impression of the swing. About three-quarters of the available rudder deflection was needed to counteract the swing, the forces necessary being large, but not unduly so. The remaining rudder deflection could, if necessary, be applied in an emergency with an extra effort. The aircraft left the ground cleanly after a short run and climbed away steeply. As already noted on JF317, there was a tendency for the elevator to hunt immediately after take off, particularly when the air was turbulent.

The change in directional trim with speed was still large but due to the incorporation of the balance tab the rudder control was lighter, enabling the change in trim to be more easily held. Power changes produced a slight change of trim with small changes of power having little noticeable effect. If the throttle was opened or closed quickly between the cruising power and throttle closed positions there was a marked initial yaw but the aircraft quickly returned to its original course and could be comfortably held on the rudder until there was a considerable change in speed. Under most normal conditions the aircraft could be trimmed for cruising speed and manoeuvred between 160 mph IAS and 400 mph IAS without any real necessity for re-trimming. The elevator came in for further criticism as it was considered to be heavier than was desirable, especially at high speeds and also at low speeds with maximum power. JF319 was also fitted with the enlarged horn balance elevator which had first been tested on a Spitfire V. On this installation the elevator had been noted as being slightly heavier, but on the Griffon-Spitfire this effect appeared to be much more pronounced. It was thought that a reduction in the size of the horns might be the cure. The ailerons were heavy at high speeds but not abnormally so.

Longitudinal stability tests showed that the aircraft was stable at all speeds, engine on or off. This was especially so at speeds above the normal cruising speed of 270 mph IAS, with stability increasing considerably until at full throttle (330 mph IAS) strong forces were needed to displace the aircraft from its condition of flight. On release of the control it returned quickly to its original speed. On the glide the aircraft showed stable characteristics with flaps and undercarriage both down and up. There was no tendency for the aircraft to tighten in steep turns or dive recoveries. When the aircraft was disturbed directionally and the rudder freed, it returned to its original direction of flight at all speeds with engine on. As speed was increased the degree of stability increased once again until at 300 mph IAS and over the aircraft returned immediately to its original course after a disturbance. Lateral stability was satisfactory and normal for a Spitfire.

Stall speeds were as previously noted on JF317, the characteristics at the stall being relatively benign. With flaps and undercarriage up the aircraft exhibited good control down to the stall, the control column remaining central and light. A nose high attitude was adopted prior to the stall but there was no hint of wing drop as the stall was reached, the nose merely dropping straight through about 30 degrees. With flaps and undercarriage down a slight kick was felt at the stall as though the left wing was about to drop, although this did not actually occur. In both cases the recovery was automatic as speed was increased.

The aircraft was dived with about two-thirds throttle from trimmed all-out level flight up to a maximum of 450 mph IAS (the limiting speed in the dive was 470 mph IAS). No undesirable characteristics were noted, the aircraft being steady with just a small change of directional trim which could be held on rudder, although it was found to be more convenient to re-trim. The stick force necessary to maintain the angle of dive tended to increase as speed was built up but was never excessive. All controls could be used at 450 mph IAS with no undesirable effects, the aircraft returning quickly to a steady course following a directional disturbance. With such excellent qualities in the dive it was felt that pilots would have little difficulty in keeping their sights on a target. Recovery also caused no problems and was effected quickly when a light pull force was used.

Aerobatic manoeuvres could be performed with little difficulty although there was a tendency for the aircraft to wander a little due to torque effects as speed dropped off at the top of a loop. It was also found that the aircraft did not respond as quickly as was desirable when pulling out from loops and up to 1,000 ft could be lost from the original entry height. Rolls were normal and satisfactory. In their conclusions, A&AEE pilots were unanimous that the balance tab fitted to the rudder had caused a significant improvement in the aircraft's directional characteristics as the changes in trim could be comfortably held on the rudder without the need for constant re-trimming.

Following the trials carried out with the batch of converted Spitfire VIIIs, the first production Spitfire XIV to be tested at A&AEE was RB141 from 14–20 November 1943. This aircraft featured a revised fin that was much more aesthetically pleasing than the straight-edged fin of the prototypes. As much information had already been gathered on the Spitfire XIV, the report into RB141 only commented on the modifications that had been introduced on production aircraft.

In general the cockpit layout was similar to that on other marks of Spitfire, however, there was one major change. A new type of box was fitted for the engine controls which gave a much bigger throttle lever travel and incorporated the carburettor cut-out control and a new type of friction locking device. In operation, the new system was very much liked and it was found that the throttle controlled the boost smoothly and fine adjustments were possible. The controls were so arranged that the throttle and propeller control levers could be grasped and moved together, enabling power changes to be made much more quickly. The friction lock worked very well and the cut-out control was in a more convenient position.

One item on the Spitfire XIV that came in for criticism, however, was the lack of mechanical visual-indicators that protruded through the wings to tell the pilot that the undercarriage leg was in the down position. These had been a feature on previous aircraft, but on the Mark

XIV the only indication that the undercarriage was down was by the electrical indicators in the cockpit. It was felt that a direct indication of undercarriage position was of great benefit to the pilot, particularly in times of emergency, and their reintroduction was recommended.

As on other marks of Spitfire which incorporated a Bendix carburettor, engine starting was a matter of practice and dexterity. After priming the engine, the wobble pump had to be used to obtain the required fuel pressure, however, the pressure tended to drop as soon as the pilot stopped pumping which required periodic re-pumping. The cut-out, which was spring loaded, had to be held back whilst the Coffman starter button was pressed and as the engine fired, the throttle needed to be adjusted. While all this was going on the stick had to be held fully back with the knees. Although this technique would become natural with time, it was felt by A&AEE that any simplification would be welcome.

The handling characteristics of RB141 were very similar to those of JF319 except that there was a decrease in the directional trim change with speed as a result of the revised fin. This was most noticeable during all-out dives to 470 mph IAS as it was found that the reduced trim change could easily be held on the rudder which made re-trimming unnecessary. Despite the absence of reflexing on the ailerons, lateral control was heavier than expected. This was put down to manufacturing differences between individual sets of ailerons as it was quite common for the weight to vary quite significantly. This did not go down too well with the test pilots at A&AEE who felt that the heavy lateral control caused by an inferior pair of ailerons should have been picked up during production testing.

After spending time at Boscombe Down, RB141 was delivered to AFDU at Wittering on 28 January 1944, but as this aircraft was not up to full production standard a tactical trial had to be put on hold for a month pending the arrival of RB179. When the trial eventually got underway AFDU pilots found the handling characteristics to be similar to the Spitfire IX in most respects although the need to trim directionally, and to a lesser extent longitudinally, following throttle alterations was still apparent despite the use of servo-operated trim tabs. To prevent loss of control on take off it was recommended that the initial take off run be made using +6 lbs/sq.in boost, with full power being selected when the aircraft was nearly airborne. Elevator control had also to be used with care as there was very little propeller clearance in the tail-up attitude.

In the air the Mark XIV exhibited many of the standard Spitfire characteristics although the buffet that set in before the stall occurred a little later and consequently there was less warning. The landing run was longer and the increased weight of the XIV meant that it was less likely to float at touchdown. Unlike the Spitfire XII tested previously by AFDU, night flying was carried out with the XIV with and without exhaust blinkers fitted. The exhaust glow was brighter than that from a Spitfire IX, being a brilliant blue in colour, but in conditions of half moon it was found that the aircraft could be flown without blinkers in place, provided that the pilot's seating position was not too high. On darker nights blinkers were recommended, although these tended to restrict vision over the nose which was a particular concern at touchdown, and also made taxying at night extremely difficult. The best approach speed was found to be 120 mph IAS, engine on, which allowed the flarepath to be seen and the aircraft positioned for landing.

The bulk of the trial carried out by AFDU consisted of comparisons with other aircraft with the Spitfire IX being used to gauge the amount by which the XIV had advanced in performance terms. At all heights the Spitfire XIV was discovered to be 30–35 mph faster than the IX and it also had a slightly better climb rate which was the best that had been seen by AFDU up to that time. Due to its increased power and weight the XIV was also superior in the dive. As regards turning circle and rate of roll, the two aircraft were virtually identical.

The Spitfire XIV was also compared with a Tempest V. As the Tempest was in its prime at low to medium levels, it was no great surprise when it proved to be the quicker of the two aircraft by around 20 mph up to 10,000 ft. Both aircraft were evenly matched from this height up to 22,000 ft, but at higher altitudes the Spitfire XIV showed a marked superiority, being 30–40 mph faster. It also had a much higher service ceiling and was still effective at 40,000 ft whereas the Tempest had reached its limit at 30,000 ft. The climb rate of the Spitfire XIV was also vastly superior, although the Tempest did hold the advantage during zoom climbs and it could also pull away in the dive. The Spitfire XIV could out-perform the Tempest with ease during sustained turns and it also possessed a better rate of roll at speeds below 300 mph IAS, although this advantage was reversed at speeds above 350 mph IAS. Comparative test with a Mustang III showed both aircraft to be virtually identical in terms of top speed. The Spitfire XIV had a better climb rate but lost out in the dive, although the Mustang's advantage was not as marked as that of the Tempest. Turning circles and rate of roll also favoured the Spitfire XIV but it could not compare when it came to range, the Mustang having twice the endurance of the Spitfire when both were fitted with overload tanks, two 62½ gal drop tanks for the Mustang and one 90 gal slipper tank for the Spitfire.

The opportunity was also taken to test the Spitfire XIV against captured examples of the Messerschmitt Bf 109G and Focke-Wulf Fw 190A. Although both these machines had been 'acquired' some time before, the results at least gave some indication as to how a Spitfire XIV was likely to fare when confronted with the latest variants in combat. Compared with the Bf 109G, the Spitfire XIV was around 25 mph faster up to 16,000 ft, but at this height, which was the rated altitude of the 109, its advantage was cut to only 10 mph. Above this height the Spitfire's superiority was reasserted and by 30,000 ft it was nearly 50 mph faster. The Spitfire XIV also had a markedly superior rate of climb at all heights except when operating near to the 109's rated altitude when there was little to choose between the two. When both aircraft were placed in a dive with engines throttled back and then put into a climbing attitude, their rate of climb was virtually identical. When using maximum power in the dive, however, the Spitfire XIV easily left the 109 when a climb was initiated. Comparative dives showed the 109 to have an initial edge but this advantage was lost as speed built up above 380 mph IAS. As was to be expected, the Spitfire XIV was much the better of the two when it came to turning circles, the degree of superiority being even more marked when turning to the right due to the greater power of the Griffon and the fact that the airscrews rotated in opposite directions. In the rolling plane the Spitfire was again superior at all speeds.

Against the Fw 190 the Spitfire XIV was faster at all heights by up to 60 mph, although this advantage was cut to 20 mph from sea level up to 5,000 ft and in the height band 15–20,000 ft. The Spitfire XIV had a much better rate of climb and it could also out-turn the 190 with ease. The Focke-Wulf fared better in the dive, pulling away in the initial stages, and its rate of roll was very much quicker thanks to its large ailerons and excellent lateral control. However, in air combat these advantages were largely of a defensive nature and any Spitfire XIV pilot (assuming he avoided being bounced) had little to fear if he used his aircraft's speed, rate of climb and turn performance to the full.

Further spinning trials were carried out at Boscombe Down in March 1944 using RB146 which was specially fitted for the occasion with a tail parachute and a guard around the rudder horn. Spins of up to three turns were made at three different CG positions representing a normal fighter loading, the design forward limit and the aftmost loading as determined by trials carried out by Supermarine. All spins were entered from a straight stall followed by the application of full rudder in the direction of the intended spin. In all cases when the rudder was applied the aircraft rolled well over through about 135 degrees with the nose well down. It then rolled back to an even keel while pitching longitudinally, the periods of pitch and roll being identical. The spin was fast for the first three-quarters of a spin with the nose well below the horizon but it then began to rise and the rotation almost stopped at the end of the turn, by which time the nose was just above the horizon. There was a tendency for the opposite wing to drop and for the aircraft to yaw in the opposite sense to the direction of the spin before the nose dropped again and a replica of the first turn occurred.

Recovery was easily accomplished by applying full opposite rudder and easing the control column forward. If recovery was initiated at the end of the turn, when rotation had momentarily stopped, it was immediate and straightforward. If, however, it was initiated at any other phase of the spin when rotation was appreciable, up to three-quarters of a turn was needed before recovery was complete. Control forces were rated as being moderate during all phases of the spin. A certain amount of buffeting was noted coming from the elevators and rudder on the entry to the spin, and also towards the end of each turn when the nose was at its highest position. Aileron buffet was also apparent in the nose-high attitude following each turn. The spinning characteristics were not noticeably affected by movement of the CG or the height at which the spin was initiated. Spinning to the right was slightly more violent than spinning to the left, the entry being steeper and quicker, the characteristics otherwise being identical.

The Spitfire XIV was also adapted for the fighter-reconnaissance role as the FR.XIV which featured clipped wings, a rear-mounted fuel tank of 33 gallons capacity and an F.24 camera installation also housed in the rear fuselage for oblique photography. Late production examples were also delivered with cut-back rear fuselages and teardrop canopies. As this variant regularly flew with external 'slipper' tanks of up to 90 gallons under the centre section to extend its range, further testing was necessary to determine the extent to which the aircraft's handling characteristics had been affected by the increase in all-up weight and the change in CG position. With the rear tank full of fuel, the FR.XIV weighed in at 8,970 lbs and with a full drop tank in addition it weighed 9,760 lbs.

Trials were carried out at Boscombe Down in March/April 1945 with Spitfire FR.XIV MV247 to assess its suitability as a fighter-reconnaissance aircraft, particularly its behaviour at low altitude. With full internal fuel (including the rear fuselage tank) the aircraft was longitudinally stable at all speeds up to 15,000 ft. Above this height it became less stable and a tendency for it to tighten in turns, which had first been apparent when tested at 12,000 ft, was noticeably worse. With the rear tank full, the FR.XIV was considered unsatisfactory for service use above 15,000 ft as it exhibited light stick forces per 'g' and the degree of tightening in turns was unacceptable. If fuel from the rear tank was used up, however, the aircraft became progressively more stable in all manoeuvres. By the time that only a few gallons remained in the rear tank there was no sign of tightening in turns, even up to 25,000 ft. Directionally, there was a large change in trim with power and a still larger change with speed. There was also considerable interaction between yaw and pitch, similar to that experienced with initial testing of the Spitfire F.21 (see Chapter Six). Although the directional characteristics of the FR.XIV were far from ideal, overall it was felt that there were no particular features that might render the aircraft dangerous in service.

With the 90 gallon drop tank in place there was little change in longitudinal stability and if the rear tank was used from take off, stability was satisfactory at all altitudes up to 28,000 ft. Directional stability was a different matter and required very accurate flying to keep the aircraft in balanced flight. When the aircraft was climbed at 2,600 rpm and +9 lbs/sq.in boost, full left rudder trim was required to keep at a trimmed speed of 170 mph IAS. If speed was increased to 180 mph IAS the aircraft yawed strongly to the left and a large rudder force was needed to check this. If on the other hand speed was reduced to 160 mph IAS there was a yaw to the right which required a moderately heavy rudder force to maintain flight without sideslip. A fine balance was thus needed to fly straight with constant re-trimming of the rudder.

When a left hand climbing turn with feet off was made, and the bank reversed to the right by use of opposite aileron, the rudder tended to move over to nearly full left as the aircraft started to bank to the right. In this condition the aircraft was banking to the right while turning to the left. Further cases of rudder overbalance were noted during trimmed climbs at best climbing speed resulting in the trimmer being centralised and the aircraft flown with a continuous foot load. This was extremely tiring for the pilot and made the aircraft unpleasant to fly. When the aircraft was trimmed for cruising flight at 240 mph IAS it tended to yaw from side to side, accompanied by a rolling motion. Continuous re-trimming was necessary during flight as a small change of speed had a large effect on directional trim.

The aircraft was also dived to 320 mph IAS with the drop tank fitted. In this condition directional stability improved slightly but the rudder was still found to be very light. At low altitudes buffeting began to be felt from the tank as speed was built up to 380 mph IAS and this had become severe by the time that 400 mph IAS was reached. Although A&AEE concluded that the Spitfire FR.XIV equipped with a 90 gallon drop tank could be used safely up to 15,000 ft, it was recommended that flying in this configuration be limited to conditions of good visibility as the adverse effects on directional stability made it dangerous to fly in close formation or when instrument flying was required.

One of the last handling trials to be carried out on the Spitfire XIV at A&AEE involved RB146 which by March 1945 had been fitted with piano-hinge type ailerons with geared tabs to provide the necessary balance in lieu of the normal nose balance. It was hoped that this new type of aileron would provide a substantial improvement in the Mark

XIV's manoeuvrability and lateral control. The aircraft was flown at a take off weight of 8,560 lbs and the tests comprised the assessment of lateral control throughout the full speed range and at heights up to 40,000 ft. It was found that aileron control at low speeds, although still satisfactory, was not as good as that obtained on previous aircraft and at speeds near the stall the ailerons became rather sloppy and were much less effective than the standard ailerons. As speed was increased, however, up to 360 mph IAS, the ailerons became light and effective, although they tended to become heavier at speeds approaching 450 mph IAS. At speeds above 400 mph IAS it was also noticed that more force was required to turn to the right than to the left. In general, except at low speeds, the ailerons were lighter and more effective than the standard nose-balanced ailerons.

# CHAPTER FOUR

# Spitfire XVIII

Although the Spitfire was to be developed to a greater degree than any other aircraft of the period, this process was anything but orderly with operational requirements taking priority and resulting in the adaptation of existing variants to perform specific tasks as temporary stop-gaps. Just as the Spitfire IX had been produced quickly pending development of the Mark VIII, so the Spitfire XIV was rushed into service and was produced in significantly greater numbers than the Mark XVIII which was specifically designed around the Griffon engine. Such was the workload at Supermarine that the Spitfire XVIII did not appear until shortly before the end of the war and a total of 300 were eventually made, these being shipped overseas for use in the fighter-reconnaissance and fighter-bomber roles.

Externally the Spitfire XVIII was virtually indistinguishable from a late low-back Mark XIV with teardrop canopy, however, there were significant differences as far as the mainplane was concerned. The wing of the Spitfire XIV could be traced back to that of the Mark VC but that of the XVIII was entirely new and much stronger, consisting of solid spar booms instead of tubular booms of laminated square section. The undercarriage was also strengthened to cater for an increase in all-up weight brought about by the use of two rear-mounted fuel tanks of 33 gallons in the fighter version. This was reduced to one extra fuel tank in the FR variant to allow two F.24 cameras to be fitted vertically in the rear fuselage, with another for oblique photography, or one vertical F.52. Early Spitfire XVIIIs were powered by a Griffon 65 as fitted to the Mark XIV but later aircraft featured a Griffon 67 of 2,340 hp which turned a Rotol constant-speed propeller of 35 degree pitch range.

Armament for both the fighter and fighter-reconnaissance versions comprised two 20 mm Hispano cannon and two 0.50 in Browning machine-guns. The ammunition boxes were built into the wings and held 250 rounds for each 0.50 in gun and 120 rounds for each 20 mm cannon. Provision was also made for the Spitfire XVIII to carry up to three 500-lb bombs, one under each wing and one on an adapter in the drop tank fitting under the fuselage. The fuselage was of standard all-metal, stressed-skin construction with four main longerons, oval and U-shaped frames and intercostals for stiffening the light alloy skin. The tail end of the fuselage was a separate unit with an integral fin and was bolted to the main structure. The wings were also of all-metal, stressed-skin construction with a main and auxiliary spar, and were attached direct to the fuselage as there was no centre section. Split flaps were fitted between the inboard end of the ailerons and the wing roots. The tailplane was of similar construction to the wings, the two halves being bolted to the fuselage. Rudder and elevator surfaces were metal and fitted with trimming tabs.

The undercarriage consisted of two separate cantilever main wheels and a tail wheel unit, the latter being retractable. The shock absorber struts were oleo-pneumatic and the main wheels had pneumatic brakes. When retracted, the main units were enclosed by fairings on the struts and the tail wheel by doors in the fuselage. The flying controls had a conventional spade-grip type control column with individual rudder pedals and were connected to the ailerons, elevators and rudder by cables. The rudder pedals had two positions and were adjustable for reach. Trimming tabs for the rudder and elevator were controlled via hand wheels mounted on the port side of the cockpit and operated through chains and cables. The flaps were pneumatically operated.

The Griffon 67 engine was mounted on two cantilever beams constructed of extruded channel booms and light-alloy side plates. Each beam was attached to a lug on the datum (top) longeron and was supported by a stay tube fitted to each beam and the bottom of the bulkhead. It had a two-speed, two-stage supercharger with intercooler and was interchangeable. The two main fuel tanks were housed one above the other between the cockpit and the bulkhead with two auxiliary tanks located in the leading edge of each wing near the root end. The F.XVIII had two further tanks in the rear fuselage just aft of the cockpit, these being mounted in similar fashion to the main tanks, however, on the FR.XVIII the lower tank of the two was deleted to allow space for a camera installation. In addition a long-range drop tank of 30, 45, 50 or 90 gallon capacity could be fitted under the fuselage and jettisoned when empty. The oil tank was mounted in the top of the fuselage between the top main fuel tank and the bulkhead.

The pneumatic system was supplied with compressed air from two storage bottles which were kept charged by an engine driven compressor. This operated the split flaps, the gun cocking and firing mechanism, the supercharger gear change, cine camera, radiator flaps and the main wheel brakes. The hydraulic system was powered by an engine driven pump and worked the undercarriage retraction system, the tail wheel doors being opened and closed automatically by mechanical links. A back-up system was provided which used compressed carbon dioxide to lower the main wheels in an emergency. Electrical services were powered via an engine driven generator and the aircraft was fitted with an R/T set capable of beam approach and an IFF (Identification, Friend or Foe) box. Other equipment included windscreen de-icing, oxygen supply and provision for a signal discharger in the rear fuselage.

The radiators for the main cooling system were carried in identical fairings under each wing. On the port wing the main radiator was located in front of the oil cooler, the corresponding radiator on the starboard wing being mounted behind the intercooler radiator. Both radiators were served by a thermostatically controlled flap to regulate the flow of air, the header tank for the main cooling system being positioned over the reduction gear casing at the front of the engine. The coolant used was a mixture of 70 per cent distilled water and 30 per cent ethylene glycol, and passed from the header tank, along each side of the engine, then through the leading edge fillets to the radiator situated under each wing. From the radiators, return pipes led to the coolant pump on the engine. Coolant from the pump then passed through the engine and back to the header tank.

The intercooling system reduced the temperature of the fuel-air mixture from the supercharger before it reached the cylinders. From the header tank, which was incorporated with the intercooler itself at the rear of the engine, a pipe led to an auxiliary coolant pump on the starboard side of the engine. The pump delivered coolant to the same specification as that of the main system through the supercharger casing and through a pipe to the intercooler radiator under the starboard wing. On return from the radiator the coolant passed through the intercooler before returning to the header tank.

In the cockpit the controls for the throttle, fuel cut-off and propeller were in a single quadrant bolted to the datum longeron and located on the pilot's left. The top edge of the quadrant carried a rail to provide a hand rest to assist him in making smooth throttle movements. Also located on the throttle lever hand grip was a gyro gunsight range control, together with a bomb and RP firing button, the latter also being used to operate the oblique camera on fighter-reconnaissance aircraft. A friction damper was provided for the throttle control and was operated by means of a lever on the inboard end of the spindle. The propeller control consisted of a lever on the inboard side of the throttle quadrant and was connected to the constant-speed unit on the engine by a Teleflex cable. Fuel cut-off was via a spring-loaded lever on the outboard side of the throttle quadrant which was linked to the throttle by a Bowden cable. A stop was provided at the aft end of the gate for the fuel cut-off position [for the layout of all controls and instruments of the Spitfire XVIII, see the cockpit diagrams at the end of this chapter].

The supercharger was operated automatically by an altitude switch. This energised a solenoid and caused it to admit compressed air to a pneumatic ram which was connected to the supercharger gear change lever. When the aircraft was climbing, the supercharger gear changed from medium (MS) to full supercharge (FS) when it reached the height for which the altitude switch was set, the gear then changing back to MS again when descending through the same level. The two main fuel tanks were interconnected, as were the two rear tanks on the F.XVIII. Electrical fuel booster pumps were fitted in the bases of the bottom main and rear tanks and were controlled from the cockpit. Contents gauges were fitted, one showing the combined contents of the two main tanks, and the other the total amount of fuel remaining in the rear tanks. The top main fuel tank was rectangular in plan, but semi-circular in front elevation, and was mounted on four brackets on the top longerons. It held 36 gallons of fuel but was not self-sealing, a 10 SWG detachable fairing panel over the top affording armour protection. The bottom main tank held 48 gallons and was self-sealing. The other fuel tanks were all self-sealing, the rear tanks holding 33 gallons each and the wings tanks, which were situated between ribs 5 and 8 in the leading edge, each holding 12½ gallons. Cockpit controls for the drop tank consisted of two levers in a quadrant mounted low down to the pilot's right, one lever for jettisoning the tank and the other to control the fuel cock. These two levers were interconnected to make it impossible to jettison the tank with the fuel cock lever in anything other than the OFF position.

The reconnaissance version of the Spitfire XVIII carried three F.24 cameras, one oblique and two vertical, in the rear fuselage between frames 13 and 15. These were electrically operated and were controlled from the cockpit. To prevent misting of the camera windows, warm air was passed through ducts from the aft end of the starboard radiator to the camera positions in the fuselage. This warm air was then retained in the camera compartment by plywood bulkheads and temperature could be monitored by the pilot on a gauge mounted on the starboard side of the cockpit. The vertical cameras were carried on Type 45 mountings, each attached to two rails which were fixed in turn to lateral bearers secured to the fuselage frames. Apertures were built into the underside of the fuselage, the forward camera facing 10 degrees to starboard and the aft camera 10 degrees to port of the aircraft centreline.

Above the vertical camera installation was the oblique camera which could be mounted to face either port or starboard. The mounting assembly consisted of a ring hinged between two vertical channel brackets to give angular adjustment in the vertical plane. This was then attached to a base tray, the tray having circular slots to permit the mounting assembly to be similarly adjusted horizontally. The tray itself

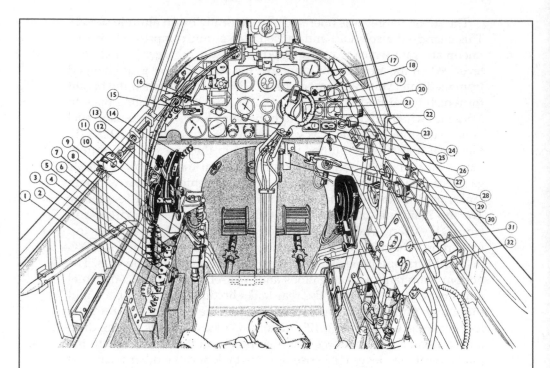

Fig 1 – Engine Controls and Instruments

1  Fuel pump master switch
2  Main tank booster pump test button
3  Rear tank booster pump test button
4  Booster pump test socket
5  Supercharger ground test button
6  Radiator flap test button
7  Oil dilution system button
8  Air intake control: FILTER – forward;
                   NON-FILTER – AFT
9  Rear tank fuel cock
10 Throttle lever: SHUT – aft; TAKE OFF – At stop;
             COMBAT – Forward
11 Throttle damper
12 Fuel transfer selector cock
13 Fuel cut-off; FOR CUT-OFF – Aft into gate
14 Propeller (interconnected with throttle)
     AUTOMATIC – At stop
     INCREASE RPM – (Without increased boost)
     Forward
     REDUCE RPM – (Emergency only). Aft beyond
     stop. When in this position, throttle must not be
     moved forward.

15 Ignition switches
16 Starter button
17 Engine speed indicator
18 Fuel pressure warning lamp (set at 10 lbs/sq.in)
19 Supercharger gear change switch and warning lamp
20 Boost gauge
21 Oil temperature gauge
22 Radiator temperature gauge
23 Oil pressure gauge
24 Low fuel level warning lamp
25 Main fuel tanks contents gauge
26 Rear fuel tanks contents gauge
27 Priming selector cock
28 Starter breech control
29 Priming pump
30 Main fuel cock control
31 Drop tank cock control
32 Drop tank jettison handle PULL – (with cock
control forward)

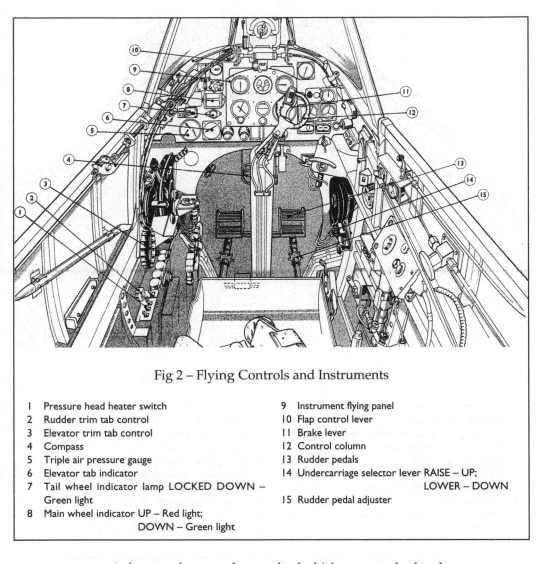

Fig 2 – Flying Controls and Instruments

| | | | |
|---|---|---|---|
| 1 | Pressure head heater switch | 9 | Instrument flying panel |
| 2 | Rudder trim tab control | 10 | Flap control lever |
| 3 | Elevator trim tab control | 11 | Brake lever |
| 4 | Compass | 12 | Control column |
| 5 | Triple air pressure gauge | 13 | Rudder pedals |
| 6 | Elevator tab indicator | 14 | Undercarriage selector lever RAISE – UP; |
| 7 | Tail wheel indicator lamp LOCKED DOWN – | | LOWER – DOWN |
| | Green light | 15 | Rudder pedal adjuster |
| 8 | Main wheel indicator UP – Red light; | | |
| | DOWN – Green light | | |

was carried on two bearer tubes, each of which was attached to the port and starboard datum longerons.

In marked contrast to previous versions of the Spitfire, the Mark XVIII underwent only limited testing at Boscombe Down as its performance and handling were virtually identical to the earlier Spitfire XIV. NH872 underwent brief handling trials in August 1945 with a 99-gallon drop tank and to determine the aftmost CG when both of the rear fuselage fuel tanks were full. Three months later TP279 was used for camera installation and gun heating trials in which some vibration was noted in the camera assembly which was liable to come into contact with the

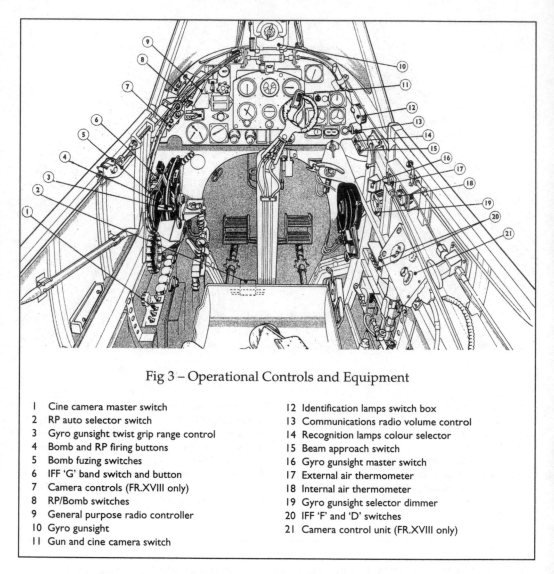

Fig 3 – Operational Controls and Equipment

1   Cine camera master switch
2   RP auto selector switch
3   Gyro gunsight twist grip range control
4   Bomb and RP firing buttons
5   Bomb fuzing switches
6   IFF 'G' band switch and button
7   Camera controls (FR.XVIII only)
8   RP/Bomb switches
9   General purpose radio controller
10  Gyro gunsight
11  Gun and cine camera switch

12  Identification lamps switch box
13  Communications radio volume control
14  Recognition lamps colour selector
15  Beam approach switch
16  Gyro gunsight master switch
17  External air thermometer
18  Internal air thermometer
19  Gyro gunsight selector dimmer
20  IFF 'F' and 'D' switches
21  Camera control unit (FR.XVIII only)

viewing windows. In May 1948 TP423 carried out a trial of the Mark 4B gyro gunsight which was considered satisfactory.

As regards performance, the Spitfire XVIII had maximum speeds of 402 mph TAS at 11,000 ft in MS gear and 437 mph TAS at 24,500 ft in FS gear. The sea level rate of climb in MS gear was 4,120 ft/min and in FS gear was 3,480 ft/min at 17,500 ft. Thereafter the climb rate fell away significantly so that at 30,000 ft it was only 480 ft/min. The normal take off weight was 8,861 lbs with a maximum permissible weight of 9,100 lbs, however, in certain circumstances the aircraft could be flown at the

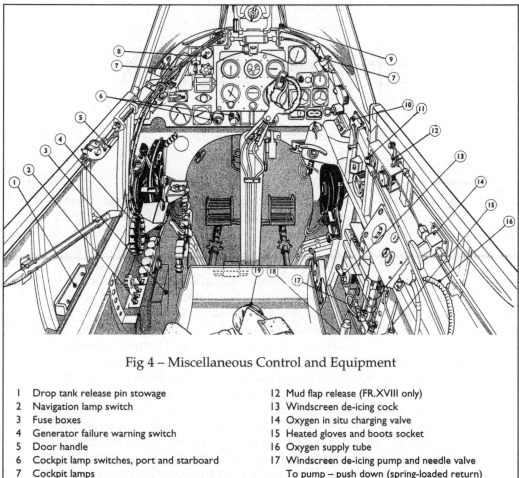

Fig 4 – Miscellaneous Control and Equipment

| | |
|---|---|
| 1 Drop tank release pin stowage | 12 Mud flap release (FR.XVIII only) |
| 2 Navigation lamp switch | 13 Windscreen de-icing cock |
| 3 Fuse boxes | 14 Oxygen in situ charging valve |
| 4 Generator failure warning switch | 15 Heated gloves and boots socket |
| 5 Door handle | 16 Oxygen supply tube |
| 6 Cockpit lamp switches, port and starboard | 17 Windscreen de-icing pump and needle valve |
| 7 Cockpit lamps | To pump – push down (spring-loaded return) |
| 8 Oxygen regulator | 18 Seat adjusting handle – Depress top button to |
| 9 Spare lamps for gyro gunsight | release |
| 10 Hood winding gear – Pull inboard to unlock | 19 Safety harness |
| 11 Safety harness release | |

maximum overload figure of 11,000 lbs. Of the total production run of 300 aircraft, 200 were FR.XVIIIs and the variant saw action in the Middle and Far East before it flew its last operational sortie in Malaya on 1 January 1951.

The layout of the cockpit of the Spitfire XVIII is shown in the diagrams on pages 38–41.

# CHAPTER FIVE

# Spitfire PR.XIX

The Spitfire had not been in service with the RAF for very long when it began to be considered as a high-speed, photo-reconnaissance machine. The first PR Spitfires (N3069 and N3071) were delivered to Sidney Cotton's Heston Flight in October 1939, and were standard Mark Is with two F.24 cameras replacing the normal eight-gun armament. Following the success of high-level reconnaissance missions over Germany towards the end of 1939 a further batch of Spitfire Is were converted to carry out similar duties over occupied Europe with extra fuel tankage to increase range. By the summer of 1940 the Photographic Reconnaissance Unit had been formed and the flying carried out by PRU was to be vital to the war effort. The most numerous early PR variant of the Spitfire was the PR.Mk1D (Merlin 45) which was eventually re-designated PR.IV, production coming to an end after 229 had been built. The ultimate Merlin-engined PR Spitfire was the Mark XI which was produced in greater numbers than any other reconnaissance variant, a total of 476 eventually being built. With an internal fuel capacity of 217 gallons, which could be supplemented by a 30, 45 or 90-gallon slipper tank under the fuselage, the PR.XI had the range to carry out deep penetration missions over Germany to bring back target information and to check on the damage caused by the Allied bomber offensive.

Just as the Merlin-engined Spitfire had become one of the most significant reconnaissance machines of the period, the use of the Griffon engine opened up the tantalising prospect of being able to extend the boundaries still further. Such increased capability was urgently needed as *Luftwaffe* defences were continually being improved and were making life very difficult for PRU pilots. The PR.XIX was a development of the Spitfire XIV and all but the first twenty-two aircraft were powered by a 2,035 hp Griffon 66 which operated a Marshall XIV blower to pressurise the cockpit, a similar installation to the earlier PR.X (Merlin 64). The wings were as those of the PR.X and XI except that the 66-gallon leading edge tanks were augmented by inter-spar tanks of 19 gallons which gave an overall internal fuel capacity of 254 gallons (three times that of the Spitfire I). It was normal operational procedure to fly with a slipper tank of up to 90 gallons capacity, and even the oversized 170 gallon tank was carried on occasion. As befitting a photo-reconnaissance machine, no armament was fitted, the camera installation comprising two F.52, two F.8 or two F.24 vertical cameras. With the latter an oblique F.24 could also be carried, generally viewing to port although it could be made to face to starboard if required.

The first non-pressurised PR.XIXs (Griffon 65) were delivered to 541 and 542 Squadrons in May/June 1944 to supplement the PR.Xs and PR.XIs which were already being used on deep penetration sorties into Germany. The first definitive PR.XIX was SW777 which was used as the prototype for all subsequent machines. On 5 February 1945 Spitfire PR.XIX PS858 was delivered to A&AEE for handling trials with and without 90 and 170 gallon slipper tanks. The latter was an oversize drop tank which had first been developed for the delivery of Spitfires direct from Gibraltar to Malta in late 1942. In the clean configuration PS858 was tested with full internal fuel at a take off weight of 8,985 lbs (loading 1) and with the wing leading edge tanks empty at a weight of 8,025 lbs which was the aft CG position (loading 2). With full internal fuel and the 90 gallon slipper tank in place weight had gone up to 9,750 lbs (loading 3) and with the 170 gallon tank fitted it was 10,400 lbs (loading 4).

On arrival at Boscombe Down the external condition of PS858 was found to be good with all panels and cowlings fitting tightly. It featured circular camera windows in the fuselage, one underneath and one in each side, just aft of the cockpit and came complete with a pressure cabin and Malcolm-type hood. The tail unit was similar to that fitted to the Spitfire XIV with a fabric-covered, horn-balanced rudder which was fitted with a combined trimmer and balance tab. Friction in the rudder circuit was such that a force of 15 lbs was required to move the rudder pedals steadily backwards or forwards. The elevators were also fabric-covered with trimmer tabs and on the ground the pilot had to apply a 5½ lbs force to bring the control column fully back. The ailerons were metal with the usual nose-balance, requiring a 3 lb force to over-come friction and move the controls to their fullest extent.

The trials conducted were made up of general handling to test the suitability of the PR.XIX for the photo-reconnaissance role to include take off, climb, level flight and dives. Particular attention was paid to the behaviour of the aircraft at high altitudes and at high Mach numbers. Some brief quantitative stick free static stability tests, consisting of measuring the stick forces required to change speed at various trimmed conditions, were also carried out at 10,000 ft and 25,000 ft with the aircraft in the clean configuration.

The results of qualitative handling tests showed that the PR.XIX was easy to taxy at all loadings with good all-round visibility and effective brakes. Take off was normal even at the heaviest weight although it was recommended that a runway be used when the 90 or 170 gallon drop tanks were fitted as acceleration was poor and the run was long. During the initial climb the 'hunting' that had been reported on earlier Griffon Spitfires was still apparent in bumpy air, although in the report on the PR.XIX it was referred to as 'twitching'. At loading 1 when flying at low altitude the aircraft could be trimmed to fly 'hands off' for long periods at 170 mph IAS, the best climbing speed. At 33,000 ft with the aircraft trimmed for the best climbing speed at that height (150 mph IAS) small oscillations in pitch were noted when the control column was released. With the control column held at this speed there was a tendency to pitch which made the aircraft rather unpleasant to fly, but this characteristic gradually eased with increase in speed until it had disappeared altogether at 170 mph IAS. Tests at loading 2 were similar, except that the pitching oscillations at high altitude were slightly worse. Once again these tended to diminish with increase in speed but a considerable loss in climb performance was incurred as a result.

At loading 3 with the 90 gallon drop tank in place there was a definite deterioration in the aircraft's directional handling characteristics and its longitudinal behaviour was also slightly worse than the previous loadings. In rough air at low altitudes there was a slight tendency to oscillate in pitch and yaw but this was easily controllable. At high altitudes longitudinal and directional behaviour became much worse and above 35,000 ft the rudder had to be used continually to correct a strong tendency to sideslip in either direction. On one occasion the controls were released with the aircraft at 36,000 ft and trimmed to climb at 160 mph IAS. This led to a series of undamped oscillations in pitch, yaw and roll so that the pilot had to resume control within 5–6 seconds. The same characteristics were apparent when the aircraft was flown with the 170 gallon tank, but in each case the effects were more pronounced which made it more tiring to fly, particularly at high altitude and in rough air.

In level flight the aircraft behaved normally throughout the entire speed range at low altitudes when flown at loadings 1 and 2. At 39,000 ft it could be trimmed to fly 'hands off' at 200 mph IAS, but at 160 mph IAS it behaved as in the climb, oscillating slowly in pitch. In steep turns at low speeds there was a slight tendency to tighten up but this was not present above 200 mph IAS. The pull force required in sustained turns in either direction was noticeably less at loading 2 (aft CG) than loading 1. The minimum comfortable continuous cruising speed at 35,000 ft was about 170 mph IAS at both loadings. As in the climb, at loadings 3 and 4 continuous correction for sideslip was required when cruising at 200 mph IAS at 36,000 ft and in rough air the aircraft tended to oscillate in yaw. Even with the most careful trimming, if the controls were released, oscillations in pitch, roll and yaw quickly set in, requiring the pilot to resume control to prevent the aircraft from stalling or diving.

As the Spitfire PR.XIX was unarmed, its only method of defence was to try to stay out of range of intercepting fighters. Due to the fact that it could operate at altitudes of over 40,000 ft the PR.XIX was a very difficult target for the most advanced piston-engined fighters of the day, and even for the first generation of jet fighters. Should it be intercepted, however, the best tactic for the Spitfire pilot to adopt was to try to maintain or extend range by carrying out an elongated dive at high speed. At the high altitudes involved this brought into question the aircraft's handling characteristics at high Mach numbers and during the trial at Boscombe Down a number of dives were made at each of the four loadings.

From previous testing at RAE Farnborough with a Merlin-engined Spitfire PR.XI, it was known that the aircraft's qualities at high Mach numbers were exceptional due to the low thickness/chord ratio of the wing. Dives had been made up to Mach 0.89 (not without mishap it has to be said) which was far in excess of any other piston-engined fighter of the period. The PR.XIX was to prove to be just as good. At loading 1 the aircraft was trimmed for level flight at 220 mph IAS (+2 lbs/sq.in boost, 2,600 rpm) before being put into a dive from 39,000 ft. At 270 mph the push force needed to maintain the angle of dive was heavy and at 350 mph IAS (30,000 ft, Mach 0.80) it was considered to be excessive. On releasing the control column at 350 mph IAS, normal acceleration built up rapidly and the accelerometer reading would have exceeded 5g if the pilot had not taken over control. The push force needed to limit the increase in 'g' was moderate. Dives were also carried out with the aircraft trimmed into the dive. Starting from level flight at 35,000 ft and 240 mph IAS (+4 lbs/sq.in boost, 2,600 rpm, trimmer set to 1½ divisions nose heavy) the aircraft was dived to 350 mph IAS at which speed 4 divisions of nose heavy trim was required. Recovery was effected by a moderate pull force resulting in accelerations of no more than 3g.

The highest Mach number attained during the dives was about 0.825 [for comparison the Meteor F.4 was limited in service to Mach 0.78]. This was obtained at a speed of 345 mph IAS at 32,500 ft, the aircraft showing no adverse handling characteristics at all. No buffeting was apparent during any of the dives or recoveries. One aspect of handling was commented upon, the fact that aileron control was much lighter at high altitudes than it was below 10,000 ft. There was also a tendency for the control to overbalance at speeds above 250 mph IAS. In an attempt to remedy this it was recommended that the droop of the ailerons be increased. This would tend to make the control heavier at low altitudes, but it would improve the harmony between the elevator and aileron controls which was considered to be poor, particularly at high altitudes.

Quantitative handling tests were also carried out in which measurements of the stick force required to change speed at 10,000 ft and 25,000 ft were made with the aircraft trimmed for various speeds, with CG at the forward and aft positions. These proved the aircraft to be statically stable, stick free, at nearly all of the conditions tested. The only exception occurred with the aft CG loading at 25,000 ft at speeds below 175 mph IAS, although above this speed it was stable.

In its summing up, A&AEE reported that the PR.XIX was pleasant to fly over its normal speed and height range without external tanks. With the 90 gallon tank fitted, however, there was a large change of directional trim with speed and its behaviour in the yawing plane at high altitude was bad. With the 170 gallon tank in place handling characteristics deteriorated even further. Although the aircraft was unpleasant to fly in this condition it was not considered to be dangerous in the hands of an experienced pilot. Manoeuvres with either drop tank had to be gentle and ideally the fuel contained in the tanks was to be used immediately after take off so that the tanks could be jettisoned as soon as possible.

Unlike its fighter equivalent, the PR.XIX saw widespread use by front line units after the end of the Second World War and was finally retired by 81 Squadron on 1 April 1954 when the last operational sortie by an RAF Spitfire was made in Malaya. The point should be made that this photo-reconnaissance version of the Spitfire was fulfilling the role on merit during this period, and not because it had been forced to linger on as there was nothing else available. Although jet-powered fighters had taken over at lower levels, it was a different story at 40,000 ft plus, the heights at which the PR.XIX normally operated. At these heights Meteor pilots were having to tread very carefully as indicated airspeed was beginning to fall rather alarmingly (even though true airspeed remained the same) and any significant manoeuvring was likely to lead to a further reduction in IAS and a possible stall/spin situation. With its lower wing loading the PR.XIX was much happier at altitude and on a good day could even be coaxed up to 49,000 ft which endowed it with fair degree of invulnerability over the first generation of jet fighters which also had a relatively short endurance. In addition, radar cover at such heights was not complete which placed even more of a burden on the fighter.

To discover more about the best way to deal with high-flying photo-reconnaissance aircraft (and also to determine the best defensive tactics for such machines), the Central Fighter Establishment (CFE) at West Raynham conducted a trial in 1949 in which Spitfire PR.XIXs were intercepted by Meteors and Vampires. To give the intercepting fighters a chance, PR pilots drawn from 541 Squadron were asked to overfly prearranged targets at 40,000 ft at a speed of 160 kts IAS. One of the most effective defensive tactics adopted by the Spitfires was to fly just above any layer in which condensation trails were likely to form so that any attacking aircraft would have to climb through this layer and could be seen relatively easily. The best tactics for the fighters were to fly as a pair and to manoeuvre so as to approach the Spitfire from its blind area below and behind, and to position themselves so as to remain out of the condensation layer 4,000 ft below and 2,000 yards astern at a speed of 0.72 Mach. At this stage the No.2 was required to move into a close echelon formation to avoid detection by the PR pilot, before the pair commenced a 'snap up' climb at full throttle to place the aircraft within firing range and slightly below the target. Although speed would be lost in the climb, by the time that an attack could be commenced a Meteor was likely to be flying at 170–180 kts IAS so it would still have a small overtake capability.

Although this type of attack was carried out successfully during the trial, it still required a high degree of co-operation between the radar controllers on the ground and the fighters. It was also found that if the condensation trail layer was thicker than 6,000 ft the fighters tended to lose too much speed during the zoom climb and were thus unable to close to gun firing range. If the fighters were able to close on the target without being seen a good tactic was for the pair to spread out in a wide line abreast formation so that whichever way the Spitfire turned, it was bound to present a relatively easy shot to one or the other. Should the fighters be seen it was best for them not to attempt to follow the Spitfire in a turn, but to maintain their speed and, if possible, to gain height before repositioning for another attack.

From the PR pilots' point of view it was best to operate at heights above 40,000 ft as much as possible as the chances of being intercepted were greatly reduced. The performance of aircraft such as the Meteor and Vampire fell away rapidly above this height and as the climb rate fell, the amount of time taken to position for an attack was such that fuel remaining was likely to become of ever-increasing importance. The Spitfire was, not surprisingly, much more manoeuvrable at altitude, although it was easy to lose height which might play into the hands of the attacking fighters. It was imperative therefore to evade any attacks, but at the same time to maintain, or even increase height if possible. Good lookout for the PR pilot was essential, especially in the vulnerable area to the rear and here it was a good idea to weave occasionally to check for fighters climbing up in the six o'clock position. As already mentioned, condensation trails were to be avoided at all costs. Occasionally these were short and non-persistent which could easily be missed, however they were just as much of a giveaway to the fighter pilot as a longer trail. If the fighters were seen in good time, PR pilots could render their attack abortive by turning through 180 degrees before range had been reduced to 800 yards which would mean that the attackers would have to spend considerable time re-positioning for another go. During this time the Spitfire pilot could either seek cloud cover or decide upon his tactics to counter the next attack.

Although it had been proved that the Spitfire PR.XIX could be successfully attacked at heights of around 40,000 ft, the chances of it being able to escape increased significantly if it could be flown higher still, as the performance of the early jet fighters and the capabilities of the ground radar organisation left a lot to be desired. It would not be until the second generation of jet fighters came along, as epitomised by the F-86 Sabre and MiG-15, that the days of the Spitfire would be numbered. Even so, a PR.XIX flying at its absolute ceiling would not have been an easy target for an F-86 which would still have been faced with a zoom climb up to the Spitfire's level and a limited amount of time to effect a successful interception before the speed fell away and it was time to head back down again. The fact that the Spitifre PR.XIX was to fulfil a useful role until the mid 1950s was a remarkable achievement for an aircraft conceived twenty years before and was testimony to the genius of its designer, R.J. Mitchell, and the skill of the team at Supermarine, led by Joe Smith, which had developed it.

# CHAPTER SIX

# Spitfire F.21/22/24

The last major re-design of the Spitfire airframe resulted in the F.21 which was to cause severe difficulties for Supermarine as some of the fine handling qualities that pilots had become accustomed to were no longer apparent. Although the earlier Griffon-powered Spitfires possessed adequate performance in terms of speed and rate of climb, it was felt that certain aspects of the aircraft's handling needed to be improved. The Spitfire had always been supreme as regards turning circles but its rate of roll was poor, particularly when compared with the Fw 190 which was able to initiate rolling manoeuvres that a Spitfire had difficulty following. This situation had been improved to an extent by clipping the wings of some variants intended for low to medium altitude operations, but it had long been recognised that the Spitfire's wing would need to be made considerably stiffer.

The basic problem was one of 'aileron-reversal' caused by the wing twisting in the opposite direction to aileron deflection due to a lack of torsional rigidity. The main structural element of the Spitfire wing was the D-shaped torsion box formed by the single spar and heavy-duty leading edge skinning. On the Mark 21 this was augmented by a number of torque-boxes behind the spar that increased stiffness by 47 per cent and upped the theoretical aileron reversal speed from 580 mph to 850 mph. As well as having a strengthened wing structure, the F.21 also featured ailerons of increased span which were attached by piano-type hinges with inset balance tabs. The main undercarriage legs were revised, the oleos being extended by 4 in to allow sufficient ground clearance for a five-blade Rotol propeller of 11 ft diameter (7 in greater than the Spitfire XIV). The legs were also placed further apart, increasing track from 5 ft 9 in to 6 ft 8 in. Fairing doors, operated hydraulically, covered the lower part of the wheel that had previously been exposed when the undercarriage was retracted. The underwing radiators of the F.21 reversed the layout as seen on the Spitfire XIV in that the oil cooler was positioned behind the main radiator under the starboard wing with the intercooler radiator ahead of the other main radiator under the port wing. Armament for the F.21 was standardised at four 20 mm Hispano cannon with power coming from a Griffon 61 of 2,035 hp, although a number were to be fitted with a Griffon 85 with a six-blade contra-rotating propeller.

The 'interim' Spitfire F.21 prototype was DP851 which had begun life as the second Spitfire XX powered by a Griffon II. With a Griffon 61 in place of the earlier engine, it re-appeared in December 1942 but still possessed standard wings, albeit modified internally and covered in thicker gauge skinning. After this aircraft was written off when it crashed on landing on 13 May 1943, the first true prototype F.21 was PP139 which was flown for the first time two months later. Like its immediate predecessor, PP139 was fitted with extended wing tips similar to those of the high-altitude Spitfire VII, however, subsequent machines had rounded tips giving a span of 36 ft 11 in. It also featured a modified windscreen with a curved front forward of the normal screen (a rear view mirror was not fitted) and a straight edged fin of greater area, together with a larger rudder.

Right from the first flight of DP851 it had been apparent that the Spitfire F.21 was likely to hit trouble. Its directional and longitudinal handling characteristics were described by Jeffrey Quill as 'appalling' and it was clear that a lot of work would be required before the aircraft could be considered suitable for an average squadron pilot to fly. The progressive lengthening of the nose to accommodate the Griffon, together with the use of larger propellers of increased blade area to absorb the extra power available, had destabilised the aircraft to an unacceptable degree. The obvious solution was to carry out a total re-design of the tailplane, but this would take time and would have a detrimental effect on production. As a short term measure Supermarine began investigating modifications to the existing tailplane, but in the meantime the trials programme for the Spitfire F.21 got underway at A&AEE at Boscombe Down and AFDU at Wittering.

As the new variant was a completely different aircraft from the original Merlin-powered Spitfire a new name was proposed and for a time it was referred to as the Victor, however, this was soon dropped and it was henceforth known merely as the Spitfire F.21. Following the demise of DP851, the first aircraft to be delivered to A&AEE was PP139 which arrived in September 1943 for an assessment of its performance [the serial number allotted to the Spitfire F.21 prototype was actually compromised as it was also carried by a Sunderland III flying-boat]. The trials were not without incident as PP139 suffered two engine failures during the two months it was at Boscombe Down, eventually being fitted with a Griffon 65 which differed from the failed engines (Griffon 61) in having 0.51 to 1 reduction gearing instead of 0.45 to 1. This tended to disrupt the trial somewhat and as a result some of the level speed data had to be obtained from just a single flight. Confirmatory flights could not be made to back up the results obtained with the Griffon 61 due to the Griffon 65's higher reduction gearing. Normally climb performance would also have been tested during the trial but, due to the engine problems that were experienced, this was not possible.

All of the tests were made at a take off weight of 9,125 lbs which was the normal weight of the aircraft when carrying full fuel and service equipment. The maximum speed of the aircraft was measured with the radiator flaps closed in MS gear at heights between 4,000 ft and 22,000 ft, and in FS gear at heights between 18,000 ft and 38,000 ft. The results achieved were as follows

| Height | 4,000 ft | 8,000 ft | 12,000 ft | 16,000 ft | 20,000 ft |
|---|---|---|---|---|---|
| TAS – mph | 390 | 412 | 434 | 433 | 430 |
| IAS – mph | 378 | 377 | 375 | 351 | 327 |

| Height | 24,000 ft | 28,000 ft | 32,000 ft | 36,000 ft | 38,000 ft |
|---|---|---|---|---|---|
| TAS – mph | 449 | 454 | 448 | 440 | 434 |
| IAS – mph | 320 | 302 | 276 | 250 | 235 |

The maximum true airspeed in MS gear was thus 434 mph at the full throttle height of 12,000 ft, and the equivalent speed in FS gear was 457 mph at 25,800 ft. It is interesting to note that with the extremely high altitudes now being attained by piston-engined fighters and the use of propellers of increased diameter, the propeller tip speed at 38,000 ft, the highest altitude tested, was extremely close to the speed of sound at Mach 0.99.

The first production Spitfire F.21 was LA187 which commenced a series of trials with the manufacturers in early 1944 prior to being delivered to A&AEE. It was immediately apparent that longitudinal stability was much worse than had been previously encountered with the earlier Griffon-Spitfires and was unlikely to be accepted by the service test pilots at Boscombe Down. For a time the aircraft also had a tendency to fly right wing low and during a terminal velocity dive on 16 August the cockpit hood and the side door departed, leaving the unfortunate pilot to endure a battering from the slipstream. In November 1944 LA187 was delivered to Boscombe Down for handling trials which included some quantitative measurements of stick forces and accelerations in high speed flight. This was the first Spitfire F.21 to be tested at A&AEE for its handling as PP139 had not been assessed in this way due to the fact that it differed in several respects from production aircraft. Unfortunately LA187 displayed undesirable handling characteristics as regards its directional behaviour. Interaction was noted between longitudinal and directional changes of trim which were considered to make it unsuitable for high altitude operation. Although Supermarine had known about this situation for some time, the level of criticism by A&AEE pilots took the firm by surprise and many in the company felt that the service was being overly critical. It was known by the RAF that modifications were already in hand at the time of the trial which was eventually abandoned pending their development, A&AEE not wishing to continue flying the machine in its original condition because of its undesirable handling qualities which were considered to be dangerous at its upper limits.

The result of qualitative testing showed that longitudinal stability was very difficult to assess due the strong interaction between directional and longitudinal changes of trim. Any yawing was accompanied by pitching, and any change of directional trim was followed by a change in longitudinal trim. The overall effect as far as the pilot was concerned was to make the aircraft very difficult to trim longitudinally. Particular difficulty was encountered during the recovery from trimmed or untrimmed dives as the aircraft could not be kept on a constant heading when 'g' was applied due to the fact that it yawed either to the left or right, together with longitudinal pitching. These tendencies became worse as height was gained and also with aft movement of the CG, but even at a normal fighter loading with full service equipment, fuel and ammunition they were sufficiently marked above 25,000 ft as to cause safety concerns. Pitching was also experienced immediately after take off during the initial climb away. Although no quantitative measurements were taken during dives at speeds in excess of 470 mph IAS, pilots found that they had to apply a heavy push force on the control column to increase speed any further, and to reach the maximum permissible speed of 520 mph IAS appreciable re-trimming in a nose-down sense was necessary.

The ailerons on LA187 had piano hinges and balance tabs as first tested on Spitfire XIV RB146 and these provided excellent lateral control, although this tended to be spoilt as the aircraft was affected laterally by the poor directional stability noted above. In straight flight without sideslip, there was no appreciable change of lateral trim with increase in speed. At high altitudes and particularly at the aftmost CG loading, quick application of aileron tended to produce initial yaw away from the direction of the ensuing turn, but in general, aileron control was considered to be good from the point of view of effectiveness and lightness of the control.

Directional stability, or lack of it, produced the most criticism, although it was felt that if it could be improved, some of the other adverse handling characteristics would be improved as well. Despite the fact that the rudder was moderately heavy, at high speeds large angles of sideslip could easily be induced inadvertently. The rudder trimmer was extremely sensitive and required a very delicate touch to prevent the aircraft from yawing. This latter characteristic was accentuated by the large change of directional trim with variations in speed, power and applied acceleration, rendering it necessary for the pilot to re-trim the aircraft frequently during manoeuvres in order to avoid what appeared to be dangerous angles of sideslip. At higher altitudes these adverse directional qualities affected longitudinal control and gave rise to a peculiar corkscrewing behaviour, particularly at high Mach numbers. The pilot did not feel comfortable at any of the loadings tested (3 in to 6 in aft of datum) when carrying out combat manoeuvres at 25,000 ft which was the aircraft's optimum performance altitude. Due to its poor directional control which also affected longitudinal handling, LA187 was considered to be unsatisfactory as a high altitude fighter.

The Spitfire F.21 was first flown by AFDU towards the end of 1944 when LA201, an early production machine, was delivered to Wittering for a tactical trial, during which it was also compared with a Spitfire XIV operating at +18 lbs/sq.in boost pressure. Although it was the most potent Spitfire yet tested by the establishment, its potential could not be utilised to the full and, like the trial already carried out at Boscombe Down, the subsequent report was highly critical in several respects.

Initial impressions at least were favourable as take off swing was found to be not quite as pronounced as that of the Spitfire XIV and with full port rudder trim set the swing could be controlled with ease, assuming the throttle was opened slowly. Using +12 lbs/sq.in boost, take of run was approximately 400 yards. Once in the air however, the first of the F.21's adverse handling characteristics became apparent as the need to re-trim directionally, together with extreme sensitivity in pitch, made it difficult to hold the aircraft in a steady climb until a speed of 180 mph IAS had been attained. Landing was straightforward, the wide track undercarriage and increased all-up weight helping to keep the aircraft on the ground.

Once again, the Spitfire F.21's instability in the yawing plane, especially at altitude and at high speed, was its biggest deficiency. The rudder was extremely sensitive to small movements and very careful flying was necessary to avoid slipping and skidding. Elevator control was better and although it was positive in action, the pilot needed to apply constant corrections to maintain attitude, particularly at low speeds and at high altitude at all speeds. In marked contrast the ailerons were superior to any previous Spitfire variant being light and positive at all heights and at all speeds up to 350 mph IAS. Above this speed aileron control did begin to become heavy, especially above 400 mph IAS. Trim tabs were fitted to the elevators and rudder and, because of the sensitivity of these controls, pilots spent much time trying to fine-tune the aircraft, especially as there was a marked reaction to changes of throttle and any speed alteration during climbs and dives.

Although the Spitfire F.21 was not unstable in pitch, above 25,000 ft the instability in yaw made it behave as though it was unstable about all three axes. All previous Spitfires had been at their best during sustained level turns, but during steep turns in the F.21 the general feeling of instability, together with critical trimming characteristics and an earlier high speed stall (due to its increased weight), combined to make for an unpleasant experience for the pilot. These undesirable qualities meant that the aircraft was difficult to fly accurately and compared unfavourably with most other fighters of the period. The excellent aileron control was spoilt by the F.21's instability in yaw and its constant need for re-trimming and as a result aerobatics were not as easy, or as pleasant, as previous marks of Spitfire. For the same reasons, formation flying was also more difficult than earlier Spitfires.

The all-round view was similar to that of the Spitfire XIV, being particularly poor straight ahead due to the longer nose of all Griffon-powered variants. This aspect was at its worst when flying at low level in poor visibility, the aircraft's basic instability only serving to increase the pilot's workload at a time when he least needed it. The slightest movement of the elevators was sufficient to cause a variation in height which in bad weather could lead to a dangerous situation developing, one which may have gone unnoticed until it was too late. During the trial at AFDU night flying was also carried out under conditions of moonlight. To avoid excessive glare when landing, it was necessary to maintain engine-on as a fully throttled back approach produced a bright exhaust glow and a stream of sparks which was liable to affect the pilot's night vision. The exhaust glow could be seen from the ground at a range of 1,000 ft and it was recommended that blinkers be fitted when flying in dark conditions.

In simulated air combat, the significant improvement made with aileron control on the Spitfire F.21 was nullified by its instability in yaw as it proved to be difficult to hold the gunsight on a target, especially if the other aircraft carried out rapid changes of direction. It was also felt that the aircraft's instability would lead to a deterioration of its capabilities as a sighting platform when it was fitted with a gyro gunsight. Although simulated ground attack could be flown successfully under trial conditions with experienced pilots, it was considered that the F.21's tendency to wander directionally would have been beyond the skills of an average pilot and, as a result, it was unsuitable for the ground attack role.

The Spitfire F.21 was compared with a Mark XIV and was found to have a slightly better range and endurance as a result of having an extra 11 gallons of internal fuel. This resulted in an improvement of 15 miles in terms of radius of action and 10 minutes in endurance. Speed tests carried out by AFDU showed that the F.21 was approximately 10–12 mph faster than the Mark XIV at all altitudes. The two aircraft were accelerated in straight and level flight from maximum cruise settings (2,400 rpm and +7 lbs/sq.in boost) and each took around 2 minutes 30 seconds to reach maximum speed. There was also little to choose between the two during climbs at maximum power (2,750 rpm and +18 lbs/sq.in boost). Up to 15,000 ft the Spitfire XIV had a slight advantage but above this height the F.21 was slightly superior. During zoom climbs, however, the F.21 had the advantage over the XIV.

In dives the F.21 pulled away from the XIV in the early stages but when a speed of 350 mph IAS had been reached the gap between the two aircraft stabilised and no further advantage was gained. Due to the F.21's undesirable handling characteristics in the turn it was inferior to the Mark XIV at all speeds and was out-turned at will. Rate of roll was similar up to 300 mph IAS but the F.21 became increasingly superior above this speed due to its lighter ailerons. Despite the F.21 being superior in several aspects of performance, the Spitfire XIV was considered to be the better all-round fighter as the handling qualities of the former meant that the pilot could not exploit its capabilities fully. In conclusion AFDU went so far as to suggest that the Spitfire F.21 be withdrawn from service and replaced by the Mark XIV or Tempest V until the instability in the yawing plane could be eradicated. Failing this it was felt that the F.21 was unlikely to become a satisfactory fighter and although it was felt that it was not a dangerous aircraft to fly, pilots would have to be warned that its handling qualities were different in many respects to any other mark of Spitfire that they might have flown. In its parting shot, AFDU stated that no further attempts should be made to perpetuate the Spitfire family.

The long term solution was, of course, to fit an enlarged tail unit but with aircraft already coming off the production lines, a temporary fix would have to suffice. The over-sensitive rudder was attended to by removing the balance action of the rudder trim tab. This tended to increase the foot load necessary to produce a given amount of sideslip. At the same time the elevator trim tab gearing was reduced by 50 per cent to reduce the sensitivity of the trimmer control, i.e. a larger movement of the control wheel was now necessary for a given change of tab setting. The final alteration was a metal-covered elevator with rounded off horn of reduced area to reduce the interaction of yaw and pitch, and also to reduce the change of longitudinal trim with speed, especially at the high end of the speed range. A modified Spitfire F.21 (LA211) was delivered to A&AEE in February 1945 for handling trials to discover how successful the fixes had been in curing the aircraft's undesirable handling characteristics. After a few hours flying, however, LA211 suffered an engine failure which meant that the trial had to be completed using LA215.

It was found that the modifications to the tail unit of the Spitfire F.21 had improved the general handling characteristics of the aircraft in several respects. The interaction between pitch and yaw was greatly reduced with the result that the unpleasant corkscrewing behaviour during dives at high altitudes was no longer apparent. The aircraft was dived to a Mach number of 0.82 and rudder applied to produce changes of direction of around 5 degrees. The resultant pitching was relatively mild and the oscillations could be steadied by holding all controls fixed, the aircraft resuming its original dive path after about four oscillations. This behaviour was far less disturbing than that noted on LA187 under the same conditions and did not give the pilot the impression that he was about to lose control, as had been the case with the previous aircraft. The change of longitudinal trim with speed was also reduced, in particular the rapid change in stick forces in out-of-trim dives above speeds of about 470 mph IAS which had been completely eliminated. The tendency for the aircraft to develop large angles of involuntary sideslip during manoeuvres at high altitudes was also reduced to a tolerable degree and the gearing of the elevator trimmer control was considered satisfactory.

Although the modifications had improved the Spitfire F.21's handling significantly, its fundamental directional instability was still present which gave rise to a number of adverse characteristics. The application of reasonably large aileron deflections still produced yaw in the opposite direction to the applied bank. The aircraft also tended to yaw to the left when subject to normal accelerations, although this could be checked by the use of rudder, and large angles of sideslip could be induced with light foot loads, especially at low speeds. In view of the general improvement in the aircraft's behaviour at high altitude, it was recommended that the Spitfire F.21 be cleared for service use without restriction, however, it was considered that further attempts should be made to improve its instability in yaw. As testing with a Spitfire XIV with a cut-down rear fuselage and teardrop hood had shown there to be a reduction in directional stability, it was felt that if a similar version of the Spitfire F.21 was planned, the level of directional stability would have to be substantially improved. In the event the low-back fuselage was adopted for the Spitfire F.22 and F.24, but all service aircraft were to feature the enlarged Spiteful-type tail.

After the trial at Boscombe Down, LA215 was delivered to Wittering for an assessment by AFDU. The subsequent report also noted a distinct improvement in the handling of the modified aircraft. The hunting which was previously experienced as a result of the extreme sensitivity of the elevator control was no longer apparent and it was possible to put the aircraft into a quick turn in either direction quite easily. Much less trimming was involved and the elevator and rudder together felt more in harmony. This was felt throughout all aspects of flight and was particularly appreciated when approaching to land. The reduced gearing of the elevator trimmer made for smooth and accurate flying, however, the rudder trimmer was still very sensitive to small movements and any misuse of the control could result in a skid developing. Aileron control was unaffected by the modifications and remained excellent at all times.

As a result of the changes the Spitfire F.21 was much more pleasant to fly at low level, even in conditions of bad visibility when it was necessary to manoeuvre the aircraft constantly to avoid obstacles. There was also a big improvement in handling qualities during aerobatics to the point where the F.21 compared favourably with previous marks of Spitfire, although care still had to be taken with the sensitive rudder. Formation flying was also much easier and it was considered that an average squadron pilot would have no difficulty in maintaining position during all normal manoeuvres. The modifications did not alter the high speed stall which still occurred before that of earlier Spitfires, but with the usual pre-stall buffet.

The reduced sensitivity of the elevator control was particularly appreciated during instrument flying as pilots were able to fly much more smoothly. The modified Spitfire F.21 was also easier to handle when flying in formation for cloud penetration purposes. A steady rate of climb was obtained even when the pilot's hand was removed from the control column, but it was still recommended that no sudden throttle movements be made to avoid inducing a strong yawing moment. The aircraft was also much improved as a sighting platform and it was considered that an average pilot would be able to hold his gunsight on a target throughout all normal combat manoeuvres. The rudder was noticeably heavier which tended to reduce unintentional sideslip, except at speeds in excess of 400 mph IAS when the pilot was liable to over-correct.

In marked contrast to the damning criticism of the Spitfire F.21 just three months before, AFDU considered the modified aircraft to be acceptable for service use as the trimming characteristics reported previously had largely been eliminated. It was now thought to be suitable for all aspects of flight, including instrument and low flying, and quite capable of being flown by even the most junior of squadron pilots. As such a big improvement had been made to the aircraft's controllability it was recommended that all production F.21's should have the modifications incorporated immediately and that all aircraft in service should be modified retrospectively.

As PP139, the prototype Spitfire F.21, differed from production aircraft in several respects, a further series of climb and level speed performance trials were carried out at Boscombe Down from March to July 1945 using LA187. By this time the aircraft had been engaged on a long programme of tests, both at A&AEE and with the manufacturers, so that its external condition had deteriorated considerably. The paint-work was chipped in many places and some of the filler used to ensure flush joints in the wing leading edges had worked loose. Once again the trial was disrupted by engine problems when the original Griffon 61 in LA187 failed before the tests had been completed, the replacement motor showing a slightly reduced performance during level speed runs. The engine limitations were +9 lbs/sq.in boost at 2,600 rpm in the climb with +21 lbs/sq.in boost at 2,750 rpm as a combat rating, normally limited to a maximum of 5 minutes, although A&AEE had been granted a concession to allow this boost setting to be used continuously to deter-mine the maximum rate of climb.

For the climb tests an automatic observer was installed in the radio compartment, the pilot's instruments being used for level speed runs only. The observer consisted of a panel, containing a watch, altimeter, airspeed indicator and boost gauge, which were photographed by a camera at intervals of about ten seconds during the climb. Climbs were made to 40,000 ft at both normal and combat rating at the best climbing speed of 170 mph IAS up to 25,000 ft, falling off linearly to 140 mph IAS at 40,000 ft. To obtain optimum performance the supercharger gear was changed from MS to FS gear when the boost was 6¼ lbs/sq.in at normal rating and 14½ lbs/sq.in at combat rating. Climb performance of the Spitfire F.21 at combat power was as follows

| Height | 4,000 ft | 8,000 ft | 12,000 ft | 16,000 ft | 20,000 ft |
|---|---|---|---|---|---|
| Rate of climb – ft/min | 4,440 | 4,000 | 3,570 | 3,595 | 3,490 |
| Time from start – mins | 0.90 | 1.85 | 2.90 | 4.05 | 5.15 |

| Height | 24,000 ft | 28,000 ft | 32,000 ft | 36,000 ft | 40,000 ft |
|---|---|---|---|---|---|
| Rate of climb – ft/min | 2,905 | 2,320 | 1,740 | 1,155 | 575 |
| Time from start – mins | 6.40 | 7.95 | 9.90 | 12.70 | 17.45 |

Maximum rate of climb at full throttle height in MS gear was 4,440 ft/min at 4,900 ft which compared with a figure of 2,740 ft/min at 14,200 ft when using the normal climb rating of +9 lbs/sq.in boost. In FS gear at combat power the best climb rate was 3,615 ft/min at full throttle height of 19,200 ft (2,125 ft/min at 29,000 ft at the normal rating). The estimated service ceiling at 2,750 rpm was 43,400 ft.

Normal procedure was followed for the level speed performance tests, the figures being corrected to ICAN standard atmosphere condi-tions and to 95 per cent of the take off weight (9,305 lbs). The results obtained were as follows

| Height | 4,000 ft | 8,000 ft | 12,000 ft | 16,000 ft | 20,000 ft |
|---|---|---|---|---|---|
| TAS – mph | 389 | 407 | 411 | 421 | 435 |
| IAS – mph | 378 | 375 | 356 | 341 | 335 |

| Height | 24,000 ft | 28,000 ft | 32,000 ft | 36,000 ft | 40,000 ft |
|---|---|---|---|---|---|
| TAS – mph | 440 | 438 | 434 | 428 | 407 |
| IAS – mph | 313 | 290 | 267 | 243 | 209 |

Maximum speeds at the full throttle heights of 7,000 ft (MS gear) and 21,800 ft (FS gear) were 406 mph and 442 mph respectively. These figures were obtained with the replacement Griffon 61 which produced slightly lower performance levels, the maximum speed being achieved with the original engine at 446 mph in FS gear at a full throttle height of 22,600 ft. These results were somewhat lower than those achieved with PP139 eighteen months before, LA187 being 15 mph slower in FS gear and 20 mph slower in MS gear. This was put down to a number of reasons. Part of the difference could be attributed to the fact that LA187 was fitted with a flat windscreen as opposed to the curved type on PP139, the former aircraft also having an external circular rear-view mirror which was not fitted to the prototype. From tests carried out at RAE Farnborough on a Spitfire IX it was known that the loss in performance at full throttle heights by the inclusion of these two items amounted to 9 mph TAS in MS gear and 13 mph TAS in FS gear. The remaining speed loss of the production aircraft compared with the prototype could be attributed to differences of surface finish, engine powers and propeller efficiencies.

Although the adverse handling characteristics of the Spitfire F.21 had been improved somewhat by the tailplane modifications already discussed, the ultimate cure was the fitment of a larger Spiteful-type tail to the later F.22 and F.24 variants. This increased tailplane/elevator area by 27 per cent and fin/rudder area by 28 per cent compared with the F.21. Just as the tail was being re-designed, major benefits in controllability were being achieved through the use of contra-rotating propellers which eliminated torque effects and made the aircraft much easier to fly. This type of propeller had first been fitted in 1943 to Spitfire HF.IX AB505 (a converted Mark V) powered by a Merlin 77. The trials programme was continued using several Spitfire XIVs including the sixth prototype JF321 and RB144 so that by early 1945 the system had largely been proved. On 23 March Spitfire F.21 LA218 fitted with a Griffon 85 and a six-blade Rotol contra-rotating propeller was delivered to AFDS at Tangmere [AFDU changed its name to the Air Fighting Development Squadron and moved to Tangmere from Wittering in February 1945]. As the aircraft was only available for one day, it was not possible to carry out a comprehensive test but initial impressions were so good, it was hoped that a similar aircraft would be attached for a more exhaustive tactical trial. This occurred later in the year when LA215 and LA217 were delivered.

Both aircraft were identical to the normal Spitfire F.21 except for the contra-prop mechanism which reduced the maximum power available by some 135 hp. During the trial in which LA215 and LA217 were flown for 30 hours and 41 hours respectively, no difficulties were experienced. As the aircraft did not have the enlarged tail a speed limitation of 470 mph IAS was imposed in view of the destabilising effect of the contra-prop at high speed. Longitudinal stability showed a definite improvement over the standard five-blade F.21 and the aircraft was stable fore-and-aft at all speeds from 125–450 mph IAS at low to medium altitudes and at 30,000 ft down to 140 mph IAS. There was no tendency to tighten up in turns, although the aircraft could be easily held in the turn with light stick forces. Large forward stick forces were only required in a prolonged dive if no trimming was used. In terms of lateral stability the contra-prop had no effect, the aircraft being just stable in the rolling plane at low altitude and just unstable above 30,000 ft. The ailerons were light and effective over the whole speed range.

Despite the increased density of the propeller disc there was no worsening of the forward view. Some concern had been expressed at 'ghost images' which had been clearly visible from the rear of the aircraft when it was run up at low revs on the ground. Throughout the trial, however, there were no adverse comments regarding this phenomenon and unless specifically brought to a pilot's attention he was unlikely to notice it. All forms of aerobatics were greatly enhanced by the contra-prop due to the complete absence of change of directional trim with speed or throttle setting and a uniform rate of roll in either direction. Instrument flying was also much simplified by the elimination of the need for any change of directional trim as was night flying, the absence of swing on take off and the improved stability at low speed being major advantages. It was noted, however, that the height at which the climb rate fell below 1,000 ft/min was 4,000 ft below that for a standard F.21 which was due mainly to the reduced diameter of the propeller. Pilots were unanimous in their praise for the contra-prop F.21 as a sighting platform for air-to-air and air-to-ground firing due to the lack of skid and it was easy to hold the sight on another aircraft, even if it took violent evasive action.

The opportunity was also taken to compare the contra-prop Spitfire F.21 with a standard five-blade F.21 using +18 lbs/sq.in boost. For all practicable purposes the aircraft were identical in terms of speed up to their operational ceilings, although the standard aircraft had slightly better acceleration, particularly at low level. Climb performance on the contra-prop F.21 was also not as good, the climb rate being around 100 ft/min less at sea level and 300 ft/min less at 21,500 ft. Once again this was mainly due to the reduced propeller diameter. Zoom climbs showed no appreciable difference, although the standard aircraft held a slight advantage at full throttle, and in dives both machines were identical. The rate of roll was difficult to measure although the standard aircraft appeared to have a slight advantage below 300 mph IAS, the contra-prop F.21 being superior above this speed. The most significant advantage for the latter was a better rate of turn, particularly at high altitude and in turns to the left, the improved 'feel' of the aircraft being most marked when carrying out tight turns.

The Spitfire F.21 was followed by the F.22 which was closely related but featured a cut-back rear fuselage and a teardrop canopy. It also introduced a 24-volt electrical system, all previous Spitfires having had a 12-volt supply. The first F.22 was PK312 which took to the air for the first time in March 1945. Initially it had the same tail dimensions as the F.21, but towards the end of 1945 it received the enlarged tail which was fitted to all subsequent F.22s. Armament was four 20 mm Hispano cannon plus wing pick up points for zero-length rocket projectile launchers. Total production of the F.22 amounted to 263 aircraft which were built at Castle Bromwich and South Marston [production of the F.21 had amounted to 120].

Just as the name 'Victor' was at first applied to the F.21, the Spitfire F.23 was initially referred to as the 'Valiant'. Two machines (JG204, a former Mark VIII, and PP139, the F.21 prototype) were modified with a high-speed aerofoil with a raised leading edge, new root fillets and tab-assisted ailerons with piano hinges. A curved windscreen and a balloon hood were fitted but the aircraft proved to be longitudinally unstable and the project was abandoned, all future work on high-speed flight being concentrated on the laminar-flow wing Spiteful (see Chapter Ten).

The final Spitfire variant was the F.24 which was adapted from the F.22. It featured increased internal fuel with two additional fuel tanks mounted in the rear fuselage, each containing 33 gallons. Armament differed from the F.22 in that the four 20 mm Hispano cannon were of the short-barrelled Mark V type. In 1947 flight trials were carried out using VN302 under various loading conditions. With four 300-lb rocket projectiles and a full 90-gallon slipper tank, all-up weight was 12,120 lbs which resulted in a wing loading of approximately 50 lbs/sq.ft, or more than double that of the Spitfire prototype. Even at this extreme weight, the aircraft's handling qualities were deemed acceptable although it was recommended that take off be made on paved runways instead of from grass surfaces, as bumps were liable to launch it into the air too soon resulting in excessive strain on the undercarriage. A total of 78 Spitfire F.24s were built, the variant seeing service in the Far East with No.80 Squadron. After this unit converted to the de Havilland Hornet in 1952 some of its Spitfires were taken over by the Hong Kong Auxiliary Air Force which used then until 1955.

# CHAPTER SEVEN

# Seafire XV

Although the Fleet Air Arm had been slow to recognise the potential of a navalised Spitfire, by the time that the Griffon-Spitfire appeared, the equivalent Seafire was not far behind. The first aircraft delivered to the Royal Navy were 48 Seafire IBs converted from ex RAF Spitfire VBs in 1942. Apart from a retractable A-frame arrester hook and strengthening of the rear fuselage to cater for the increased loadings imposed by deck landings, these aircraft were virtually identical to a standard Spitfire V. A further batch of 118 Seafire IBs was produced and these were followed by 260 examples of the Seafire IIC which were further strengthened for the installation of catapult spools and the use of RATOG (rocket-assisted take off gear). The definitive Merlin-engined Seafire was the Mark III, the first variant to feature folding wings. Over 1,100 Seafire IIIs were produced by Cunliffe Owen and Westland Aircraft and this variant saw widespread service from early 1943.

The first Griffon powered variant for the Fleet Air Arm was the Seafire XV, six prototypes being built to Specification N.4/43 (NS487, NS490, NS493, PK240, PK243 and PK245). The engine chosen for the new aircraft was the single-stage Griffon VI of 1,750 hp driving a four-blade Rotol propeller. The installation was similar to that of the Spitfire XII except that the cooling system was to be suitable for operations in the tropics. In view of this both underwing radiators were full size, even though the Griffon VI did not have an intercooler. The starboard duct carried a coolant radiator, with a further coolant radiator being located in the port duct, together with the oil cooler. Early aircraft were fitted with an A-frame arrester hook, however, this arrangement tended to produce a nose down pitch on landing and later machines had an improved sting-type hook which was spring loaded and, on release, extended aft by about 18 inches. In the lowered position it was prevented from bouncing on hitting the deck by an oleo-pneumatic damper. It could also pivot laterally through about 30 degrees. To prevent the tail wheel being fouled by the arrester wires, it was protected by a tubular guard.

The arrival of a Griffon-powered Seafire was not greeted with universal acclaim within the Navy hierarchy as some believed it to be inferior to US fighters designed specifically for naval operations, namely the Grumman Hellcat and Vought Corsair. Other voices, however, were adamant that the Seafire XV was superior to anything that the Americans possessed, perhaps with the exception of the Hellcat, and that its performance would be the equal of any land-based fighters that the Fleet Air Arm were likely to encounter. Production was again carried out by Cunliffe-Owen and Westland, but as it turned out disruption caused by the changeover from the Mark III meant that delivery of the XV to operational units was delayed until May 1945 and so it did not see action during the Second World War. In the meantime service testing had commenced at Boscombe Down in March 1944 when NS487 was delivered for handling trials and to determine the aftmost CG position.

As a naval development of the Spitfire XII, the Seafire XV showed few major changes from its land-based equivalent. The only aerodynamic differences were an enlarged rudder balance tab and the additional radiator under the port wing, the other changes being due to its navalisation, i.e. the fitment of an under-fuselage arrester hook and folding wings. On arrival the external finish of the aircraft was extremely good the skin being flush-riveted throughout with all joints filled with compound and the surface polished to give a smooth finish. As the first prototype, NS487 did not feature emergency flap operation which was to be incorporated on production aircraft. Most of the flying completed throughout the trial was carried out at an all-up weight of 7,865 lbs which represented a normal service load with full fuel and ammunition. Airframe limitations included a maximum diving speed of 470 mph IAS, with 160 mph IAS being the upper limit for flight with either flaps or undercarriage down.

Despite a strong swing to the right on take off, it was found that this could be controlled with a moderate foot load on the rudder when using +9 lbs/sq.in boost and full left rudder trim.. If the aircraft was taken off at the maximum boost setting of +15 lbs/sq.in the swing was rather stronger leading to a heavy foot load, but this was not considered to be excessive. There was a marked drop of the right wing due to torque reaction and although this could be somewhat disconcerting for the pilot, it was not serious. The tail tended to rise quickly and the aircraft left the ground after a short run and climbed away steeply.

Once in the air the controls were assessed as follows. The elevator displayed the usual characteristics for the type, being slightly heavy throughout the speed range with engine on, particularly at low airspeeds at high power settings. It was noted once again that the elevator tended to hunt at low speeds in rough air conditions, this minor defect being typical of the elevator with the enlarged horn balance. When gliding with flaps and undercarriage down the elevator was very light over the mid-part of its range, but became considerably heavier when large control movements were made.

The fitting of a rudder balance tab of increased area resulted in a considerable improvement in directional control compared with the Spitfire XII. The rudder was effective throughout the speed range and was very light at low speeds. It tended to become heavier as speed was increased, but still remained reasonably light for the small movements that were necessary at high speeds. It was also found that the changes of directional trim with speed and power could easily be held on the rudder bar without the need to retrim. The ailerons displayed the normal Spitfire characteristics, though it was noted that the set fitted to NS487 were rather heavy which led to the ailerons becoming excessively heavy above 400 mph IAS.

An assessment of the aircraft's longitudinal stability showed it to be satisfactory under all conditions of flight, although it became noticeably less stable at the lower end of the speed range when climbing or gliding with flaps and undercarriage up. When the aircraft was disturbed on the climb, one or two oscillations occurred followed by speed decreasing to the stall, and in the glide the oscillations again increased in amplitude. When flying straight and level at slow cruising speeds any disturbance was followed by a slow return to the trimmed condition through a damped oscillation. None of these phugoids were violent in character. Laterally and directionally the Seafire XV was similar to all previous marks of Seafire and Spitfire. Stalling speeds with flaps and undercarriage up and down were 80 mph IAS and 68 mph IAS respectively, the characteristics being normal except for a slight 'twitching' of the ailerons just before the stall with the gear and flaps down.

Having been trimmed for all-out level flight, the Seafire XV was dived to 450 mph IAS requiring a heavy push force on the control column as speed increased towards the upper limit. When the pilot released the controls the aircraft recovered quickly without excessive normal accelerations and there was no tendency to tighten up automatically. When trimmed into the dive the pull force needed to recover was moderate and again no tightening was experienced. One characteristic of the Seafire XV noted during the dives was that the wing-folding doors tended to lift slightly but this was in no way dangerous.

Simulated deck landings were carried out on both a runway and a grass airfield without the assistance of a batsman. The view forwards on the Seafire XV was considered to be rather better than that on earlier Seafires as the aircraft was fitted with single ejector exhausts in place of the broad triple ejectors employed on some of the previous marks. Approaches were made at 75 mph IAS, but it was found that the aircraft was more comfortable to fly at 80 mph IAS, the pilot having more control over attitude and the rate of descent. Compared with the earlier Merlin-powered Seafires pilots found more difficulty in maintaining the correct approach speed and the lack of drag was more noticeable. This lack of speed control was probably due to the fact that only small throttle movements were needed for considerable increases in power and hence it was not easy to check any sink without either increasing the approach speed or causing a nose-up change of attitude. On NS487 the harmony of the controls was poor at low speeds, the ailerons being rather heavy and the elevator and rudder very light. Despite the problems that were encountered the Seafire XV was deemed suitable for operations from aircraft carriers as the deck landing characteristics were not appreciably different from the Seafires already in service.

Handling trials were also carried out at aft CG settings, the aircraft in general behaving in similar fashion to the normal CG loading. Exceptions occurred on take off, however, when 1–1½ divisions extra nose-down elevator trim was required, the tail rising quickly with very little force being needed on the control column. On the initial climb the aircraft felt slightly less stable than previously and the elevator tended to hunt rather more at low speeds. Compared with the normal CG loading, longitudinal stability showed a progressive deterioration and the impression gained by the pilot was that the aircraft was unstable over the whole speed range, engine on or engine off. Dives at aft CG settings showed that there was a tendency for the recovery to become automatic once a pull-out had been initiated when flown at a CG of 8.5 in aft of datum (the normal CG was 6.6 in aft of datum). It was for this reason, and the fact that any further movement aft of CG would cause a serious deterioration in longitudinal stability, that A&AEE recommended the aft CG limit on the Seafire XV be fixed at 8.25 in aft of datum for all forms of flying.

Level speed performance of the Seafire XV was assessed by A&AEE in June 1944 using NS493, the third prototype which was more representative of late production Seafire XVs and differed from NS487 principally in having a curved windscreen, a teardrop hood, and a cutback rear fuselage. Maximum level speeds were measured at heights up to 32,000 ft as follows

| Height | Sea level | 2,000 ft | 4,500 ft | 8,000 ft | 12,000 ft |
|---|---|---|---|---|---|
| TAS – mph | 356 | 366 | 380 | 380 | 378 |
| IAS – mph | 367 | 368 | 369 | 350 | 327 |

| Height | 16,000 ft | 20,000 ft | 24,000 ft | 28,000 ft | 32,000 ft |
|---|---|---|---|---|---|
| TAS – mph | 394 | 390 | 383 | 373 | 358 |
| IAS – mph | 321 | 298 | 272 | 248 | 218 |

The best speed achieved in MS gear was 380 mph TAS at a full throttle height of 4,500 ft, whilst in FS gear it was 395 mph TAS at full throttle height of 12,800 ft. For optimum level speed performance FS gear was to be used when the boost in MS gear had fallen to +10½ lbs/sq.in.

Data on the Seafire XV as regards climb performance up to 30,000 ft was obtained using SR448 in May 1945. Tests were carried out at an all-up weight of 7,950 lbs using a best climbing speed of 160 mph IAS up to 10,000 ft, decreasing by 2 mph IAS per 1,000 ft thereafter with the following results

| Height | 2,000 ft | 4,000 ft | 6,000 ft | 8,000 ft | 12,000 ft |
|---|---|---|---|---|---|
| Rate of climb – ft/min | 4,340 | 4,040 | 3,760 | 3,640 | 3,360 |
| Time from start – mins | 0.40 | 0.90 | 1.40 | 2.00 | 3.30 |

| Height | 16,000 ft | 20,000 ft | 24,000 ft | 28,000 ft | 30,000 ft |
|---|---|---|---|---|---|
| Rate of climb – ft/min | 2,800 | 2,260 | 1,720 | 1,180 | 880 |
| Time from start – mins | 4.60 | 6.20 | 8.10 | 11.00 | 13.20 |

The maximum rate of climb in MS gear was 4,340 ft/min at full throttle height of 2,000 ft, the equivalent figure in FS gear being 3,640 ft/min at 10,000 ft. Service ceiling was estimated at 35,800 ft.

At the same time as NS493 was being used to determine its level speed peformance, it was also given a brief trial to ascertain whether the low-back fuselage had altered the aircraft's handling characteristics in any way. The cockpit layout was essentially the same as that of NS487 but differed in one important respect. An operating lever to the right of the pilot provided for emergency flap operation which was provided by injecting carbon dioxide into the normal pneumatic system. Although the system was not tested at the time, it was known from previous experience that it operated independently of the flap selector position.

NS493 featured a teardrop hood and the curved windscreen. It was not the first time that Boscombe Down had seen these as they had already been reported on favourably following the trial with Spitfire VIII JF299. The all-round field of vision was excellent with no apparent distortion in the hood or the curved windscreen, the only criticism being the view directly astern which was adversely affected by the acute line of sight to the hood surface and by small scratches of the transparent surface. Some difficulty was experienced in locking the hood open in flight and if the pilot attempted to push it as far back as he could with his elbow it did not engage with the lock. It was felt that this could become a serious deficiency during deck-landing as the hood was liable to slide forward and strike the pilot on the back of the head. A winding mechanism capable of being locked in a variety of positions would have been preferable. The maximum speed at which the hood could be opened in flight was 220 mph IAS.

In general, the flying characteristics of NS493 were similar to those of NS487 and the reduction in fuselage depth aft of the cockpit caused no worsening in the longitudinal and directional behaviour of the type. Some deficiencies in engine handling were noted, however. When operating at engine speeds below 1,900 rpm there was a certain amount of vibration and although this was not considered to be serious, during long transit flights the pilot suffered discomfort after a period of time. The engine also tended to cut when running in weak mixture when subject to the application of 'g'. The worst condition occurred at 2,000 rpm and +2 lbs/sq.in boost when an acceleration of only 2½ g would lead to the engine cutting. As soon as the pilot relaxed his pull on the control column the engine picked up once again.

As the major sub-contractor, Westland Aircraft had a long history of Spitfire/Seafire production stretching back to an initial order for 300 Spitfire IAs in August 1940 [this order was subsequently amended to include Mark VBs and VCs]. The first production Seafire XV to emerge from the Westland factory at Yeovil was SR446 which was tested at Boscombe Down in November 1944. Although the intention was to fit metal elevators to the Seafire XV, SR446 retained fabric-covered surfaces. The metal-covered ailerons were adversely commented upon and certain aspects of the aircraft's lateral characteristics were poor enough as to almost place it in the rogue category.

At relatively low speeds (up to 100 mph IAS) the aircraft was in trim laterally but as speed was increased there was a slight tendency to fly left wing low. At about 200 mph IAS this tendency was still apparent even though there was an upfloat of the starboard aileron of about ¼ in at its trailing edge. Above 360 mph IAS the aircraft's desire to fly left wing low became progressively more noticeable, so that at 450 mph IAS a lateral stick force of 10 lb was required to hold the wing up. By this stage the starboard aileron upfloat was approximately 1 in, while the port aileron remained level. When banking to the right by applying full aileron at 160 mph IAS the starboard aileron was seen (and felt) to vibrate. At higher speeds the vibration occurred at a smaller stick displacement but at the same approximate force (25–30 lbs). During dives at 450 mph IAS, although only half aileron could be applied, the vibration was still evident, however, if the pilot exerted enough force, the ailerons could be moved far enough past the range where the vibration was apparent, to feel a decrease in force, which suggested a degree of over-balance. None of these undesirable characteristics were apparent at normal deck landing speeds (70–80 mph IAS), the ailerons being classed as light and effective.

Rudder control had all the typical Seafire characteristics, the forces being light enough to allow the aircraft to be yawed 3 degrees in either direction (as measured on the directional gyro) at 450 mph IAS with little difficulty. An unwanted further effect of yaw, however, was a nose-down pitch. In addition, slight rudder movement involved large angles of skid and these two features together constituted a major criticism of the aircraft. The rudder trimmer was geared in such a way that even a slight trimmer adjustment was enough to overtrim the rudder. This was not in itself a great inconvenience for the pilot, but it meant that the aircraft's pitching tendency was brought into play which was undesirable. If the rudder was left free, directional changes of trim with speed were sufficient, especially at low speeds and high power settings (as in the climb), to induce considerable skidding which led to the unwanted pitching.

A number of dives were made up to the limit speed of 470 mph IAS. When trimmed in level flight at 300 mph IAS at climbing power, the aircraft was dived at one-third throttle to 450 mph IAS without requiring excessive push force. Trimmed into the dive at this speed, a pull force of around 15 lb was required to pull out at an accelerometer reading of 4g. At no time did the aircraft show any tendency to tighten up during dive recovery.

The stalling speed with flaps and undercarriage up was 79 mph IAS. With the aircraft trimmed to fly at 115 mph IAS, the control column was pulled gradually back with vibration beginning at 85 mph IAS. The pull force on the control column at this stage was about 2 lb and the stick was at approximately mid-position. At the stall there was a sharp shudder and the nose dropped through about 5 degrees. Thereafter the aircraft entered a stalled glide and lateral control was maintained. On release of the stick, recovery was immediate. With flaps and under-carriage down the stall came at 65 mph IAS. From a trimmed glide at 80 mph IAS the stick was brought back until it was just aft of the mid-position and at the point of stall there was a small amount of port wing drop, accompanied by buffeting. Once again the subsequent stalled glide could be held and recovery began as soon as the stick was released.

On the approach to land SR446 showed typical Seafire landing characteristics with all controls being light and effective. It was felt, however, that it had too little drag for a deck landing aircraft. The best approach speed with engine off was 90–100 mph IAS but with engine on, as for a deck landing, this figure could be reduced to 70–80 mph IAS. The aircraft was also tested as in the case of a baulked landing. When trimmed in the glide at 100 mph IAS with flaps and undercarriage down, heavy left rudder and stick push force were necessary on opening the throttle to climbing conditions, but this was considered to be acceptable.

In conclusion, A&AEE, on the basis of its qualitative testing, found this particular example of the Seafire XV to be unsatisfactory for service use due to the reasons given above. Further testing with the third production aircraft (SR448) from the same manufacturer showed its ailerons to be rather better and it was felt that if production aircraft conformed to the standards shown on this machine, then the Seafire XV could be cleared for use by the Fleet Air Arm. Subsequent to the trial with SR446 the propeller was fined off from 30 degrees to 28 degrees in an attempt to provide more drag in the landing configuration.

In March/April 1945 SR448 also undertook a series of spinning trials to provide a comparative assessment with NS490, the second Seafire XV prototype, which had since been fitted with a sting-type arrester hook and cut-away rudder. At the time of the test SR448 was equipped with an A-frame under-fuselage arrester hook and a Spitfire XII type rudder. Of the two types of rudder, pilots generally preferred the revised design fitted to NS490. The principal differences were that the rudder on NS490 was considerably heavier and rather less effective than that of SR448 and so the pitching and rolling moments accompanying yaw were smaller. The trimmer gearing on NS490 was lower than the same control on SR448, in which only a quarter of the total trimmer movement was actually required, and was much less likely to lead to excessive yaw (and resultant pitch) if adjusted in the dive. With both types of rudder the standard method of spin recovery (full opposite rudder and moving the control column to the mid-position) was satisfactory, however, care had to be taken to centralise the rudder as soon as the spin stopped to prevent a spin developing in the opposite direction. It was also important that the stick be eased forward to the mid-position and not beyond, as any movement further forward was likely to lead to the dive becoming unnecessarily steep.

During the same period A&AEE also carried out a handling trial with PK245 which was fitted with 22½ gallon flush-fitting combat tanks one fitted on the undersurface of each wing, outboard of the cannon installation. The tanks did not have any appreciable effect on handling characteristics but as in the case of SR446, the aircraft required an increasing lateral stick force to the right to maintain straight and level flight. As a result the maximum practicable diving speed was deemed to be 440 mph IAS. Metal elevators began to be fitted to Seafire XVs towards the end of the production run but it was found that discrepancies in the standard of manufacture resulted in unacceptable handling qualities on some aircraft. To get round this problem Seafire mod 601 was introduced which consisted of a length of beading fitted to the trailing edge of the elevator. This was tested at Boscombe Down in September 1945 using SR490, the effect of the modification being to restore the aircraft from an unpleasant condition in which there was a (longitudinal) region of dead movement in the control column, to a condition in which it could be recommended as suitable for deck landing.

After a protracted development period, the Seafire XV finally entered service with No. 802 Squadron at Arbroath in May 1945 before flying from the aircraft carriers *Premier, Berwick* and *Vengeance*. Other units to operate the type operationally included No. 803 Squadron, which later flew with the Royal Canadian Navy from the carrier *Warrior*, and No. 804 Squadron which re-formed at Eglinton in October 1946 and embarked on HMS *Theseus* and *Ocean*. Seafire XVs were also flown by No. 805 Squadron which also flew from *Ocean* and No. 806 Squadron from *Berwick* and *Glory*.

# CHAPTER EIGHT

# Seafire XVII

Externally, the Seafire XVII was virtually indistinguishable from a late low-back Mark XV, the main differences being under the skin. One of the most significant was the use of a 24-volt electrical system in place of the 12-volt system used on all previous Spitfires and Seafires. For extra range a 33-gallon fuel tank was mounted in the rear fuselage, this being replaced by two F.24 cameras for vertical and oblique photography on the FR.XVII. The Seafire XVII was capable of using Rocket Assisted Take-off Gear (RATOG) to improve take off performance, two rocket motors being carried adjacent to the wing/fuselage fillet. Firing time was four seconds and the rockets were jettisoned when safely airborne.

Because of its narrow track undercarriage, deck handling had always been a problem with the Seafire but this was improved with the Mark XVII by the use of a long-stroke undercarriage, the shock-absorber struts having a travel of 8 inches. This allowed a revised landing technique whereby the aircraft could be dropped onto the deck to take a wire rather than the pilot having to fly it on. Intensive deck landing trials were conducted from HMS *Triumph* in June 1945 using SX311 and SX314. In the course of 100 arrested landings the shock absorption qualities of the Seafire XVII undercarriage was found to be a vast improvement over that of the earlier Seafires with rebound being virtually eliminated. The Seafire XVII was also capable of carrying external stores including eight 60-lb rocket-projectiles in addition to the normal armament of two 20 mm Hispano cannon and four 0.303 in Browning machine-guns. Production was once again split between Cunliffe-Owen and Westland Aircraft, however, in this case the latter firm produced the vast majority, being responsible for 212 out of 232 examples (not including NS493, the former Seafire XV which was converted to act as a prototype).

As the Seafire XVII was so closely related to the later Seafire XVs the amount of testing carried out at Boscombe Down was limited, however, brief handling trials were carried out in October 1945 using SX153 to ascertain whether there was any appreciable difference in the two variants. The aircraft featured the now standard features of a cut-down rear fuselage with teardrop hood, a sting-type arrester hook and a whip aerial. The retractable tail wheel was fitted with a guard but no bomb rack or external load was carried. The aircraft skin was flush riveted throughout, the finish being classed as moderately good, although some unevenness was noted on the upper surface of each wing at the root.

SX153 differed from the early examples of the Seafire XV on which type clearance had been made in having a 3½ lb inertia weight fitted to the elevator control circuit. This modification had first been used on the prototype Spitfire III which suffered from a serious lack of longitudinal stability. Following the demise of the Mark III the idea was later employed retrospectively on the Mark V which was running into stability problems as more and more service equipment was being added which had the effect of moving the CG backwards and worsening the aircraft's longitudinal behaviour. The elevators were metal-covered with approximately 7½ in of beading (Seafire mod 601) fitted to the trailing edge of the trimmer tabs each side. The fabric-covered rudder was fitted with a trim tab but there was no indicator in the cockpit to show the trimmer position, the wheel, which was adjusted in the vertical plane, being wound fully back or forward to give full left or right trim respectively. The ailerons were metal-covered but did not have a cockpit-adjustable trimmer.

The aircraft was flown under all normal conditions of flight including climb, slow and fast cruise, diving to limiting speed of 470 mph IAS, landing and baulked landing, to investigate whether the modificatons had introduced any undesirable characteristics liable to render the aircraft unsatisfactory for service use. Results showed that the Spitfire XVII did not exhibit any adverse characteristics in any condition of flight, its longitudinal and lateral behaviour being virtually identical to the Seafire XV. The only difference that was noticed was an increase in the amount of pre-stall buffet, irrespective of whether the undercarriage was up or down. It was thought, however, that this may have been caused by the slightly rough nature of the wing surface near the root and was not considered serious. Directionally the aircraft's behaviour was satisfactory although the impression of pilots that flew SX153 was that directional stability had decreased slightly, resulting in increased responsiveness and lightness of the rudder in the dive. The degree of lookout from the cockpit was particularly praised as the view above and rearwards was excellent, the whole of the fin and rudder and the upper surface of the tail plane being visible to the pilot. As the handling of the Seafire XVII was virtually identical to that of the XV, A&AEE had no hesitation in clearing it for use by the Fleet Air Arm.

In February 1946 Seafire XVII SX157 was delivered to Boscombe Down for spinning trials to clear the aircraft for intentional spinning (without external stores) by the FAA. The tests comprised one, two and three turn spins in either direction at heights of 15,000 ft and 25,000 ft at two CG positions, namely 8.2 in and 9.0 in aft of datum (undercarriage down). These CG positions represented the aftmost loadings for the fighter and fighter-reconnaissance versions of the Seafire XVII respectively. The take off weights in each condition were 7,825 lbs and 7,870 lbs. The control surfaces as fitted to SX157 at the time of test included metal-covered ailerons. The horn-balanced, metal-covered elevators were fitted with trimmer tabs with metal beading extending along the trailing edge of the elevator for 6 in at both the outboard and inboard edges of each tab. A 3½ lb inertia weight was fitted in the elevator control circuit just behind the pilot's seat. This weight exerted a moment of 40 lb/ins about the elevator hinge and tended to depress the trailing edge of the elevator. The rudder was fabric-covered and was fitted with a fabric-covered trimmer tab.

Before entering the spin, the aircraft was trimmed to glide, flaps and undercarriage up, engine off, at 100 mph IAS. Accurate longitudinal trimming was difficult, but the aircraft was approximately in trim with the elevator trimmer reading 1½ divisions nose up. The aircraft was stalled by easing the control column back against a light stick force, and, as soon as the buffeting associated with the stall was observed (at approximately 83 mph IAS), full rudder was applied and the control column pulled back the remaining short distance needed to produce full up elevator movement. The stick was held back during the spins and was not moved forward again until recovery was initiated.

When spinning in either direction the first half turn of the spin was always steeply banked with a high rate of rotation, and with the nose depressed about 70–80 degrees at the bottom of the spiral. In the second half of the turn the nose came up, the rate of rotation decreased, as did the angle of bank. At the end of a whole turn the nose was almost up to the horizontal and the spin had practically ceased. The aircraft then tended, momentarily, to bank away from the turn. This opposite bank was about 10 degrees and it felt as if another spin was about to start, but in the opposite direction. As soon as the nose dropped again, however, the spin tightened and the original wing dropped steeply.

Throughout all of the spins there was severe buffeting which caused the whole aircraft to shudder. This buffeting was particularly violent around the cockpit canopy, and on one occasion was severe enough as to cause the canopy operating handle to unlock which allowed the canopy to be sucked open. Buffeting over the tail unit could be felt in the form of 'twitching' on the control column and the rudder pedals, and it was necessary to grip the control column firmly and keep the rudder pedals firmly depressed. The spin characteristics of the Seafire XVII were similar in both directions except that spins to the left seemed to be slightly tighter and less erratic than spins to the right. In the second half of each turn of a left hand spin the nose did not come up quite as high as in the case of a spin to the right. In the former, the nose stopped about 20 degrees below the horizon, and in the latter reached almost to the horizontal position.

The normal recovery method of full opposite rudder followed by forward movement of the control column brought a rapid recovery on every occasion, one that was thought to be rather more positive than that of the Seafire XV. From one, two and three turn spins, recovery always took less than one half of a turn and in many cases the spin stopped almost as soon as opposite rudder was applied – on average, in one quarter of a turn. A slight initial push on the control column was necessary during recovery, after which the stick force became fairly light. The control column did not have to be pushed further forward than the mid position to unstall the aircraft and there was no tendency for a spin to develop in the opposite direction. Recoveries were similar from spins in either direction. During the recovery dive very severe buffeting was experienced and this persisted until approximately 160 mph IAS had been reached in the pull out manoeuvre. The total height lost during a three turn spin from 15,000 ft was around 3,000 ft, this figure increasing to nearly 4,000 ft when the spin was commenced from 25,000 ft, however, there was no noticeable difference in the rate of recovery at either height.

When the Seafire XVII was flown at a CG loading representing that of the FR version, the spinning characteristics were found to be very little different to those of the fighter variant. Recovery was extremely rapid but it was noticed that it was necessary to push the control column almost to the fully forward position to unstall the aircraft. This left very little down elevator movement in hand, though in the circumstances it was unlikely to be needed. As the Seafire XVII had displayed very predictable spinning characteristics and was quickly recoverable, A&AEE were able to pass the aircraft for intentional spins of up to three turns in either direction.

Like its immediate forebear, the Seafire XVII had a relatively short operational life but it was to play a significant role in the post war Fleet Air Arm as it equipped many second-line and reserve squadrons. It was to outlast all other Griffon-Seafire variants in terms of length of service, the last unit to fly the aircraft being No.764 Squadron at Yeovilton which retired its Seafire XVIIs on 23 November 1954. Of the 232 production examples, only SX137 survives at the Fleet Air Arm Museum at Yeovilton.

# CHAPTER NINE

# Seafire F.45/46/47

The Seafire F.45 was the Fleet Air Arm equivalent of the Spitfire F.21 and was powered by a Griffon 61 driving a five-blade Rotol propeller. As the wings had not been modified in any way from those of the RAF machine, this variant did not feature wing folding. Armament comprised four 20 mm Hispano cannon, the first Seafire to be so equipped.

Admiralty interest in a navalised version of the Spitfire F.21 resulted in the issue of Specification N.7/44, the end product of which was regarded very much as an interim type, pending development of a more advanced variant with laminar flow wing (this was a proposed version of the Spitfire 23 which was subsequently abandoned). The prototype Seafire F.45 was a converted Spitfire 21 (TM379), the main modifications comprising the fitting of a sting-type arrester hook, which increased overall length to 33 ft 4 in, and the incorporation of a guard for the tail-wheel. Due to its non-folding wings and the strong swing on take off as a result of the extra power of the Griffon 61, the Seafire 45 tended to be flown from shore based establishments only, although a number were fitted with a Griffon 85 and six-bladed contra-rotating propeller which eliminated the swing on take off due to engine torque.

The handling section in Pilot's Notes for the Seafire 45 fitted with a Griffon 61 warned that the aircraft was likely to be nose-heavy during taxying, extreme care having to be taken when applying the brakes to avoid nosing over. Concentration was also required on take off as the use of high power levels not only caused a pronounced swing to the right, but the aircraft was also likely to crab in the initial stages of the take off run and tyre wear when operating from runways could be severe. A boost setting of +7 lbs/sq.in was found to be quite adequate for take off, with full power being selected when safely airborne. After take off the wheels could be braked and the undercarriage retracted, however, any failure of the gear to retract was likely to lead to excessive engine temperatures as the airflow to the underwing radiators and oil cooler was likely to be interrupted.

Once in the air and in the climb the recommended speed was 150 kts

IAS up to 25,000 ft, reducing speed by 3 knots for every 1,000 ft gained thereafter. Normally during a combat climb the supercharger would change into high gear automatically at around 11,000 ft, however, the maximum rate of climb could be obtained manually by delaying the changeover until boost had dropped to +6¼ lbs/sq.in. Some deterioration in longitudinal stability was noted when climbing at low airspeeds, otherwise stability about all axes was satisfactory. Control forces throughout the speed range were generally light, movements in pitch and yaw being assisted by elevator and rudder trimmers which were very effective in operation. This sensitivity could be a problem during high speed dives as any sudden application of rudder or its associated trimmer was likely to cause the aircraft to skid violently. When diving, the aircraft also tended to become increasingly tail heavy as speed was increased and it was recommended that it should be trimmed into the dive. The elevator trimmer could be used to assist recovery but this had to be handled with care as it was very effective and there was a distinct possibility that excessive accelerations could result.

Stalling speed at a typical service load with engine off and flaps and undercarriage up was 80 kts IAS (85 kts IAS when fully loaded) and 72 kts IAS (76 kts IAS fully loaded) with flaps and undercarriage down. The stall was preceded by airframe buffet which became noticeable 5–10 knots before the stall with aileron snatch in the latter stages. At the stall either wing was liable to go down followed by the nose, but recovery was immediate if the back pressure on the control column was relaxed. Intentional spinning was prohibited but the aircraft usually responded to normal recovery action. All normal aerobatic manoeuvres could be performed except flick rolls and sustained inverted flying. The recommended entry speed for a loop was 320–340 kts IAS and upward rolls could be carried out from an initial speed of 360–400 kts IAS.

When approaching to land the recommended speed with engine on and flaps down was 85 kts IAS increasing to 90 kts IAS with flaps up. With the engine off 10–15 kts IAS had to be added. If the aircraft was at light weight with ammunition expended and minimal fuel, 5 knots could be reduced from the above speeds. For deck landing the recommended final approach speed was 75 kts IAS, a considerably improved view of the deck being obtained if a curved approach was made. During the approach the aircraft was subject to a number of trim changes as its configuration was changed. When the undercarriage was lowered a nose down trim change occurred, the opposite occurring when the flaps were lowered. A nose up trim change also occurred when the radiator shutters were opened. Landing was straightforward, the only possible problem occurring when a missed approach resulted in a go around situation. It was important not to select full power when close to the stall due to a strong tendency to roll and turn to the right. At low airspeeds even full opposite aileron and rudder would be insufficient to counteract this effect and control could well be lost.

Development of the later Spitfires to incorporate a Griffon 87 engine with contra-rotating propellers was potentially of more importance in a naval environment, the close confines of an aircraft carrier leaving little room for error. The absence of torque effects with such an installation was a clear benefit and trials soon commenced at A&AEE to assess the aircraft's suitability for deck operations. Having already been tested with a Griffon 61 and a five-blade propeller, the prototype Seafire F.45 TM379 was returned to Boscombe Down in June 1945 with a Griffon 87 and a six-blade Rotol contra-prop. Certain aspects of its control surfaces were non-standard and the fabric-covered elevator was not modified to current Spitfire F.21 standards in that the alteration to the horn balance and the trimmer tab gearing had not been made. The fabric-covered rudder had a revised trimmer tab which was split into two parts and splayed 1.6 in at the trailing edge, this also being thickened to about 0.25 in. Above and below the trimmer tab there were fixed split tabs. The ailerons and balance tabs were metal-covered and were fitted with piano-type hinges on the bottom surface.

During the trial TM379 was loaded to a typical service take off weight of 9,385 lbs. Ground handling tests showed that the aircraft could be held against the chocks without the tail lifting up to an engine boost pressure of +1 lb/sq.in. Compared with the single rotating propeller with which the aircraft was fitted on its last visit, there was no tendency to swing or for one wheel to lift during the take off run. There appeared to be improved thrust in the early stages of the run, but otherwise the take off characteristics were normal for the type. To evaluate the stall, the aircraft was trimmed in the glide at 80 mph IAS with flaps and undercarriage down, the speed then being gradually reduced. At speeds below 80 mph IAS a vibration of small magnitude was noticed which had not been apparent when the aircraft had been tested previously. This was not considered serious, however, and the stall occurred at 66 mph IAS, with a normal recovery.

The contra-prop installation on TM379 came into its own on the approach to land and during a baulked landing. Directional changes of trim with speed and power, and the pitching associated with yaw, were very small, which was in marked contrast to the findings of the test when the aircraft was fitted with a normal five-bladed propeller. The rudder appeared to be a little heavier, but this was considered to be an improvement. Some difficulty was experienced in keeping the approach speed down and it was felt that more drag would be advantageous when in the landing configuration. Baulked landings in particular showed a significant improvement as large power changes merely led to a small directional trim change which was easily controlled by the pilot. As the fitting of contra-rotating propellers had considerably improved the aircraft's handling characteristics, especially during take off and landing, A&AEE were able to approve the installation for carrier operation without any restriction. Spinning trials were carried out in September 1945 using TM383, its behaviour being typical of other Spitfire/Seafire aircraft with normal recovery characteristics.

Towards the end of 1945 a more comprehensive handling trial was carried out at Boscombe Down using Seafire F.45 LA446 so that clearance could be given for the service to conduct intensive flying trials. This aircraft was also fitted with a six-blade contra-rotating propeller (Griffon 85) but at the time of test it was limited by the manufacturers to a maximum speed of 403 mph IAS (350 knots) due to concern about directional instability at higher speeds. The results of qualitative testing showed the aircraft to be pleasant and easy to fly and without any serious fault up to the limiting speed.

Although the advantages of the contra-prop installation were mainly apparent when in the air, it was also noted that ground handling was very much better than the Seafire F.45 fitted with the normal five-bladed propeller. As the rudder was more effective, the brakes did not have to be used as much which made taxying much easier. With the throttle open, the rudder centred rapidly when freed. The tendency for the tail to lift on opening the throttle was no different from previous Seafire F.45s. For take off, the rudder and elevator trimmers could be set to neutral and the whole process was extremely simple as there was no swing and the rudder could be held fixed in the central position.

The aircraft was then climbed at 170 mph IAS with 2,600 rpm and +9 lbs/sq.in boost, the elevator trimmer being set to 1½ divisions nose up, with the rudder trimmer an eighth of a turn forward of neutral. When the speed was displaced by +/-10 mph and the control column released, a slow damped oscillation of small amplitude was set up. Rudder centring from small displacements was good, but there was a slight tendency to overbalance at larger displacements when the aircraft was kept laterally level by applying opposite aileron. From full starboard displacement the rudder centred slowly on release, but from full port displacement there was little or no tendency to centralise.

At a fast cruise speed of 270 mph IAS at 25,000 ft with the engine set to 2,400 rpm and +7 lbs/sq.in boost, the trimmer settings were – rudder neutral and elevator ½ division nose up. In this condition static longitudinal stability (stick free) was positive, a speed displacement of +/-10 mph requiring the application of a moderate push or pull force on the control column. On release of the stick after such a displacement the aircraft returned slowly to its trimmed speed, never taking more than two cycles to return. When the rudder was freed after displacement and the wings were held level by ailerons, a fast oscillation ensued which damped out in about six cycles. All the controls were moderately light and responsive inducing powerful roll, but no pitch with yaw. Use of rudder gave accurate turns in both directions with the ailerons held fixed, but turns made with ailerons only resulted in slight slipping in.

From the pilot's viewpoint the ailerons appeared to float up about a quarter of an inch at the trailing edge in level flight. Rate of roll was extremely high and the ailerons were described as being very light and crisp. On previous tests with the Seafire F.45 pilots had criticised excessively high static friction in the aileron circuits. Although this was considerably reduced on LA446 it was still higher than the recommended value and the ailerons did not centre when displaced and freed. At 35,000 ft, with the engine operating at 2,400 rpm and +2 lbs/sq.in boost, the longitudinal stability was satisfactory and directional stability appeared to be substantially the same as at 25,000 ft.

The aircraft was also dived up to the limiting speed of 403 mph IAS with trim and engine controls set as for fast cruise. There was no change of directional trim of any note, but a push force of around 20 lb was required on the control column. The controls were fairly light and positive, the rudder centring rapidly after being freed following a displacement. At no point did any unpleasant characteristics become apparent and on release of the stick the maximum reading measured on the accelerometer was 3g. A slight swing to starboard was noticed when the throttle was closed at the maximum speed attained, but this was easily counteracted by a very small rudder movement.

At the opposite end of the speed range, with power off and the elevator trimmer wheel fully back (flaps and undercarriage up), the aircraft was put into a glide with the control column free at 106 mph IAS. When displaced +/-10 mph from the trimmed speed, the aircraft returned to this speed with a slow damped oscillation on release of the control column. Directionally the contra-prop F.45 appeared to be no different from normal Griffon-Seafires but when the control column was displaced laterally and released, a lateral oscillation commenced, together with oscillation of the ailerons, which showed no sign of damping out. In circumstances when the control column was held, rather than released, these oscillations were not present. Neither were they present during power off glides at 92 mph IAS with the flaps and undercarriage down. Pilots also reported that longitudinal stability was slightly better in this configuration.

Stalls were carried out which showed that at a take off weight of 9,510 lbs and with a typical service CG loading, LA446 stalled at 88 mph IAS with flaps and undercarriage up and 78 mph IAS with flaps and undercarriage down. The characteristics at the stall were virtually identical to a standard Seafire F.45. To simulate a baulked landing, the aircraft was put into a glide with power off, flaps and undercarriage down, radiator flaps closed, elevator trimmer fully back and the rudder trimmer neutral. The engine was then opened up to full power and a climb was made at 140 mph IAS. No directional change of trim was encountered and the longitudinal change was counteracted by a push force on the control column estimated at 25 lb.

Landings with power off were straightforward. When landing from a powered approach pilots found that this was much easier to perform as any amount of power could be added to adjust the rate of descent without incurring strong changes in directional trim. In view of this it was considered that the contra-prop Seafire F.45 had vastly improved deck landing characteristics, although it still suffered from a poor forward view and a tendency to float. In certain conditions of visibility dark segments were visible in the propeller disc at low engine speeds but this did not worsen the forward view to any extent.

Although it did much to develop the engine/propeller combination of the ultimate Seafire, the F.47, the only F.45's to serve with the Fleet Air Arm were fitted with a Griffon 61 and five-bladed propeller. Only fifty were produced at the Vickers-Armstrong factory at Castle Bromwich, some of these aircraft seeing service with Nos. 771 and 778 Squadrons at Ford from October 1946. The penultimate Seafire was the F.46 which was of low-back configuration (unlike the F.45) and was essentially similar to the Spitfire F.22. Early aircraft tended to have the original empennage, whereas later machines had the Spiteful-type tail. Most examples of this variant were powered by a Griffon 61 with a five-blade propeller, although a few were fitted with a Griffon 87 and contra-props. Production was once again centred on Castle Bromwich but only twenty-four were to be produced, a few being designated FR.46 following the installation of an F.24 oblique camera. The Seafire F.46 entered service in early 1947 with No.781 Squadron at Lee-on-Solent and the variant also flew with No.1832 Squadron at Culham until retired in 1952.

The last of the Spitfire/Seafire line was the Seafire F.47, the first of which (PS944) was taken into the air for its maiden flight on 25 April 1946. As much of the development work had already been carried out on the contra-prop versions of the Seafire F.45 and F.46, there was no prototype as such and PS944 was followed by another thirteen aircraft in the same serial batch (PS945–PS957). Subsequent batches were VP427–VP465, VP471–VP495 and VR961–VR971. The aircraft in the PS batch were powered by a Griffon 87 but those machines that followed were fitted with a Griffon 88 which had a Rolls-Royce developed fuel injection and transfer pump instead of the Bendix-Stromberg induction-injection carburettor used on previous versions of the Griffon engine. Although this had the effect of adding 70 lbs to all-up weight, a significant advantage was gained in that power was maintained under all conditions of 'g'. Wing folding was incorporated in the Seafire F.47, consisting of a single break point outboard of the cannon installation.

In December 1946 a deck landing assessment was carried out at Boscombe Down using PS944, the main aim of which was to determine the rate of descent and touchdown speed. Apart from the provision of wing folding, the Seafire F.47 differed from the F.46 seen previously in that it had a redesigned air intake in an elongated duct under the nose, long stroke, anti-rebound oleo struts and flaps of increased chord. All the control surfaces and trimmers were metal-covered. Each aileron had a balance tab and a trimmer tab was fitted to the port and starboard sides of the elevator. The rudder was fitted with a combined trimmer and anti-balance tab. The latter was approximately 18 in long and was split about 7 in from the lower end, the upper part being displaced 15.25 degrees from the lower part of the tab. A 6½ lb inertia weight was fitted in the elevator control circuit which exerted a moment of +66 lb/ins about the elevator hinge with the elevator neutral and fuselage datum horizontal.

In a series of simulated deck landings on a runway, made with and without the aid of a batsman, it was considered that the best approach speed was 81 mph IAS (70 knots). The engine conditions for an approach at this speed were -4½ lbs/sq.in with the propeller set to fully fine, these resulting in a steady rate of descent of around 600 ft/min. On closing the throttle just prior to touchdown (normally on the batsman's signal) the aircraft sank in a three-point attitude. During testing of the Seafire F.46 a certain amount of nose drop had been apparent when the throttle was closed but this was not experienced with the F.47. In the case of a misjudged, engine off approach, if power had to be fed in to avoid an undershoot developing, a slight nose-down trim change occurred requiring a light pull force. Directional and lateral changes of trim were negligible.

In the case of a baulked landing the engine could be opened up to 2,600 rpm and +9 lbs/sq.in boost with little difficulty following an approach at the above speed. On retracting the undercarriage there was a very slight nose-up change of trim requiring a push force of 1–2 lbs to hold, however, the trim change when raising the flaps at 115 mph IAS was in the opposite sense and needed a pull force of 7–10 lbs to maintain the aircraft's correct climbing attitude. This nose-down change of trim was most marked when the flaps were moving from the 'take off' to the 'up' position, the trim change when they were being raised from 'landing' to 'take off' being small and easily held. It was discovered, however, that a climb out with the flaps in the 'take off' position held no problems so that if another circuit had to be made after being given the 'wave off', the flaps need not be fully retracted.

Other approach speeds were attempted for a comparative assessment. At a speed of 86 mph IAS (75 knots) the aircraft tended to touch down slightly main wheels first, but with the long stroke oleo undercarriage there was little or no bounce. At 75 mph IAS (65 knots) the approach was rather uncomfortable due to aileron twitching and buffeting as the aircraft was getting close to the stall. At this speed a relatively large amount of power had to be maintained to prevent an excessively large rate of descent.

Rates of descent and (true) touchdown speeds were measured during a series of simulated deck landings controlled by a batsman, the engine being cut on his signal when the aircraft was very near to the ground. From an approach speed of 81 mph IAS the rates of descent on touchdown varied somewhat up to a maximum of 7.2 ft/sec. The average true touchdown speed was 93½ mph thus giving a correction to indicated values of 12½ mph. An investigation was also made on the effect of engine power on the rate of descent by measuring height against time at various boost pressures (flaps and undercarriage down). The results obtained varied from a rate of descent of 8½ ft/sec at -4 lbs/sq.in boost to 29 ft/sec with the engine off.

The recommended approach speed of 81 mph IAS for Aerodrome Dummy Deck Landings (ADDLs) on the Seafire F.47 compared favourably with that of 86–92 mph IAS for the Seafire F.46 and was most likely due to the increase in flap area on the F.47. The latter was also easier to land in a three-point attitude due to the fact that the nose did not drop when the throttle was closed. One aspect of the Seafire F.47's landing performance that became apparent after the Boscombe Down trial was that although 81 mph IAS was a satisfactory approach speed during ADDLs, for actual deck landings on an aircraft carrier it was best to increase approach speed to 92 mph IAS (80 knots). The reason for this was subject to some conjecture, but Service Trial Unit pilots were adamant that the higher figure produced a more controllable touchdown during actual deck landings.

Following its deck landing assessment PS944 was retained by A&AEE for further handling trials which showed that attitudes were beginning to change within the testing establishments. The aircraft was evaluated at a loaded weight of 10,394 lbs and was subject to limiting speeds based upon a Mach number of 0.77. At the beginning of the trial, however, the limit was at the higher figure of 0.85M, but continuing tests using a Spitfire F.22 highlighted a violent and rapid pitching or 'porpoising' at a true Mach number of 0.77 (0.82 indicated) and so this lower figure was imposed. At 25–30,000 ft 0.77M represented an indicated airspeed of 345 mph (300 knots) rising to 520 mph (450 knots) at 5–10,000 ft. The reason for the test was to obtain sufficient knowledge of handling characteristics to decide whether the aircraft could be cleared for service use in what was now a post-war environment. The Seafire F.47 was put through a variety of manoeuvres including stalls, dives, baulked landings and a full range of aerobatic manoeuvres including loops, half rolls off the top of loops, rolls and climbing rolls.

Ground handling was straightforward and the aircraft was easily controlled in cross winds of up to 10 knots. The brakes were effective and the engine could be opened up to 2,800 rpm with +8 lbs/sq.in boost without them slipping. This power setting was also the maximum in which the aircraft could be run up against the chocks without the tail lifting. Turns on the ground could be made in calm air without brakes by application of rudder and bursts of power up to zero boost. Take off was easily accomplished using a power setting of 2,750 rpm and +12 lbs/sq.in boost and the rate of climb was good. It was during the climb, however, that the first criticism of the aircraft was made which showed that handling characteristics that had been deemed acceptable during the war would be coming in for much tighter scrutiny in the future.

When trimmed into the climb at 180 mph IAS (156 knots) the aircraft showed neutral longitudinal stability (stick free) and if disturbed it tended to diverge either to a dive or a stall. At the higher speed of 200 mph IAS (174 knots) the stability became positive but the post-war requirements were for an aircraft to have positive stability at all speeds. In all other conditions of flight the Seafire F.47 had excellent longitudinal stability, particularly on the glide with the flaps and under-carriage down. Certain aspects of the aircraft's directional stability were also remarked upon. Generally the degree of directional stability was good and when the rudder was displaced and then released in any trimmed condition of flight the aircraft quickly returned to straight flight. However, during flat turns that introduced sideslip, the rudder tended to overbalance so that the rudder control force did not increase progressively as the angle of sideslip was increased up to the maximum obtainable. Again this was outside the current requirements and was considered to be unsatisfactory.

Dives were carried out in both 'out of trim' and 'in trim' conditions. With the aircraft trimmed to fly level at 300 mph IAS (260 knots) with climbing power at 12,000 ft, the speed was increased in a dive to 525 mph IAS (455 knots) at 5,000 ft when a push force of 30 lb on the stick and a left foot force of 15 lb on the rudder pedal was required to maintain the dive and keep the aircraft straight. On release of the stick in this dive the aircraft recovered with an accelerometer reading of 4.1g. The aircraft was also dived in trim from 20,000 ft to 7,000 ft up to 525 mph IAS. The foot force needed on the rudder pedal to generate 5 degrees of sideslip as measured on the directional gyro was measured at 50 lb and a pull force on the stick of 45 lb was needed to recover from the dive with an accelerometer reading of 4g. Stick force per 'g' at 20,000 ft was 2½ lbs/g at a speed of 325 mph IAS (282 knots), rising to 15 lbs/g at 430 mph IAS (374 knots). These figures were also not in accordance with the recommended values, being outside the upper and lower limits as laid down in the requirements of the time. As the Seafire F.47 was likely to be a first-line fighter for some time to come and would probably be flown by relatively inexperienced pilots in the event of a national emergency, A&AEE felt that it should be made to comply fully with the requirements, particularly with regard to its deficiencies in relation to longitudinal stability and the inconsistent forces that were encountered during use of the rudder.

The problems that the later versions of the Spitfire/Seafire had encountered during testing at high Mach numbers caused considerable concern at A&AEE and the rapid imposition of a flight restriction limiting high speed flight to a True Mach Number (TMN) of 0.77. High speed dives in a Spitfire F.22 had resulted in an extremely uncomfortable pitching motion setting in at 0.77 TMN (0.82 IMN or 420–430 mph IAS at 20,000 ft). Supermarine produced a modification (Seafire mod 971) to increase the critical Mach number and this took the form of 9 in of angle strip which were mounted above and below the trailing edge of each side of the elevator. The total depth of the angle was about 0.75 in. PS944 was tested at Boscombe Down without modification to ascertain the limiting Mach number and it was then sent to the manufacturers to have the strips fitted.

In its pre-modification state, PS944 showed a slight fore-and-aft oscillation at a TMN of 0.78-0.79 (0.83-0.83 IMN), however, this became violent with just a slight increase of speed, the top of the control column then moving 3–4 in forwards and backwards. After returning from Supermarine PS944 was tested with the angle strips in place at a normal service take off load, with full internal fuel tanks and wing combat tanks. The rear fuselage tank was used in the climb so that at the commencement of the dive, CG was approximately 7.5 in aft of datum (this represented the forward CG limit of the Seafire F.47). During the dive an auto observer recorded height and airspeed.

In the second set of dives with the modified elevators the aircraft behaved normally up to a TMN of 0.82 at 25,000 ft (0.87 IMN), the only trim change being a slight nose-down tendency which was easily trimmed out. With a slight increase in Mach number the ailerons snatched sharply and the aircraft started to roll to port. This was restrained by the ailerons which were effective, but without any appreciable increase in Mach number the aircraft started a pitching motion that rapidly became violent. A brief handling check was made to ascertain the modified aircraft's handling at 5,000 ft with a full service load and the CG at 9.4 in aft of datum (the aftmost acceptable CG for the type). A qualitative assessment at moderate Mach numbers and at low speed showed the aircraft to have handling that was virtually unchanged from the unmodified case with no loss of stability. As the modification raised the maximum Mach number without any apparent deterioration in general handling characteristics, A&AEE recommended that mod 971 be applied retrospectively to all Seafire F.47 aircraft and that for modified aircraft the limiting speeds should be raised and based on a true Mach number of 0.81.

Following the criticism of the Seafire F.47 as regards a) its neutral longitudinal stability at the best climb speed, b) the variable foot loads experienced during sideslips and c) unacceptable stick force per 'g', Supermarine attempted to improve the situation by fitting a larger inertia weight of 15½ lbs to the elevator circuit of PS952. This produced a moment of +143 lb/ins about the elevator hinge (the corresponding figures for the standard weight were 6½ lbs and +66 lb/ins). In addition a spring tab was fitted to the starboard side of the elevator immediately outboard of the trimmer tab. These two modifications were intended to improve items (a) and (c) above, however, despite attempts to remedy item (b), it was eventually decided that the only way this aspect of directional control could be improved was for the fin to be re-modelled to include a dorsal fillet. As this would have required extensive modification work, the Seafire F.47's inadequacy as regards rudder control had to be accepted, albeit reluctantly. PS952 was delivered to Boscombe Down in September 1948 but unfortunately it had not been tested prior to modification to compare it with PS944. Because of this the results of the subsequent trial were somewhat speculative in certain areas as it was quite possible that PS952 in its unmodified state was slightly less stable than PS944 had been [throughout its service life, the Seafire F.47 was inevitably made to carry more weight which tended to reduce longitudinal stability].

The outcome of the trial was extremely disappointing as the larger inertia weight and modified elevator gave no appreciable improvement in longitudinal stability on the climb at the best climbing speed compared with PS944, indeed there appeared to be some deterioration in longitudinal handling in various other respects. Even when using fuel from the rear tank first (as was normal practice) no improvement was apparent and the aircraft was difficult to trim acurately during climbs at any altitude. There was some improvement, however, in the stick force per 'g' characteristics, but at high altitudes and at aft CG, stick force per 'g' was still too low at low speeds and too high at high speeds. The eventual conclusion from the trial was that the advantages of the modifications, such as they were, did not warrant action being taken, particularly since production of the type was drawing to a close. [In view of the recent modification to the elevators to improve the

Seafire F.47's limiting Mach number, several dives were carried out in PS952 to evaluate its handling at high IMN. Despite the fact that mod 971 had been incorporated on the aircraft, the porpoising started at only 0.82 IMN (0.78 TMN) or slightly earlier than on PS944 before it was modified].

One A&AEE trial that did proceed more or less to plan was an investigation into the spinning characteristics of the Seafire F.47 at take off weights up to 10,885 lbs. In this condition wing combat tanks were carried (during tests at two lower weights they were not) and fuel in the rear tanks was used up during the climb to height to maintain CG as far as possible at 9.4 in aft of datum. As the trial took place in February 1948, mod 971 had been incorporated in the trials aircraft (PS944). In each spin the aircraft was allowed to make two complete turns (this was visually assessed by the pilot) before standard recovery action was taken consisting of the application of full opposite rudder, a pause, and then forward stick.

In general, the Seafire F.47 was reluctant to enter a spin, full pro-spin controls being required both before and during the spin, indeed pilots gained the impression that even a relaxation of the controls would have been sufficient encouragement for the aircraft to begin its recovery. There was no tendency for the aircraft to depart into a spin in the other direction after recovery and when it was flick rolled into a spin from a stalled turn entry there was no sign at any stage of an inverted spin being the result. Once the Seafire F.47 had settled down into the spin, the rate of rotation was fast with a steep nose-down attitude, although the longitudinal pitching that had been apparent on previous Seafire variants was still present. There was also a certain amount of lateral wallowing and both of these characteristics were accentuated with altitude. Spins to the right and left were similar, except that the aircraft was prone to dropping its port wing at the stall entry which meant that a spin to the left was entered rather more readily than one to the right.

With the wing combat tanks fitted two spins were made in each direction from 30,000 ft following straight stalls (engine off) and from stalls off turns. The entries into the turns were made at approximately 208 mph IAS (180 knots) and the stick was eased back until the aircraft stalled, the throttle then being closed. Entry to the spin was by a flick roll which was followed by a steep fast spin with considerable longitudinal pitching and lateral wallowing, with buffet being felt from the tail surfaces. From the straight stall the entry was slow and flat but after about half a turn the spin got faster and steeper, again with pitching and wallowing. The amount of height lost from the commencement of the spin to the achievement of full recovery was of the order of 6,000 ft [recovery from spins at reduced take off weight from 15,000 ft was in the order of 3–4,000 ft].

Towards the end of its development life the later Spitfire/Seafire variants carried significantly more fuel than the early aircraft and the Seafire F.47 was no exception. The main internal fuel tanks mounted forward of the cockpit held a total of 85 gallons which were supplemented by a rear fuselage tank of 33 gallons and two leading edge tanks with a combined total of 36 gallons. In addition, two underwing combat tanks could be carried, each holding 22½ gallons, and the aircraft was also capable of accommodating a 90-gallon overload tank on the fuselage centreline. Total fuel capacity was thus 289 gallons, sufficient for a range of around 1,000 miles. With full fuel and a full warload the Seafire F.47 weighed a prodigious 12,450 lbs, although it was capable of even more than this as it was cleared for gentle flying when overloaded to 12,900 lbs. At the latter weight wing loading was 52.95 lbs/sq.ft which compared with a wing loading of only 24.5 lbs/sq.ft on Spitfire I K9793 which had been the subject of trials at Boscombe Down in 1939. With such significant weight growth it was necessary to re-test the Seafire F.47 and in March 1949 VP463 was delivered to A&AEE for handling trials with and without the 90-gallon 'airship type' drop tank.

VP463 was flown at various loadings as follows – Loading 1 – 10,825 lbs (no external stores but combat tanks fitted); Loading 2 – 11,590 lbs (as loading 1 plus 90-gallon tank); Loading 3 – 12,645 lbs (as loading 1 plus 90-gallon tank and two 500-lb smoke bombs); Loading 4 – 12,035 lbs (as loading 1 plus 90-gallon tank and eight 60-lb rocket projectiles, but less combat tanks). The controls of the aircraft were standard Seafire F.47 and included 9.25 in of angle above and below the trailing edge of each half of the elevator. The inertia weight in the elevator control circuit was of 6½ lbs. Preliminary trials were carried out with no external stores (except for the combat tanks which were a standard fit) but these showed that the aircraft's handling characteristics were very much worse in several respects than those of PS944 which had been used to clear the Seafire F.47 for service use. The trials were continued, however, so that any serious adverse features resulting from the carriage of the 90-gallon drop tank might be brought to light at an early stage.

Without external stores (loading 1) VP463 was climbed between 3,000 ft and 10,000 ft at the recommended climbing speed of 172 mph IAS (150 knots) at the maximum permissible climb power of 2,600 rpm and +9 lbs/sq.in boost. Accurate trimming was found to be very difficult but after doing so, when the stick was released, the aircraft diverged rapidly in either direction. Other speeds were then tried and the aircraft continued to be statically unstable (stick free) up to nearly 230 mph IAS (200 knots). After trimming in level flight at 270 mph IAS (235 knots) at 10,000 ft, normal turns were made with the speed constant at 252 mph

Another view of DP845 after it had been converted to have clipped wings and a retractable tailwheel. *(Philip Jarrett)*

DP845 was the first Griffon-engined Spitfire and was first flown as a Spitfire IV before becoming the Mark XII prototype. It is pictured during trials at Boscombe Down in September 1942 with standard wings and a fixed tailwheel. *(Philip Jarrett)*

*Top:* Seen at low level where it was at its most effective, the Spitfire XII was more than a match for the Fw 190 below 15,000 ft. This is MB882 EB-B of 41 Squadron. *(via author)*

*Centre:* Spitfire XII MB882 seen on an early test flight. It later served with 41 Squadron and the Fighter Leader School at Milfield. *(Philip Jarrett)*

*Bottom:* JF318 was one of six Spitfire VIIIs fitted with Griffon engines to act as prototypes for the Mark XIV. These aircraft were often referred to by Supermarine test pilots as the Spitfire VIIIG. *(Philip Jarrett)*

The Spitfire XII was first flown by 41 Squadron which was initially based at High Ercall before moving to Hawkinge. This formation includes MB882 'B', MB858 'D', MB794 'H', MB840 'J' and MB862 'E'.

*(via author)*

JF318 in the air. This aircraft was lost on 23 September 1944 when the pilot baled out following engine failure at high level.

*(Philip Jarrett)*

Jeffrey Quill piloting the first production Spitfire XIV RB140 on an early test flight in late 1943. This aircraft later flew with 616 and 610 Squadrons but was written off following battle damage that was sustained on 30 October 1944. (*Philip Jarrett*)

Spitfire XIV RB151 pictured in December 1943. It later served with 610 Squadron. (*Philip Jarrett*)

*Above:* Spitfire XIV RM619 wears the 'AP' codes of 130 Squadron. It was shot down by flak near Aachen on 16 January 1945 when flown by 350 Squadron, Flt Lt H.J. Smets baling out to become a PoW. *(Philip Jarrett)*

*Inset:* Later Spitfire XIVs had a low-back fuselage and teardrop hood. RM784 spent much of its life at Boscombe Down where it was used for various trials work including hood jettison tests. *(Philip Jarrett)*

*Below:* Another view of RM784 taken in March 1945 when it was engaged on spin trials at Boscombe Down. *(Philip Jarrett)*

Spitfire FR.XIVE TZ112 served with 2 Squadron in the reconnaissance role in Germany in the immediate post war period. *(Philip Jarrett)*

Spitfire FR.XIVE CF-GMZ (formerly TZ138) was flown by Flt Lt J.H.G. McArthur (RCAF) in the 1949 Tinnerman Trophy Race at Cleveland, Ohio where he was placed third. *(Philip Jarrett)*

Spitfire FR.XVIII TZ203 flew with both 32 and 208 Squadrons in the Middle East. It was struck off charge on 12 December 1951. *(Philip Jarrett)*

Seen over a typical Malayan landscape in December 1947, Spitfire FR.XVIII TP377 of 28 Squadron ended its days as a decoy at Kai Tak, Hong Kong. *(Philip Jarrett)*

Rolls-Royce-owned Spitfire XIV RM689 was flown for many years in the markings of 130 Squadron with the serial RM619. *(Philip Jarrett)*

Spitfire FR.XIVE NM821 of 2 Squadron probably at Celle circa 1948. It was written off in a wheels up landing at Utersen on 20 August 1949.

Pictured at Boscombe Down in February 1945, Spitfire PR.XIX PS858 was used to test various sizes of slipper tanks including the 170-gallon tank as seen here. *(Philip Jarrett)*

During its RAF career Spitfire F.21 LA212 was flown by Nos. 91, 1 and 122 Squadrons and 3 CAACU. It was finally sold for scrap on 17 March 1954. *(Philip Jarrett)*

Preserved Spitfire PR.XIX PS915 seen on 19 March 1987 during a sortie which took in the BAe airfields of Warton and Samlesbury. *(Philip Jarrett)*

Spitfire PR.XIX of 81 Squadron having its cameras removed. This aircraft survives and has been converted to Griffon 58 power with contra-rotating propellers. *(Philip Jarrett)*

Spitfire F.21 LA232 later flew with contra-rotating propellers and was written off in a landing accident on 30 October 1949. *(Philip Jarrett)*

Spitfire F.21 LA215 was fitted with Rotol contra-rotating propellers and undertook comparative trials at Boscombe Down to assess handling and performance with the standard F.21 with a five-blade propeller. *(Philip Jarrett)*

The Spitfire F.21 formed the equipment of a number of home-based fighter squadrons in the immediate post war years. LA275 is seen here in the markings of 602 Squadron, the code letters signifying that it was part of Reserve Command. *(Philip Jarrett)*

Another view of LA232 in its final configuration and in natural metal finish.     *(Philip Jarrett)*

LA215 is seen shortly after roll out and before it had contra-props.     *(Philip Jarrett)*

*Top:* Spitfire F.21 LA188 was used for a number of compressibility trials for which it was fitted with a Machmeter and an accelerometer. *(Philip Jarrett)*

*Bottom:* Spitfire formation comprising F.22 PK312 leading two F.21s (LA217 and LA232). *(Philip Jarrett)*

Spitfire F.22 of 607 Squadron wearing the number '4' for participation in the 1948 Cooper Trophy air race. (*Philip Jarrett*)

Another view of Spitfire F.22 PK312. It was later fitted with contra-props and a Spiteful type tail unit. (*Philip Jarrett*)

Although built as an F.22, PK515 was soon converted to F.24 standard but did not see squadron service. It survived until 1956 when it was sold for scrap. (*Philip Jarrett*)

F.22 PK312 peels away into a dive and displays the revised wing planform of the later Spitfires. (*Philip Jarrett*)

Seen in the vicinity of Kai Tak, Hong Kong, Spitfire F.24 PK682 was flown by 80 Squadron before being struck off charge on 28 August 1951. *(Philip Jarrett)*

Spitfire F.24 PK713 pictured in October 1946. This view shows the higher 'sit' of the later Spitfires due to extended oleos. *(Philip Jarrett)*

Spitfire F.24 VN324 was used for gunnery acceptance trials with the Mark V Hispano cannon before being returned to Vickers for air racing purposes. It survived until June 1956. *(Philip Jarrett)*

NS487 was the Seafire XV prototype and is seen at Boscombe Down in February 1944.
*Philip Jarrett)*

Second prototype Seafire XV NS490 pictured in late 1944 after it had been fitted with a sting-type arrester hook. Trials were carried out at Farnborough and it was found that this arrangement was much superior to the A-frame hook which tended to lift the tail on landing. *(Philip Jarrett)*

Seafire XVII SX194 flew with 781 and 899
Squadrons aboard HMS *Hunter* and later flew
from Lee-on-Solent. *(Philip Jarrett)*

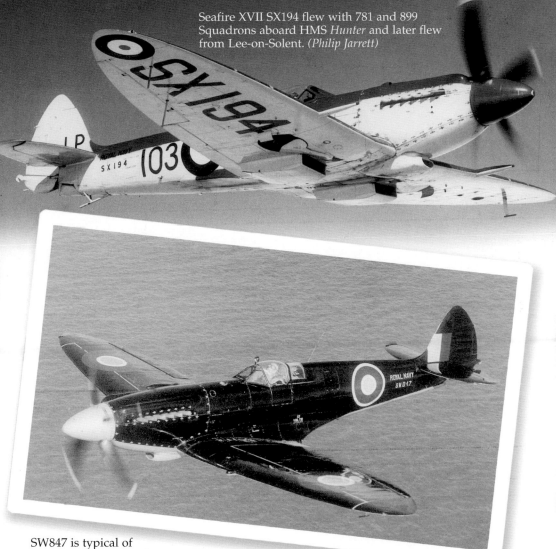

SW847 is typical of
a late production Seafire XV
and has a sting-type arrester hook. *(Philip Jarrett)*

Seafire XVII SX277 features a cut-back rear fuselage, a
feature of this mark. *(Philip Jarrett)*

A mass start up of Seafire XVIIs with Fairey Fireflies to the rear. *(Philip Jarrett)*

Seafire XVII SX235 about to land on HMS *Illustrious* on 1 September 1950. *(Philip Jarrett)*

For reconnaissance duties the Seafire FR.XVII carried two F.24 cameras in the rear fuselage in place of the rear-mounted fuel tank carried on standard Mark XVIIs. SX334 displays its camera ports and is pictured in August 1947. (*Philip Jarrett*)

Seafire F.45 LA443 passed through Boscombe Down in August 1946 for carbon monoxide contamination tests. It was also used for trials with 500 lb bombs fitted under the fuselage centreline. (*Philip Jarrett*)

Seafire F.45 prototype TM379 seen on an early test flight before it had its rudder altered to incorporate Mod 429 which introduced a split trim tab to help with directional control. (*Philip Jarrett*)

LA428 was the first production Seafire F.45. A total of fifty were produced and this mark was the Naval equivalent of the Spitfire F.21. *(Philip Jarrett)*

Another view of Seafire F.45 prototype TM379. *(Philip Jarrett)*

LA541 was the first of twenty-four examples of the Seafire F.46. It is seen here with contra-rotating propellers and the enlarged Spiteful-type tail unit. *(Philip Jarrett)*

A pleasant underside view of Seafire F.47 PS946. This aircraft was flown a number of times by John Derry (including a forced landing) and was also used for gunnery and fuel consumption trials at Boscombe Down. *(Philip Jarrett)*

An anonymous Seafire FR.47 of No.1833 Squadron from Bramcote displays its revised wing folding which comprised a single break point outboard of the cannon installation. *(Philip Jarrett)*

When in the fully folded position the Seafire F.47 mainplane was supported by a jury strut as seen here. *(Philip Jarrett)*

This view of Seafire F.46 LA542 illustrates well the lines of the ultimate Seafire with contra-props and enlarged tail. (*Philip Jarrett*)

NN664 was the second prototype Spiteful and was flown for the first time on 8 January 1945. It is seen here with the original Spitfire XIV tail before enlarged vertical surfaces were fitted. (*Philip Jarrett*)

Seafire F.47 VR961 was first flown from RNAS Anthorn before being delivered to No.800 Squadron. Flying from HMS *Triumph* it was used for ground attack missions in Malaya and Korea before being returned to the UK for service from Lee-on-Solent and Stretton. (*Philip Jarrett*)

The first production Spiteful was RB515 which took to the air for the first time on 2 April 1945. On 28 September 1945 it was force landed at Farnborough by Lt Patrick Shea-Simmonds after the engine exploded at high level as a result of failure of the propeller constant speed unit and the first-stage supercharger. *(Philip Jarrett)*

This view of RB515 shows to good effect the Spiteful's wide-span radiators under each wing. *(Philip Jarrett)*

After completing manufacturers trials, Spiteful RB520 was fitted with a sting-type arrester hook as part of the development programme for the Seafang. *(Philip Jarrett)* occurred at 98 mph IAS (85 knots) and on occasions the ailerons could also snatch vigorously. Stalling characteristics were similar with undercarriage and flaps down, the stall occurring at 86 mph IAS (75 knots). Just before the stall there was marked snatching of the ailerons after which the port wing dropped followed by the nose. In both cases recovery was straightforward on easing the control column forward and applying opposite rudder when stalling in the landing configuration. Paradoxically, when the same tests as noted above were carried out at loadings 3 and 4, the aircraft's handling characteristics actually showed a slight improvement, although stability on the climb was still negative.

The conclusions to the Boscombe Down report on VP463 highlighted the deterioration in longitudinal stability compared to that of PS944. At a CG only 0.1 in forward of the aft limit, PS944 had approximately neutral static stability (stick free) on the climb at normal climbing speed, whereas at a more forward CG VP463 became neutrally stable only at a speed 46 mph IAS (40 knots) higher. It was also emphasised that the longitudinal characteristics of PS944 at the time of its test were regarded by A&AEE as marginal. In comparing the two aircraft it was noted that the static friction of the elevator circuit of VP463 was approximately double that of PS944 (5–6 lbs against 3 lbs) and it was considered that this would lead to a reduction of stick free stability. Because of the basic defects in handling characteristics it was difficult to assess accurately the effect of the 90-gallon tank on handling. The main deficiencies of VP463 were summarised as follows

a)   The aircraft was statically unstable stick free on the climb at the normal climbing speed; pilots considered the behaviour to be unpleasant and potentially dangerous.

b)   Zero stick force was required to maintain 3g turns at 10,000 ft.

c)   High normal accelerations were liable to develop on release of the stick in out-of-trim dives.

d)   The aircraft tightened into the pullout beyond 3g accelerometer reading at speeds up to about 345 mph IAS (300 knots) at 10,000 ft (stick force per g values, based on tests at 3g, were low up to 460 mph IAS).

A&AEE were aware, via Supermarine, that other production Seafire F.47s were showing similar unsatisfactory characteristics so an improvement was clearly essential for all service aircraft. VP463 was later tested with a larger inertia weight in the elevator circuit and although this appeared to bring its longitudinal handling characteristics into line with those of PS944, as already noted, the experience with PS952 showed that this was not a complete cure for the aircraft's instability in pitch.

In Fleet Air Arm service most Seafire F.47s were converted to the fighter-reconnaissance role as the FR.47. Two electrically-heated F.24 cameras (one vertical and one oblique) were mounted in the rear fuselage. The aperture for the vertical camera had a spring-loaded flap for protection against debris being thrown up when on the ground. Total production of the Seafire F.47 amounted to 89 which were built at South Marston. Serial batches were PS944-PS957, VP427-VP465, VP471-495, VR961-VR971.

While the Seafire F.47 continued to cause problems at Boscombe Down, it was taken on charge by No.804 Squadron at Ford in February 1948 and later saw active service in Malaya and Korea with No.800 Squadron aboard HMS *Triumph*. Following operations against communist terrorist targets in Malaya from October 1949 until February 1950, HMS *Triumph* was in Japanese waters when the communist forces of North Korea crossed over the 38th parallel on 25 June 1950, an action which led to conflict in the area for the next three years. Together with No.827 Squadron (Firefly I), the Seafire F.47s of No.800 Squadron carried out the first naval air strikes of the war on 3 July when rocket attacks were made on the airfield at Haeju. Further strikes were launched over the coming weeks together with Combat Air Patrols and other patrols on the lookout for enemy submarines. One aircraft (VP473) was lost on 28 July when it was shot down in error by a USAF B-29 Superfortress, however, the pilot baled out and was picked up by a US destroyer.

Further strikes saw the Seafires sink a number of small vessels during operations to blockade ports on the west coast of Korea, together with attacks on railway targets near Mokpo using rockets and 20 mm cannon. By mid September the Seafires were beginning to show signs of wear and tear with several aircraft having to be taken off operations due to damage to the external skin caused by over-stressing. With more modern equipment being sent to Korea in the shape of the Hawker Sea Furies of No.807 Squadron, the decision was taken to retire the Seafire F.47 from active service. The type continued to be used by No.1833 Squadron at Bramcote before being supplanted by the Sea Fury in 1954.

# CHAPTER TEN

# Spiteful
# and Seafang

W hen the prototype Spitfire (K5054) was flown for the first time on 5 March 1936 it was powered by a Rolls-Royce Merlin 'C' of 990 hp. This engine, even at such an early stage in its development, offered half as much power again as the Rolls-Royce Kestrel and Bristol Mercury engines that had been fitted to the last of the RAF's inter-war biplane fighters, but such was the rate of progress towards the end of the 1930s that engines of 2,000 hp were being offered to manufacturers just twelve months later. Although this appeared to be the answer to every aircraft designer's dream, such a phenomenal increase in the level of power generated by piston engines did pose something of a dilemma.

As a high top speed had always been one of the priorities when designing a new fighter, the availability of much more powerful engines was to be welcomed, but on the downside, trials soon began to show that flight at the higher speeds now possible was producing some unwelcome aerodynamic and control problems. These difficulties were first experienced during high speed dives from high altitudes with many aircraft being prone to severe airframe buffet, immovable controls and uncommanded trim changes. Control was usually regained when the aircraft had descended to below 15,000 ft but in several cases aircraft had not been recovered before hitting the ground. It was also relatively easy for the pilot to overstress the airframe during the pullout manoeuvre resulting in structural failure. These were the first examples of aircraft being subjected to compressibility, a phenomenon that had been predicted by aerodynamicists from theoretical work carried out in the 1930s, but nevertheless it still came as something of a shock for test pilots when they experienced it for real.

The decision by R.J. Mitchell to incorporate a relatively thin wing endowed the Spitfire with an ability to fly at higher Mach numbers than any other piston-engined fighter of the period. Such a wing tended to delay the onset of compressibility effects and during diving trials carried out at Farnborough in 1943 a Spitfire XI was flown to Mach 0.89 in a full power dive from 40,000 ft. The sudden rise in drag that occurred as an aircraft approached and exceeded its critical Mach number (Mcrit) was the chief cause for concern for designers of the time and a number of theories were put forward on how it could be reduced.

Most conventional aerofoils, including that used on the Spitfire, are thickest at a point 25–30 per cent of wing chord measured from the leading edge. Aft of this point the airflow over the upper surface of the wing is likely to be turbulent (due to the adverse pressure gradient) which creates more drag than the laminar flow that exists over the first part of the wing. Shortly before Europe was plunged into another war, a low-drag, or laminar flow wing was schemed by the National Advisory Committee for Aeronautics (NACA) in the USA whereby the maximum thickness was moved further aft to a point close to mid chord. This held the prospect of achieving laminar flow over the first half of the wing which, it was hoped, would reduce the amount of drag created by a considerable amount.

Joe Smith first began to consider a laminar flow wing for the Spitfire in late 1942 and in November of that year Supermarine specification 470 was drafted. It was hoped that the new wing would raise Mcrit and thereby delay the drag rise experienced at transonic speeds, further aims being the reduction of profile drag and an improvement in the rate of roll. The wing was developed with the assistance of the National Physical Laboratory and eventually emerged as a two-spar tapered design with straight leading and trailing edges. At 210 sq.ft, the area of the new wing was 15 per cent less than that of the Spitfire F.21 and its thickest point occurred at 42 per cent chord. An official specification (F.1/43) was written for a new fighter, however, development was relatively slow and it was not until June 1944 that the laminar flow wing was ready to be fitted to a Spitfire XIV (NN660) so that flight tests could commence. As the aircraft was radically different from all previous Spitfires, it was felt that a change of name was necessary and shortly before it was completed the name Spiteful was chosen.

Jeffrey Quill flew NN660 for the first time on 30 June 1944. Apart from the wing planform, the other major difference when compared with the Spitfire was the wide track undercarriage which retracted inwards. This had become possible due to the use of a two-spar wing design and greatly altered the aircraft's characteristics on the ground. Right from the word go it was apparent that the handling characteristics of the Spiteful were vastly different to those of the Spitfire, especially at low speeds. The Spitfire had been renowned for its high level of controllability near the stall. This was largely due to the fact that Mitchell had designed the Spitfire wing with washout whereby the angle of incidence was reduced towards the tips so that a measure of lateral control was available right down to the stall. Effectively the wing stalled from root to tip but with the Spiteful it appeared that the opposite was the case. The laminar flow wing had been designed with a constant angle of incidence along its span, as a result of which tip stalling was much more likely to occur as the wing reached the stalling angle of attack, with resultant wing drop. A certain amount of kickback could be felt through the aileron circuits and the aircraft gave the impression that it was about to take over which, in fact, it never actually did. Even so, the Spiteful was far less predictable than the Spitfire and pilots tended to be wary of it because of its capricious handling.

Another unfortunate aspect of the Spiteful's performance was that the significant improvement in drag that had been expected with the new wing failed to materialise. This was due to the fact that the wing had to be manufactured to extremely high tolerances and had to retain its smooth surface finish at all times to obtain the desired reduction in drag. This proved to be virtually impossible during flight operations as even the smallest item of debris which adhered itself to the wing, even a squashed fly, tended to disrupt the boundary layer air and led to drag-inducing turbulence. Despite the somewhat disappointing results of the testing carried out by Supermarine the Spiteful was still faster by some margin than a standard Spitfire XIV, but not by as much as had been expected.

Flight testing continued with NN660 until 13 September 1944 when it was written off in a crash that killed Supermarine test pilot Frank Furlong. The accident occurred during a low level dogfight with a Spitfire XIV, the Spiteful suddenly rolling onto its back and diving into the ground. A thorough investigation revealed that the accident was most likely caused by jamming of the ailerons under conditions of positive 'g'. Instead of the cable-operated ailerons of the Spitfire, those of the Spiteful were operated by push-pull rods which tended to move relative to the internal wing structure when the aircraft was subject to high 'g' loads. It was found that movement of the controls could cause the ailerons to jam which may have prevented Furlong from returning the ailerons to neutral, after initiated a rolling manoeuvre at low level.

The second prototype Spiteful (NN664) was flown for the first time on 8 January 1945 but as lateral control at the stall was still poor with considerable aileron snatch, a number of palliatives were tried. These took the form of reduced span ailerons, a revised wing section at the tip and root spoilers although any variation of the basic design tended to reduce performance slightly. In its original form NN664 was flown with a Spitfire XIV rear end but this was eventually swapped for an enlarged tail which brought about a considerable improvement in lateral stability. It was first flown in this form on 24 June 1945.

In the meantime the first production Spiteful F.14 (RB515) had flown on 2 April, initially with a Spitfire F.21 tail, although the larger F.24 unit was fitted later that month at the same time as the aircraft was repaired following a forced landing, the first of several. Another unscheduled return to earth was made on 28 September when Patrick Shea-Simmonds was carrying out high level longitudinal stability tests. Failure of the propeller constant speed unit (CSU) allowed the engine to overspeed to 4,000 rpm which caused the first stage supercharger to explode, resulting in major damage to the engine and cowlings and covering the windscreen in oil. The general level of vibration indicated that there was a distinct possibility that the Griffon would break free from its mountings. The only chance Shea-Simmonds had of saving his aircraft was to stall it so that the runaway propeller would cease turning. Having achieved this, the vibration stopped and he was left to fly the Spiteful as a glider to nearby Farnborough where he made a successful (wheels-up) landing, the wide-span radiator ducts under each wing acting as extremely efficient skid plates that prevented any further damage. After repairs, and with a replacement engine fitted, RB515 was returned to the test schedule.

With the end of the Second World War production orders for aircraft were slashed and a further nail in the Spiteful's coffin was the performance of the first jet fighters, the Gloster Meteor and de Havilland Vampire which were superior to any piston-engined design. Development of the Spiteful did, however, continue for a time but of the original order of 650 (subsequently cut to 190), only nineteen were built (not including the three prototypes) although of these the last few examples were not flown. The Spiteful F.15 was fitted with a Griffon 89/90 driving a six-blade contra-rotating propeller and the one-off F.16 (RB518) had a three-speed, two-stage supercharged Griffon 101 with 25 lbs/sq.in boost. RB518 set a speed record for British piston-engined aircraft at 494 mph at 28,000 ft, but only at the expense of a number of engine failures and a total of seven forced landings. Even then the aircraft was only written off when it was dropped from a crane while being moved after its last premature return to earth.

In early 1946 the third prototype Spiteful (NN667) was delivered to Boscombe Down for an engineering and maintenance appraisal. It was fitted with a Griffon 69 driving a five-bladed Rotol propeller, this engine differing little from the Griffon 61 except that it was modified to operate at a maximum of 25 lbs/sq.in boost when using 150 octane fuel. When 100 octane fuel was used the boost had to be restricted to 18 lbs/sq.in by the fitment of appropriate throttle stops. The general condition of NN667 was found to be poor in several respects and the design of the cockpit came in for particular criticism. It was also found that servicing tasks and maintenance were not easy to perform.

For an aircraft that was supposed to extend the performance bound-aries of piston-engined fighters close to the ultimate, the external condition of the Spiteful was something of a disappointment. The butt-jointing of the light alloy skinning was not very smooth in several places, particularly at the joint forward of the leading edge of the fin and that to the rear of the cockpit. This resulted in a gap which had then been filled with stopper but after a relatively short amount of time this had become loose. It was recommended that the joints could be overlapped with the top sheet then being chamfered and this was incorporated on the fin/fuselage joint of later aircraft. Another cause for complaint was the large size of the engine cowlings and the large number of fasteners that needed to be removed and then reinserted, many of which worked loose in flight due to the vibration of badly fitting cowls and panels.

Criticism was also levelled at the workmanship in the area of the cowlings, in particular the very crude packing on the formers to which the cowlings were attached. This packing consisted of thick heavy webbing with slots hacked into it at intervals to correspond approxi-mately to the position of the fasteners. The webbing was secured, rather ineffectively, to the formers by a liquid adhesive but in as little as fifteen hours flying time it was discovered that the webbing had become detached from the stringers. This defect was general throughout the aircraft and it was considered that an alternative packing such as heavy synthetic rubber beading positively secured to the stringers be employed.

Some degree of over-elaboration was also noted on the wings, the panels that provided access to the guns being secured by no less than twenty-two fasteners and nine sets of screws. These, together with numerous other panels in the wings, made it extremely difficult for a smooth finish to be obtained. Theoretically, the fasteners were locked when their heads were flush with the skin plating, but in a number of cases they finished up below the level of the metal skinning which would have done little to help the smooth flow of air over the laminar flow wing. It was also felt that re-arming would take an excessively long time which was an obvious disadvantage for a fighter aircraft.

Other areas of the airframe which came in for adverse comment were the wing tips and the trailing edges of the rudder and elevators. 'Anti-crack' holes were very much in evidence in the vicinity of any awkward bends or abrupt changes of section, which on an aircraft that had only flown 14 hours 55 minutes on arrival was not a good sign. Although all control and balance surfaces were metal-covered, the elevator horns were made from laminations of wood bolted together which were tending to come apart. Poor workmanship was also evident where the navigation light was mounted on a boss on the trailing edge of the rudder. The latter had been crudely welded and was already cracking badly.

The fuel system consisted of four tanks situated forward of the pilot's cockpit and two saddle tanks fitted one in each wing root end. The four fuselage tanks comprised one large tank with a small tank beneath it and two smaller tanks, one on each side. All were interconnected and were filled through the main filler neck on the coaming forward of the windscreen. Total capacity of these tanks was 99½ gallons with each wing tank having a capacity of 8 gallons [later aircraft had additional tankage in the rear fuselage].

From an engineering and maintenance point of view it was felt that the layout of the cockpit was one of the worst aspects of the aircraft. All items of equipment seemed to be situated either in a series of ledges or in deep cavities which would become a trap for dirt and any other contaminants, thus making it very difficult to keep the cockpit reasonably clean. The positioning of the oxygen bottles underneath the pilot's seat was particularly criticised as they tended to foul items of equipment on the port side of the structure and the seat had to be removed each time the bottles or accumulators needed changing. It was also noted that hydraulic fluid tended to drip on the top of the oxygen bottles and adjacent piping with an attendant risk of the oxygen supply becoming contaminated. There was also a risk to the pilot in any crash-landing as he was not protected by any armour plate should the bottles explode. A particularly large cavity existed in the vicinity of the control column which would tend to collect dirt and sand etc which would lead to undue wear on the controls. Of even further concern was the fact that the controls might become jammed by the ingress of some foreign body.

Generally, the cockpit was full of projecting details that were likely to catch the clothes of both pilot and ground crew. Access to the cockpit was inadequate as no non-slip surface was provided on the wing root and there was only one foot hold on the port side of the fuselage. In their summing up, A&AEE found that normal servicing of the Spiteful was extremely difficult and even relatively simple tasks such as refuelling and rearming took an inordinate amount of time due to the inaccessibility of essential services.

Throughout the year of 1946 Air Ministry interest in the Spiteful continued to wane until December when the order was cancelled. As the laminar flow wing was also being used on the Attacker jet fighter for the Royal Navy, test flying continued for a time but all remaining Spiteful aircraft were sold for scrap in July 1948. Although it was obvious that the future lay with jet-powered fighters, the relatively low power of the early jets and their slow response led many to the view that they would be unsuitable for operations from aircraft carriers. The Seafang, a naval equivalent of the Spiteful, had been developed in parallel with the RAF fighter and for a time appeared to have more chances of succeeding. In the event it went the same way as the Spiteful as doubts about operating jet fighters from carriers proved to be somewhat overstated.

The Seafang can be traced back to 7 October 1943 when Supermarine produced Specification 474 for the Type 382 which was a development of the Seafire XV featuring the laminar flow wing and a two-stage Griffon 61 engine. The design was submitted to the Royal Navy and the Ministry of Aircraft Production, but despite an estimated top speed of 488 mph, an initial rate of climb of 4,900 ft/min and a service ceiling of 41,750 ft, at first little interest was shown in the project. Nothing was heard, in fact, until 21 April 1945 when the Air Ministry issued Specification N.5/45 for a single-seat fighter for the Fleet Air Arm, the performance of which closely matched that of Supermarine's proposal eighteen months before. Two Seafangs (VB893 and VB895) were requested, but with the cancellation of the order for Spitefuls, came an instruction to proceed with the production of the Seafang to utilise, as far as possible, the materials and components that had already been allocated to the Spiteful order. The serial numbers given to this batch were VG471–505, 540–589, 602–650, 664–679.

The first Seafang was in effect a 'navalized' Spiteful F.14 (RB520) fitted with a sting-type arrester hook. This aircraft undertook flight trials with Supermarine during the summer of 1945 but it was already becoming evident that the Navy was lukewarm to the Seafang as RB520 remained with the manufacturers after its test schedule had been completed and was not collected by the service until 1947, whereupon it was immediately struck off charge. In the event only one prototype Seafang was to fly (VB895), however, the next to make it into the air was VG471 which had started life as the sixth production Spiteful. As such it had no wing folding mechanism, a five-bladed propeller and was delivered to the RAE at Farnborough in January 1946 as the Seafang F.31. As the first true Seafang, VB895 (designated F.32) was flown for the first time in early 1946. It was powered by a Griffon 89 driving a contra-rotating propeller and featured wing folding, although on the Seafang only the outer portions of the wings were made to fold.

After abortive attempts to interest the Royal Netherlands Navy in the Seafang in August 1946, VB895 was used for deck landing trials on HMS *Illustrious* on 21 May 1947. These were carried out by Supermarine test pilot Mike Lithgow who had previously completed a series of ADDL's at Chilbolton and RNAS Ford. Although only eight landings were made on *Illustrious*, Lithgow was quite happy with the Seafang which proved to be an excellent deck landing aircraft, the best approach speed being 110 mph IAS (95 knots). The view was relatively good and the aircraft settled easily on to the deck with no float when the throttle was cut. The lack of torque from the Griffon 89 and contra-rotating propellers made the aircraft ideally suited to deck operations.

Although the Seafang had shown great promise, it ultimately lost out to the vast potential offered by the jet engine. The development sequence initiated by Frank Whittle with his series of centrifugal jet engines found its ultimate expression in the Rolls-Royce B.41 Nene which was soon offering around 4,500 lbs thrust. As a result of the research already carried out by Supermarine into the laminar flow wing, Joe Smith and his team were asked to come up with a new fighter to Specification E.1/44, an aircraft that was effectively a 'Jet Spiteful'. As the Supermarine Type 392, it featured laminar flow wings with the radiators removed and additional fuel tanks in their place. Three prototypes were eventually ordered (TS409, 413 and 416) the last two to be 'navalized' (but without any form of wing folding) and Specification E.10/44 was soon drafted around the design. Although the E.10/44 (soon to be named Attacker) at first exhibited many of the handling characteristics of the Spiteful/Seafang, it held the prospect of much improved performance and when fitted with a production Nene of 5,000 lbs thrust., it was capable of a maximum speed of 580 mph at sea level. After a comprehensive development programme to improve low speed handling, the first of 145 Attackers for the Fleet Air Arm was taken into the air on 5 April 1950 and the type remained in front-line service until replaced by Sea Hawks and Sea Venoms in 1954.

Despite the disappointment of the Seafang not being ordered by the Royal Navy, it possessed essentially the same wing as the Attacker and was therefore still of value to the Supermarine company. As part of the research effort to obtain data on the laminar flow wing, Seafang F.32 VG475 was fitted with a vertical pitot comb on a mounting behind the starboard wing trailing edge. To facilitate this arrangement aileron span had to be reduced by 15 in and the cannon armament was also removed. A camera installation was fitted in the fuselage in place of the rear fuel tank. John Derry commenced test flights on 23 June 1947 and reported his findings as follows

'The aircraft was climbed to 27,000 ft and dived to a speed of 400 mph at 20,000 ft. This speed, Mach 0.77, was attained without any noticeable compressibility or other effects. The Mach meter was reading 0.75 and a film was taken. At that moment and with no warning, the most violent pitching set up. This took the form of a high-frequency phugoid and, owing to the large angle of pitch at this frequency, the amount of positive and negative 'g' induced was considerable. The Mach meter was still reading 0.75 during this incident. It was found impossible to check the phugoid, which immediately began to diverge rapidly and it was quite impossible to hold the stick steady. The engine was throttled right back immediately, but recovery from the dive could not be attempted owing to the inadvisability of adding more 'g' to the already extreme amount to which the aircraft was being subjected at the bottom of each phugoid. Not until 16,000 ft had been reached did the pitching decrease sufficiently to allow a pull out.'

To demonstrate that this particular characteristic was Mach related Derry carried out a dive in the Seafang to 450 mph from 10,000 ft without any undesirable handling effects. Subsequent modifications to the framework holding the pitot comb and the elevator trailing edge allowed dives to be made up to Mach 0.83 in perfect safety. These experiments unfortunately confirmed that the slightest irregularities in wing surface led to the formation of turbulent flow much further forward than was desired. Debris of only 0.020 in on the surface of the wing was likely to lead to loss of laminar flow at around 10 per cent chord with a significant increase in drag.

Further experiments with the Seafang included a servodyne-assisted aileron system which was fitted to VG474 in late 1947. This led to a significant improvement in the rate of roll at cruising speeds but at limit speeds there was hardly any benefit so that the spring-tab ailerons on the Attacker were retained. Seafire F.32 VB895 was also flown with a 170-gallon under-fuselage tank of 'airship' type and undertook the service acceptance trials of the four 20 mm Mark V Hispano cannon, the same installation as used on the Attacker. During testing at Boscombe Down an explosion occurred in the port wing after firing which caused a significant amount of damage. It was discovered that this had been caused by a build up of carbon monoxide gas in the gun bay which required the fitment of ventilators above and below the wing. After this modification had been embodied the rest of the air firing trials were completed without further mishap.

The very end of the Spiteful/Seafang design stream was the Supermarine Type 391 which was first proposed in June 1944. If it had ever been built the last vestiges of the Spitfire would have vanished as the Type 391 featured a revised fuselage with an enlarged tail unit of angular proportions. Although the laminar flow wing was retained, the underwing radiators were replaced by radiators mounted in the leading edge of each wing. Power was to have come from a 3,500 hp Rolls-Royce 46H engine driving contra-rotating propellers which would have given an estimated top speed of 500 mph [this engine was later known as the Eagle and powered the Westland Wyvern prototypes].

PART TWO

# Operational
# History

CHAPTER ELEVEN

# Into Service

By early 1943 there was an urgent need to get the first Griffon-engined Spitfires into service to counter the threat posed by the Focke-Wulf Fw 190A. The Hawker Typhoon, the RAF's fastest fighter at low level up to that time, had been beset by numerous technical difficulties, in particular the unreliability of its complex 24-cylinder Napier Sabre engine which was still subject to a time between overhaul of only 25 hours. The Spitfire XII was first flown by 41 Squadron which was based at High Ercall and was under the command of Squadron Leader Tom Neil DFC and bar who had enjoyed considerable success during the Battle of Britain flying Hurricanes with 249 Squadron. He recalled his first impressions of the Spitfire XII, which involved borrowing an aircraft from AFDU at Duxford, in an article written for *Aircraft Illustrated* magazine and published in September 1971

'My recollections of that first encounter with the Mark XII are by no means vivid although I recall having trouble starting the engine. Almost all earlier Spitfires used an external battery to start up, but both the Mark II and the XII employed a Coffman cartridge starter. The trick was to prime the engine carefully before firing the gun; with a battery start the pilot could prime whilst the engine was turning over but this procedure was not, of course, possible with the Coffman. The flight itself was uneventful although I remember taking off across the grass towards the hangars and wondering whether or not I was going to make it – Duxford had no runways in those days.

Once in the air, the XII behaved much as any other Spitfire except that the engine was a good deal rougher than the Merlin – it grumbled rather than buzzed – and the beat of the big four-bladed airscrew was very pronounced. It was about 30 mph faster than the Mark V, for the same engine settings, and the nose waved about like a terrier's tail with any change of power. This tendency to fly sideways, given half a chance, was a characteristic of all Griffon-engined Spitfires (bar one) and detracted from the aircraft's performance as a gun platform. In moments of stress, a pilot could hardly be expected to fiddle about with the rudder bias, with the result that the aircraft was seldom properly in trim.'

The first Spitfire XII was delivered to 41 Squadron at the end of February 1943 and full establishment had been reached by the end of March. During the month the squadron got to know their new aircraft with formation practice, cross countries, cannon tests, practice interceptions, long range tank tests and air-to-sea firing. Aircraft also departed in pairs for air-to-air firing practice at Valley. In general the pilots rated the Spitfire XII highly, although concern was expressed at the Griffon's tendency to cut under conditions of positive or negative 'g' at low revs. Discussions took place with Rolls-Royce with the result that 'anti-g' carburettors were fitted which had the effect of curing the problem when the aircraft was pulling positive 'g', but not when it was subject to negative 'g'. As the engine behaved perfectly under all cruise and combat conditions, however, it was considered to be operationally acceptable.

On 13 April the squadron moved to Hawkinge to take over the duties of 91 Squadron which had been engaged on so-called 'Jim Crows' consisting of coastal patrols and shipping reconnaissance missions along the Channel coast. The first sortie was flown by Flt Lt T.R. Poynton on the 15th when he accompanied Sqn Ldr R.H. Harries, the C.O of 91 Squadron, on a patrol from Cap Gris Nez to Dieppe. No.41 Squadron took over the role officially on 16 April and achieved an early success the following day during an evening recce by Flg Off R. Hogarth in EN235 as recorded in his combat report

'I took off from Hawkinge at 2020 hrs on a Jim Crow recco from Calais to Ostend but there were no ships in sight. Slight flak came from points on the west side of Dunkirk. I saw a small ship in Ostend as I passed so went into a steep turn to port to look at it again more closely. I was then about two miles north of Ostend flying at 320 mph IAS at 200 ft. Halfway round my turn I saw a Ju 88 painted black crossing my path from port to starboard. In a second I found myself right on his tail so I pressed the button for a 10 second burst closing rapidly from about 500 to 100 yards. I was missing behind but hit the tail which crumpled up. I broke off to starboard and made a quarter attack closing to astern firing about 2–3 seconds of machine-gun, this being all I had left. Allowing a quarter ring deflection on this attack I set fire to his port engine and he then glided down into the sea burning well on the port side. I was hit by fire from one of the rear machine-guns and had about 3–4 bullets through the wing. I returned to base and landed at 2100 hrs.'

In the meantime, Flg Off C.R. Birbeck had been despatched on a shipping recce to Dieppe where he saw a 400 ton cargo vessel protected by a flak ship. The latter put up a formidable barrage but Birbeck dived down to sea level and launched an attack on the merchant ship which caused a fair amount of damage. This came at a price, however, as his aircraft (EN604) was hit by flak a number of times which put his airspeed indicator out of action. Flt Lt D.H. Hone took off to guide Birbeck home, both pilots landing successfully in the fast approaching darkness. Although he had only just celebrated his nineteenth birthday, Clive Birbeck, the son of a Brigadier who was serving in India, was a particularly aggressive pilot who would feature prominently for the squadron in the months to come.

With the squadron mainly operating singly or in pairs, the increased performance of the Spitfire XII was very much appreciated, particularly the ability to fly at a higher speed in the combat area. During an early morning recce to Boulogne and Dieppe on 22 April Flg Off H.B. Moffett was attacked at long range by three unidentified aircraft but he found that he was easily able to pull away from them. Even though it was a much more effective machine than the Spitfire VBs flown previously, the dangerous nature of this type of operation was brought home to everyone the following day when Flt Lt Poynton failed to return from a patrol to Dieppe in EN601. He was warned by control that eight enemy aircraft were approaching him from the north but his acknowledgement of this was the last that anyone heard from him and shortly afterwards his radar plot disappeared. Poynton had in fact been shot down by the Fw 190A of Obfw P. Fritsch of 5./JG 26, his aircraft crashing fifteen miles west of the Somme estuary. He did not survive. The squadron suffered another sad loss on 24 April when Sgt J.I. Thomas was killed after crashing near the Canterbury Road, just short of the airfield, as a result of engine failure on return from a recce to Ostend and Flushing in EN610.

On 27 April Flg Off D. Haywood (EN607) and Flg Off Birbeck (EN608) took off for a recce from Calais to the Somme estuary. Having completed their duty they had just turned for home when two Fw 190s were seen about a mile away. Haywood turned towards them with Birbeck diving down to sea level hoping to come up below the enemy aircraft. As it transpired, this was not the best tactic to use as the former became embroiled in a desperate fight for survival. His aircraft was hit repeatedly, prompting him to spiral down to sea level and escape at full boost towards Dungeness. On reaching the English coast Haywood became aware of his aircraft making a loud clanking noise which was not entirely surprising as, after making a wheels up landing, it was discovered that it had been hit thirty-three times, including three in the engine. Haywood suffered slight wounds and was taken to Canterbury hospital.

In the meantime Birbeck had pulled up in a steep climbing turn and had followed one of the 190s into thin cloud. A six second burst down to 300 yards caused damage and the Focke-Wulf began a gentle turn towards France with flames coming from the port side, forward of the cockpit. Birbeck was not able to follow as he had to take violent evasive action to avoid an attack by the other 190 which then chased him along the French coast firing five or six bursts. His indicated airspeed during the chase was 340 mph which was no mean feat considering that his long-range tank was still in place as he had forgotten to jettison it. After an anxious few minutes the 190 finally broke away, allowing Birbeck the opportunity to fly home in peace. His aircraft was undamaged apart from a nick from a single bullet.

On 3 May Flt Lt H. Parry (EN236) and Sgt W.R. East (EN612) set off for an early morning patrol along the French coast as far as Dieppe. At the furthest point of their recce they were intercepted by six Fw 190s over the sea, with another two approaching from inland. Parry jettisoned his tank and was chased for three minutes by three Fw 190s which were seen to be giving off considerable boost smoke. Pushing his throttle 'through the gate' he was eventually able to get away but saw nothing of Sgt East who had been heard to send a quick 'Mayday'. Outnumbered, he had finally fallen to the guns of Lt Radener of JG 26's 4th Staffel. His loss was keenly felt by the squadron. For some obscure reason he had been known as the 'Wing Commander', perhaps because he had expressed a wish that one day he would rise to such a lofty rank.

Over the next few days the regular shipping reconnaissance flights along the Channel coast were interspersed with defensive duties and Air Sea Rescue (ASR) escorts, however, occasional periods of bad weather brought an end to such activity. The squadron had been warned to expect the 'Hawkinge Horror', a particularly nasty type of fog which was liable to arrive without warning. On 11 May Flg Off T.A.H. Slack and Flg Off R. Lane were ordered to patrol near Dungeness but were attacked by Typhoons, the Spitfires being able to open up and get away quite easily. The following day Sqn Ldr Neil led a section of four aircraft on a scramble to investigate a report of enemy aircraft approaching Dungeness. Unfortunately control gave the wrong height and no contact was made, the 'Y' service later reporting that the German aircraft were kept fully informed of the Spitfires movements. On the 13th ASR escorts were provided all day for a

Walrus of 277 Squadron looking for the crew of a bomber reported to be in the sea thirty-five miles off North Foreland, although nothing was found.

Ground crews were kept busy around this time as two aircraft were damaged in accidents. On 14 May Sgt A. Hope hit a ridge on the airfield on take off in EN228 just prior to becoming airborne. On trying to raise the wheels he found that the selector lever would not move from the down position, and at the same time he noticed the indicator lights showing that the wheels were not locked. A visual inspection showed that the wheels appeared to be fully down but on landing the starboard oleo collapsed causing Cat B damage. On the same day Plt Off L. Prickett returning from a recce to Calais and Boulogne could not get the wheels to lower, some gentle aerobatics being required before they would come down. Three days later Sgt N.W. Heale overshot on landing in EN229, his aircraft ending up on its belly with Cat Ac damage. After the usual morning recce on the 21st the return of 91 Squadron (complete with brand new Spitfire XIIs) heralded the end of 41 Squadron's period on Jim Crows and a move was made to Biggin Hill. This particular tenure only lasted for a week however, as the squadron flew to Friston on 28 May to become part of the defences against tip-and-run raids by Fw 190s which were taking place along the south coast with increasing frequency.

Friston was not a particularly easy airfield from which to operate as its grass runways were rather bumpy and the short runway, which was only 950 yards long, ended in a sheer drop at the southern end. During fine weather the surface was acceptable enough, but with the slightest amount of rain the ground became very sticky as it was covered with about 6 in of clay. The dispersals had no permanent buildings and pilots and ground crews were required to use large marquees. To reduce scramble times, sections of two or four aircraft were held with pilots at cockpit readiness, a rather tiring business, but a necessary one as the 190s came in fast and low, and any attack was usually over in a matter of minutes. In the event it was also necessary to fly standing patrols in the area between Hastings and Brighton.

It was not long before an attack was launched and Flg Off J. Solak in MB800 (White 1) and Flg Off D.H. Smith in EN602 (White 2) were scrambled at 1120 hrs on 4 June. They soon saw a force of around eighteen Fw 190s heading for Eastbourne, both pilots attacking from the beam as the enemy aircraft came in over the coast. Flg Off Smith then attempted to get on the tail of the rearmost 190 and scored some hits before it pulled away out of range. Unfortunately Smith was at a considerable disadvantage as his engine was down on power and would only make 2,400 rpm so that he was unable to keep up (his RT had also gone unserviceable). In the meantime, Solak turned in behind the second to last machine which he had already fired at and saw its propeller hit the water. It then climbed, before rapidly losing height and diving into the sea, giving off a cloud of black smoke and spray as it plunged into the murky waters. By now, the remaining Fw 190s had reformed into a close line abreast formation prior to heading back across the Channel, but Solak found that he could not close the gap between himself and the enemy aircraft, even though he was flying at 330 mph IAS and 2,750 rpm. The standard of flying impressed him so much that he fired a burst of gunfire well out of range just to record the German aircraft on his cine gun. Damage to Eastbourne was not severe, although there were a number of fatalities. A second Fw 190 was claimed by local anti-aircraft batteries.

Another raid took place two days later and two sections of 'B' Flight were scrambled at 1330 hrs as Eastbourne was being bombed. Six Fw 190s had taken advantage of very bad visibility with low rain clouds to launch an attack, coming in over East Dean to drop their bombs before the defences could react. One of the 190s was hit by ground fire and was seen to depart trailing smoke, 41 Squadron's Spitfires also receiving attention from the local defences, although no aircraft were damaged. Friston did not escape unscathed as the station sick quarters were damaged by cannon fire. Although standing patrols were flown for the next two weeks, no further attacks were made and the threat gradually diminished. Due to the much reduced level of activity, 41 Squadron moved to Westhampnett on 21 June where they were joined by 91 Squadron to form a Spitfire XII Wing.

Westhampnett was well known to the squadron as they had been based there in early 1942. The accommodation was rather better than at Friston, the Officers residing in nearby Shopwyke Hall, whilst the Sergeant pilots and Senior NCOs were put up in the slightly less salubrious surroundings of Fishers' Cottage which at least was handily placed on the edge of the aerodrome. As the squadron had been engaged on recces and defensive patrols for the last few months, they had to get used to formation flying once again as their duties for the foreseeable future would comprise the escort of bombers attacking targets in northern France. The first operation was carried out on 26 June, providing withdrawal support to B-17 Fortresses returning from Le Mans, the squadron on this occasion being led by Wg Cdr R. Thomas DSO DFC, the Wing Commander Flying at Tangmere.

A number of similar operations were carried out over the next three weeks, together with the escort of bomb-carrying Typhoons (usually referred to as Bomphoons) to various airfield targets in northern France. The German reaction to these raids could not be predicted, most were completed uneventfully and it was not until 18 July that any significant opposition was encountered. On this day the Spitfire XIIs of the Westhampnett Wing, together with the Typhoons of 197 Squadron, were to precede an attack by Bomphoons on Abbeville aerodrome, the object being to carry out a sweep to catch any *Luftwaffe* fighters taking off from Poix. Having departed at 1745 hrs, the Wing crossed the Channel at zero feet until ten miles from France when a climb was made so that the coast was crossed at 8–10,000ft. The Typhoons of 197 Squadron took the low position, with the Spitfires of 91 and 41 Squadrons stepped up above and behind.

Shortly after crossing into France, fifteen unidentified aircraft were seen five miles ahead and 1,000 ft below and Wg Cdr Thomas, who was again leading 41 Squadron (on this occasion in MB849) turned the Wing to investigate. After chasing these aircraft as far as Abbeville, however, it was realised that they were friendly as the German ground defences opened up at them with a lively barrage. The Wing then made for Poix but when still ten miles away, a large force of 25–30 Bf 109Gs, together with a few Fw 190s, were seen approaching from the south. These aircraft gave every indication that they were looking for a fight and not long after they launched an attack out of a layer of cloud at 13,000 ft. Numerous dogfights developed during which Sqn Ldr Harries of 91 Squadron shot down two Bf 109Gs and damaged another. Blue section of 41 Squadron was badly bounced and Flg Off Hogarth (EN235) turned towards the attack but was not seen again. His No.2 (Sgt J. Fisher) dived after him and got in two short bursts at the Messerschmitt on Hogarth's tail, but his aircraft was badly shot up by an unseen 109 and he was forced to break away. Flg Off R. Johnson (Blue 3) also tried to assist but he too was engaged and was unable to see what happened to his section leader.

In the meantime, Yellow section on the right of the squadron, and the nearest to the enemy, were watching a dozen or so enemy aircraft over Abbeville which eventually joined the fray. Flg Off T.A.H. Slack (EN233 – Yellow 3) was seen going down on the tail of a 109 but he too did not return. Flt Lt H. Parry (Yellow 1) was also attacked by two Fw 190s but managed to escape after taking violent evasive action. Flg Off Birbeck (Red 3) managed to get on the tail of a Bf 109G and fired two bursts, but the German pilot caused him to miss by diving away and skidding wildly from side to side. Unfortunately Sqn Ldr Neil was not able to participate in the fight as he had been forced to return early, along with his No.2 Sgt P Wall, as his long-range tank would not jettison. Of the missing pilots it was later reported that Hogarth had been killed, but Slack survived and succeeded in evading, eventually returning to the UK via Spain and Gibraltar. The full composition of 41 Squadron on this operation was as follows

| Blue Section | Red Section | Yellow Section |
|---|---|---|
| Flg Off R. Hogarth – EN235 | Sqn Ldr T.F. Neil – EN237 | Flt Lt H. Parry – MB802 |
| Sgt J. Fisher – EN231 | Sgt P. Wall – EN603 | Flg Off H. Wagner – EN609 |
| Flg Off D. Davies – MB796 | Flg Off C. Birbeck – EN234 | Flg Off T.A.H. Slack – EN233 |
| Flg Off R. Johnson – EN238 | Flg Off H. Moffett – EN611 | Sgt A. Hope – EN226 |

Not long after this operation Sqn Ldr Neil departed for 53 OTU to be replaced by Sqn Ldr Bernard Ingham DFC who had previously flown with 234, 72 and 129 Squadrons.

By way of a change, Flg Off Birbeck (EN608) and Sgt P. Graham (EN238) carried out a Rhubarb sortie to Epreville near Rouen on 23 July, utilising poor weather conditions to look for targets of opportunity. A hutted camp was shot up, but on re-crossing the French coast on the way out, light flak hit Sgt Graham's aircraft and he was wounded in the right arm. Despite this setback, Birbeck obtained permission to carry out similar sorties and on 9 August he flew to Dieppe with F/Sgt S.H. May. A small steam locomotive was attacked just south of the town and left enveloped in steam and smoke. Whilst looking for further rail targets on the Dieppe – Fecamp line, a large German staff car was seen and attacked near Le Bourg. The car pulled up in a cloud of dust and four Army officers made a desperate bid to find cover in a ditch, one dragging his leg as though he had been hit. Both pilots continued their attack, shooting up the area where the officers had run to before finally leaving the scene with the car in flames and returning to Westhampnett, coasting out at St Aubin sur Mer.

The rest of August was mainly taken up with escort operations to medium bombers attacking *Luftwaffe* airfields, including Abbeville, Poix, Beaumont le Roger, Lille and Beauvais. This was part of the build up to Operation Starkey, a large-scale deception which was intended to disrupt German troop movements to the Russian and Italian fronts by giving the impression that a full scale invasion of northern France was about to take place. During this period Wg Cdr Thomas left for Staff College and was replaced by Ray Harries of 91 Squadron who, it was hoped, would have the knowledge to utilise the Spitfire XII to best advantage.

The sequence of attacks on airfields was broken on 27 August when 41 Squadron provided part of the escort for USAAF B-17 Fortresses attacking targets in a forest near St Omer. The objectives were described to bomber crews as 'special aeronautical facilities' and consisted of concrete structures associated with the V-1 programme, although no-one taking part realised this at the time. When about ten miles from Hardelot on the way in, Flg Off Haywood (EN611) broke away from the formation with technical trouble but was forced to bale out. Although pilots from Biggin Hill saw him in the water, when they returned later there was no sign of him [it was later confirmed that he was a PoW]. A force of around eighteen Fw 190s was seen near the target area and although they did not attack the squadron directly, Plt Off L.A. Prickett (EN236), who had become detached, did not return. The loss of two pilots without even being engaged was extremely disappointing, although news was eventually received that Prickett had also been taken prisoner.

On 4 September a busy day was rounded off in the evening when thirty-six B-26 Marauders bombed the airfield at St Pol. The Westhampnett Wing was providing top cover, but near Le Touquet on the way out twenty Fw 190s launched a fierce attack on the bombers and their close escort. Flg Off Birbeck, together with his wingman Sgt Graham, orbited the melee before picking an Fw 190 which was at 5,000 ft. Diving down, Birbeck got on the tail of the 190 but he had been seen and it immediately went into a climbing turn. Utilising his extra speed from the dive Birbeck was still able to close and commenced firing, at which point the 190 half-rolled and dived away inland. The high speed chase (up to 355 mph IAS) continued to ground level with Birbeck firing three further bursts at a range of 300–400 yards. After the last of these the 190 flew straight into some trees, cartwheeled and crashed [this aircraft was most likely that flown by Lt Ernst Heinemann of 4./JG 26 and was 41 Squadron's 150th victory of the war]. Birbeck then turned his attention to another Fw 190 which had been flying straight and level alongside without interfering in the previous combat, however, on discovering that he had run out of ammunition he quickly broke away and returned to base. In the meantime Sgt Graham had left Birbeck to follow another 190 near Etaples airfield but his aircraft was hit in the radiator by light flak and he was fortunate to be able to re-cross the Channel and land at Ford.

Two days later the Spitfires of 41 Squadron were again part of the escort cover Wing for Maruaders, this time an early morning attack on Rouen. On this occasion they failed to make the rendezvous as the bombers were early, but caught up with the 'beehive' over the target. Heavy flak was experienced over the coast and near Rouen which hit MB796 flown by Flg Off R.J. Boyd. His aircraft was seen to enter a steep dive and he was followed by Flg Off Moffett who saw the machine burst into flames before crashing near Fauville, leaving no hope that its pilot could have survived. A hectic day on 8 September saw 41 Squadron escort Mitchells to Vitry-en-Artois (from Lympne) and Venturas to Abbeville (from Hawkinge) before carrying out an offensive sweep to Boulogne. The culmination of Operation Starkey occurred on the 9th, the sense of anticipation on the British side being in marked contrast to one of almost complete apathy on the part of the Germans who appeared to be well aware that the 'invasion' was not for real. The 41 Squadron ORB describes the day in rather light-hearted fashion

'The big day dawns and the crews, pilots, medico, Intelligence Officer and Adjutant are turned out of bed at 0430 hrs. Breakfast proceeds amidst the hum and chatter of pilots speculating how many Huns they will shoot down during the day and away we go to dispersal. Then we sit and chat and make things ready for the big offensive or whatever this day will eventually be called (it was called all sorts of names when darkness eventually came!). We have heard that there is a mass of shipping in the Channel – large boats, small boats, landing craft and scores of others – it must be the invasion of the "Western Wall". Away go the squadron at 0805 hrs to cover shipping in the Channel and after stooging above for an hour looking for Huns, the squadron returns to base. Very disappointing, but perhaps the next show will bring better results.

The air is humming with dozens of planes but the squadron do not take off again until 1020 hrs and it's just a repetition of the earlier show. Back to base at 1150 hrs and to the surprise of the pilots, steaming hot tea together with ham sandwiches, tomatoes and oranges have been laid on. After all they are now getting something out of the day! At 1405 hrs we are detailed as high cover to twenty-four Bostons bombing an airfield east of St Pol but again there is no opposition and nothing to report. By now the pilots feel that the terrific build up for the day has been wasted, but we read in the evening papers that a big amphibious exercise has taken place in the Channel and the success was stupendous! One can't disbelieve the papers. The day gradually draws to a close, not one Hun has been seen and the tension of the last few weeks lapses. So ends the great day!'

If Operation Starkey proved to be something of an anti-climax for 41 Squadron, operations over the next few weeks would more than make up for it as *Luftwaffe* fighter units based in northern France finally rose to the bait. The first indication of a change of heart on the German side occurred on 16 September during Ramrod 223 to Beaumont le Roger. Shortly after the target was hit around ten Fw 190s dived on the bombers but their speed quickly took them out of range of the Westhampnett Wing. A mixed gaggle of aircraft was then seen to port at about 16,000 ft and approaching rapidly. While 41 Squadron remained with the bombers, 91 Squadron took on the German aircraft and went on to claim three as destroyed, two Bf 109Gs being credited to Flt Lt G. Stenborg and Flg Off J. Andrieux and one Fw 190 to Sqn Ldr N.A. Kynaston. When leaving the target 91 Squadron's F/Sgt B.G. Mulcahy (EN617 – Yellow 4) experienced engine trouble and was covered by his leader, F/Sgt R.A.B. Blumer. The two aircraft were soon set upon by six Fw 190s but Blumer succeeded in breaking up their attack and managed to account for one of the 190s which he chased down to tree top height. In the event Mulcahy did not get much further as he had to bale about twelve miles west of Le Havre. As it was too late in the day for ASR operations, the only assistance possible was the transmission of an International broadcast giving his approximate position in the Channel [he was later confirmed as a PoW]. The only member of 41 Squadron to fire his guns was Flt Lt B.B. Newman who had followed the first attack and subsequently damaged a Bf 109G.

On 19 September the Wing flew from Manston as part of the escort for seventy-two B-26 Marauders heading for Lille-Nord. The rendezvous was eventually made with the bombers who were seven minutes late and the French coast was crossed at Furnes. A layer of 10/10 cloud at 13,000 ft meant that the high cover squadrons were unable to function and this allowed the defending fighters an excellent opportunity. An initial group of ten Fw 190s were driven off by 91 Squadron, however, a second formation soon appeared and a series of dogfights ensued during which Wg Cdr Harries was credited with an Fw 190, with Flt Lt J.C.S. Doll claiming another with one damaged (see Chapter Fourteen). A Spitfire was seen to go down in the sea between Furnes and Dunkirk which was probably that of Flg Off G.W. Bond (MB799) who did not return. He had in fact been shot down by Hptm Karl Borris the C.O. of I/JG 26 who thus claimed his 30th victim. F/Sgt Blumer experienced engine trouble on the way home and was forced to bale out over the Channel near Deal where he was picked up by an ASR launch.

In the absence of Sqn Ldr Ingham, 41 Squadron was being led by Flt Lt A.A. Glen DFC who suspected the first attack to be a decoy. On seeing the second group of Fw 190s, he succeeded in driving them towards 91 Squadron, but quickly returned to the bombers who had been temporarily left unprotected. The squadron then had to work hard to ward off attacks by small groups of enemy fighters which persisted until the coast was reached. Having escorted the bombers as far as Dunkirk, 41 Squadron then turned back inland to carry out a sweep which was completed uneventfully, however, on landing back at Manston it was discovered that F/Sgt May was missing in MB800. German records show that the Bf 109G of Lt Ernst Todt, the Adjutant of III/JG 26 was shot down by a Spitfire, the pilot subsequently dying as a result of injuries received during a crash-landing. As no other 109 was claimed by RAF pilots at this time it appears that May was responsible, but he in turn was shot down near Poperinge shortly afterwards by the C.O. of III Gruppe, Hptm Klaus Mietusch [May was yet another 41 Squadron pilot who managed to evade capture and return to the UK].

Another Marauder escort on 22 September, this time to the airfield at Evreux, also produced a reaction with several small groups of Fw 190s attempting to get through to the bombers. On this occasion 41 Squadron was being led by Wg Cdr Harries and together with his No.2 Flg Off P. Cowell, he dived onto one of a group of six Fw 190s, sending it spinning to the ground. Before re-joining the bombers he also damaged another. Shortly after a *Schwarm* of four 190s were seen and driven off by Flt Lt Glen and Flg Off R.T.H. Collis. Flg Off Birbeck and his wingman Sgt Vann were also being kept busy, the latter claiming an Fw 190 as damaged. During this combat the two became separated and when Vann returned to the squadron, Birbeck was nowhere to be seen. Around this time Flt Lt D.H. Smith also fired at a 190 and had the satisfaction of seeing several strikes on the port side of the cockpit, plus one cannon strike on the starboard wing which produced a series of explosions as though the aircraft's magazine had been hit. A large part of the wing flew off and the 190 was last seen going down out of control and yawing wildly.

After losing his No.2 Flg Off Birbeck saw an Fw 190 in a gentle dive and opened fire from line astern at around 100 yards range. The 190 was hit a number of times around the cockpit area but took no evasive action, eventually falling away into a vertical dive. Not long after Birbeck started to experience engine trouble and, to make matters worse, he attracted the attention of a number of enemy aircraft desperate for revenge. As he had only just crossed over the Seine at Quilleboef, near Le Havre, he still had a long way to go and began to have visions of not making it home. Much to his relief the Fw 190s eventually gave up the chase and he was able to head back over the Channel, coming out of France at Trouville. The condition of his engine, however, got gradually worse and he was forced to bale out when still about twenty miles from the English coast. He was fortunate as two Typhoon pilots saw him take to his parachute and orbited while the ASR organisation was alerted and a position fix taken. On hitting the sea (the squadron ORB noted that at 16½ stones he must have made a terrific splash) Birbeck managed to get into his dinghy, but in the act of trying to clear it of water, he fell out again, his second attempt being rather more successful. After two hours bobbing up and down in the Channel he was eventually picked up by an ASR launch.

The following day the target for the Marauders was Beauvais with the Westhampnett Wing having to keep close to the bombers on this occasion as the regular close escort was under-strength. Enemy formations were seen on the run in to the target and also when leaving, 41 Squadron staying with the Marauders while 91 Squadron drove them off. A number of engagements took place between the target and the French coast with 91 Squadron eventually claiming three Fw 190s shot down, one shared by Sqn Ldr Kynaston and F/Sgt Blumer, with one each to Flt Lt Doll and Flt Lt Stenborg.

On 24 September yet another Marauder escort was laid on, the target once again being the airfield at Beauvais. On reaching the rendezvous the bombers were already on their way to France, however, the Westhampnett Wing had caught them up by the time that the French coast was crossed to the south west of Le Treport. The target was approached with 41 Squadron to the left of the Marauders at 16,000 ft but heavy flak was experienced on the run in and one B-26 was seen to go down trailing black smoke. As Beauvais was reached the Wing turned through 90 degrees to starboard, at which point ten Fw 190s were seen diving past and heading straight for the bombers 3,000 ft below. Flt Lt A.A. Glen, who was standing in for Wg Cdr Harries who had had to turn back with R/T trouble, led 41 Squadron into a turn behind the German aircraft and forced them to break away to the right, thus foiling their attack. After this initial action a general dogfight took place during which the Spitfire XII Wing claimed five enemy aircraft as destroyed. Flt Lt Glen took a shot at an Fw 190 and blew the cockpit to pieces, this aircraft's No.2 then flying into its leader causing both aircraft to disintegrate with a tremendous flash. Fw 190s were also claimed by Sqn Ldr Kynaston, Flt Lt Doll and Flt Lt Maridor of 91 Squadron. On returning to base it was found that Flt Lt H.L Parry (MB802) of 41 Squadron and Flt Lt Stenborg (MB805) of 91 Squadron had not returned. It was later confirmed that Parry was a prisoner, but it transpired that Stenborg had been killed during a head-on combat with an Fw 190 near Poix.

Beauvais was on the receiving end once more on 27 September. Wg Cdr Harries, who was leading 41 Squadron, destroyed a Bf 109G and Sgt Graham damaged another, but most of the action centred, yet again, on Flg Off Birbeck who launched an attack on a large group of fifteen Bf 109Gs. Having damaged one he was then set upon by the rest and was forced to beat a hasty retreat, fortunately without damage to his aircraft. The experience did nothing to blunt his offensive spirit, however, as shortly afterwards he spotted ten Fw 190s above him. Climbing up, he fired at one with three bursts, hitting the 190 extensively and causing it to emit dense, black smoke. As before, this woke up the others in the formation and Birbeck had to fight for his life once again, utilising the full combat potential of his Spitfire to escape.

At the end of the month two official communications were received by 41 Squadron, one welcome and one not. The first was a letter of congratulations to the Westhampnett Wing from Sir Archibald Sinclair, the Secretary of State for Air, commending 41 and 91 Squadron's achievement of destroying sixteen enemy aircraft between them during September. The second communiqué was notification that the Wing would be moving to Tangmere in the near future which meant that the officers would have to leave the opulent surroundings of Shopwyke Hall for rather more utilitarian accommodation.

The new month of October saw a continuation of bomber escorts, although the approach of winter and the reduction in daylight hours inevitably meant that the pace of recent weeks began to slacken. On 3 October the Wing flew as withdrawal cover to Bostons returning at low level from attacking targets near Paris. Although the Wing was not engaged, F/Sgt J.A.B. Gray of 41 Squadron in MB834 lost his position in the formation and was picked off by Fw 190s of JG 2. Even though large-scale operations were becoming much more infrequent there was to be one final opportunity before the year was out to cause a sensation. This occurred on 20 October during a morning fighter sweep (Rodeo 263) which took in the Triqueville – Bernay – Beaumont le Roger area.

The operation did not get off to a particularly good start as accurate flak from the defences around Le Havre hit the aircraft flown by Flg Off Birbeck who had to return to base together with his No.2, F/Sgt Graham. The remainder of the Wing crossed into France at Cap d'Antifer, climbing to 8,000 ft over Bernay before sweeping down towards Evreux. Between Rouen and Evreux a group of 25–30 Bf 109Gs and Fw 190s dived from out of the sun, requiring the Wing to pull into a climbing turn to port. The German aircraft opened fire at extreme range but did not appear to be willing to stay and fight as they soon dived away with the Westhampnett Spitfires in hot pursuit. It was not long before a large dogfight was taking place with many individual combats.

After the initial German attack, Flt Lt Newman (MB858 – Yellow 3) saw a Bf 109G by itself and dived down on it from a height of 5,000 ft closing to 50–100 yards, by which time the pair were at 500 ft. There were numerous flashes as the aircraft was hit, pieces breaking away and striking Newman's aircraft, damaging the propeller. As he broke away from his attack, he saw the 109 hit the ground and burst into flames. Shortly afterwards he witnessed another of 41 Squadron's Spitfires attacking an Fw 190 and the pilot of the latter baling out. This was the culmination of a combat involving Flg Off Cowell (MB795 – Blue 3) who had latched onto a 190 in similar fashion to Newman and fired several bursts of cannon and machine-gun down to 50 yards. The starboard oleo leg of the Focke-Wulf had dropped and the engine had become a mass of flames before its pilot finally took to his parachute. After their respective combats, Newman and Cowell returned to base together.

Flg Off Ron Collis (MB850 – Yellow 4) was also presented with an excellent firing opportunity when he turned in behind an Fw 190 at 8,000 ft. The 190 immediately rolled onto its back and dived away with Collis following, firing several short bursts which caused a thin trail of smoke to emerge from the engine. The Focke-Wulf then commenced a vertical aileron turn by which time both aircraft were at terminal velocity in the dive and passing 3,000 ft. Collis decided it was about time he should pull out, but in doing so blacked out badly and only came to at low level with his airspeed indicator hovering around the 500 mph mark. The 'g' forces in the recovery had been so severe that his aircraft's spine had been damaged and the IFF set had come adrift and was rolling free in the rear fuselage. Given his own close call, Collis considered that there would have been little chance of the German pilot pulling out in time from his dive.

Many other pilots fired their guns in the fight and most returned to base singly or in pairs. Wg Cdr Harries was credited with two more Bf 109Gs to bring his total at that time to fourteen aircraft destroyed with three shared. Sqn Ldr Kynaston shot down an Fw 190 and Bf 109Gs were credited to Flt Lt Doll, Flg Off R.S. Nash and F/Sgt Blumer, making a grand total of nine enemy aircraft shot down for no loss. This proved to be the last major operation of 1943 for the Spitfire XII Wing, a year in which the aircraft had proved itself in combat against the very best that the opposition could put up. With the prospect of even better performance from the Spitfire XIV with its two-stage supercharged Griffon 65, pilot morale was set to scale new peaks, most relishing the prospect of being able to utilise the new aircraft in the long-awaited invasion of northern France. Before this, however, they had to fight another campaign against Hitler's first vengeance weapon, the V-1 flying bomb.

# CHAPTER TWELVE

# Anti V-1 Operations

The first V-1 flying bomb to fall on Britain did so in the early hours of 13 June 1944 at Swanscombe near Gravesend. Over the next three months several thousands more were fired in the direction of London, the onslaught continuing until the launch sites in the Pas de Calais had been overrun by the advancing Allied armies. This was not quite the end of Hitler's first vengeance weapon, however, as sporadic attacks were still carried out utilising Heinkel He 111 bombers to air launch the V-1, and a number were also despatched via ramps in Holland. The last recorded V-1 to impact on British soil came down on 28 March 1945.

The V-1, or to give it its correct designation the Fieseler Fi 103, can be traced back to 1928 when Paul Schmidt, a fluid dynamicist, began work on a pulse-jet engine which could be used to power a flying bomb. Although his engines were giving 1,100 lbs thrust by 1940, Schmidt suffered from a serious lack of funding for his work and progress was slow. The *Reichsluftfahrtministerium* (RLM) favoured the Argus Motoren-Gesellschaft of Berlin to develop the pulse-jet as it had already carried out a study of this form of propulsion and Schmidt was ordered to allow his work to be viewed by the company. The official go-ahead for the missile was given on 19 June 1942 with Fieseler being responsible for the airframe, Walter KG the launching ramp and Siemens the guidance system.

Despite a difficult development period in which many V-1s failed to fly for any great distance, the system was eventually proved to the point where operations could begin. Preparations had already been taking place in northern France with the construction of launching sites but these had come in for considerable attention from the medium and heavy bombers of the RAF and USAAF which had put the V-1 programme back several months. It had been hoped that the V-1 offensive would have begun earlier so as to have some effect on preparations for the Allied invasion of northern Europe, but this was not to be and London became the principal target. The defences against the V-1 consisted of fighters, anti-aircraft guns and balloons. As it cruised at speeds of around 340–360 mph, only the fastest RAF fighters stood a chance of carrying out a successful interception which effectively meant the Tempest V, Mustang III and Spitfire XII/XIV for day interceptions with Mosquitos performing the first line of defence at night. Six squadrons of Griffon-Spitfires took part in the V-1 campaign (Nos. 41, 91, 130, 322, 402 and 610 Squadrons) and this chapter looks at their activities during this period.

## No.91 Squadron

The highest scoring unit flying Griffon-engined Spitfires was 91 Squadron which was eventually credited with the destruction of 189 V-1s. Since its involvement with the Westhampnett Wing as recorded in the previous chapter, 91 Squadron had continued with bomber escort duties until being pulled back to Drem in Scotland for a brief rest period, during which time it converted to the Spitfire XIV. It then returned south to West Malling in April 1944 where it was based for the next three months. The C.O. was still Sqn Ldr Norman Kynaston who was to become the top scoring Spitfire XIV pilot with twenty-one outright V-1 claims.

The first hint of what was to come occurred on 13 June 1944 when four Spitfire XIVs of 91 Squadron were scrambled to intercept a raid by 'pilotless aircraft' coming in over Dungeness. No interceptions were made on this occasion but it would not be long before the squadron opened its account. On the 16th ten aircraft patrolled the sector along the Thames estuary on the lookout for V-1s (code name 'Diver') and it was to be a Canadian pilot, Flt Lt H.B. Moffett, who made the first successful interception when he shot down a V-1 over Kenley in RM617 after a twenty mile chase. After a relatively slow start, the V-1 launch rate increased significantly so that by 18 June No.91 Squadron was operating at maximum intensity with a total of fifty-three sorties being flown throughout the day. By now pilots were becoming more accustomed to attacking this new type of target which generally flew at a height of around 2–3,000 ft. As the V-1 was quite small with a wingspan of only 17 ft 4 in and a length of 22 ft 7 in, it was difficult to acquire visually against a dark background, especially as the normal patrol height for the defending fighters was around 5,000 ft to allow pilots the opportunity to increase speed in a dive so as to be able to close to gun firing range.

As the warhead consisted of 1,870 lbs of explosive, the V-1 was an extremely dangerous target to attack and over the coming weeks many fighters would be hit by debris from exploding bombs. Sadly, some pilots were tempted to open fire at too close a range and died when their aircraft went out of control and crashed. One pilot from 91 Squadron brought into effect a new way of destroying 'Divers' on 23 June after he had run out of ammunition. Flg Off K.R. Collier from Glebe, New South Wales flew alongside the V-1 and managed to tip it over with his wing tip, thereby toppling the gyroscopes that were controlling its attitude. This involved very precise flying but if it could be done, it at least avoided the dangers of having to fly through the blast from the exploding warhead. On this occasion the V-1 fell away harmlessly to crash in a field near Epsom. 91 Squadron suffered its first loss of the V-1 campaign on 25 June when W/O 'Red' Blumer was killed when his aircraft (RM617) was seen to dive into the ground near West Malling after returning from the last patrol of the day.

Occasional bad weather over the next few days resulted in reduced activity but a record sixty-three sorties were flown on 29 June during which eleven V-1s were shot down. The best day for 91 Squadron, however, occurred on 7 July when twelve 'Divers' were destroyed in the course of forty-six sorties. The following is taken from Diver Report No.17 which covered the combats that occurred on this day. The courses flown by the V-1s varied from 310–340 degrees, the lowest being seen at 800 ft and the highest at 3,000 ft. Speeds varied between an estimated 320 and 370 mph. Most combats were carried out with the assistance of Kingsley 2 control and covered a large area from Dungeness on the Channel coast to Dartford on the outskirts of London.

| Time | Pilot | Place of Combat | Remarks |
|------|-------|-----------------|---------|
| 0540 | Flt Lt R.S. Nash – RB169 | South of Dartford | Sighted Diver north of Ashford and attacked from astern at 100 yards range. Saw strikes and Diver fell, exploding in a field |
| 1335 | Flt Lt A.R. Cruikshank – RB165 | Pluckley Station | Sighted Diver 4 miles west of Folkstone fired at by a Mustang but who did not get strikes. Attacked from astern at 100 yards range and Diver fell, exploding in a field near railway lines at Pluckley Station. |
| 1517 | Flg Off A.R.Elcock – RM615 | NW of Rochester | Saw Diver south of Rochester and attacked from 90 degrees to astern with one long burst at 400 yards range. Diver fell and exploded in open country. |

| Time | Pilot | Place of Combat | Remarks |
|------|-------|-----------------|---------|
| 1523 | Flg Off W.C. Marshall – NH720 | SW of Tunbridge Wells | Saw Diver south of Tunbridge Wells and attacked from line astern. Jet unit put out of action and pieces knocked off wing. Diver fell, exploding in a wood. |
| 1731 | Flg Off W.C. Marshall – NH720 | Ham Street | Sighted Diver over Dymchurch and attacked from above and astern at 300 yards closing to 200 yards range. Big pieces fell off the port wing and it spun in with jet mechanism still functioning. |
| 1859 | Sqn Ldr N.A. Kynaston – RB185 | North of Detling | Saw Diver NW of Ashford and attacked from astern at 150 yards range. Strikes caused Diver to alter course 180 degrees, after second attack it fell, exploding in a field. |
| 2039 | Flt Lt A.R. Cruikshank – RB165 | West of Wormshill | Sighted Diver north of Ashford and attacked from astern at 100 yards range. Saw strikes and Diver fell and exploded in a field. |
| 2102 | Flt Lt H.D. Johnson – NH697 | North of Appledore Station | Saw Diver over Ivychurch and attacked from astern at 100 yards range. Diver fell exploding In a field. |
| 2103 | Flg Off H.M. Neil – RB183 | West of base | Saw Diver south of Ashford and attacked from astern with two bursts from 150 yards range and it fell on a large country house where it exploded. |
| 2123 | Sqn Ldr N.A. Kynaston – RB185 | West of Ashford | Saw Diver over Rye and attacked from astern at 150 yards range and it fell, exploding in a field. |
| 2321 | Flg Off P.A. Schade – RM620 | NW of Rye | Warned of approaching Diver. Sighted it five miles out to sea being fired at by another aircraft which was not getting any strikes. Called over RT that I was going in to attack and other aircraft broke away. Attack made from astern at 250 yards closing to 100 yards range. Strikes caused Diver to descend and when I was certain that it was crashing, I broke away. |

| Time | Pilot | Place of Combat | Remarks |
|------|-------|-----------------|---------|
| 2334 | Flg Off H.M. Neil – RB174 | NNW of Dungeness | Saw Diver five miles south of Dungeness. Attacked from astern at 150–100 yards range and it fell, exploding on hitting the ground. |

On 21 July No.91 Squadron moved to Deanland, an Advanced Landing Ground (ALG) near Lewes in Sussex, where it continued its highly successful anti-Diver patrols. The unit's score rose steadily during this period but in the space of just over a week three pilots were lost in tragic circumstances. On 26 July Flt Lt E.G.A. Seghers DFC, a Belgian pilot, was killed when he collided with a V-1 in RM743 north of Dungeness and on the 31st Flg Off P.A. Schade died when his Spitfire XIV (RM654) was in collision with a Tempest V (EJ586) near Bexhill, an accident which also took the life of F/Sgt A.A. Wilson of 486 (RNZAF) Squadron. Flt Lt J-M. Maridor DFC was also killed on 3 August when attacking a V-1 near Benenden in RM656. As the flying bomb appeared to be heading straight for Beneden School, Maridor pressed home his attack which caused it to blow up, but his own aircraft was damaged by the blast and he was killed when his Spitfire crashed in the school grounds. Not long after this incident, 91 Squadron was informed that it would be fulfilling a different role in the future and on 9 August it flew to Hawkinge where it gave its Spitfire XIVs to 402 Squadron, receiving the latter unit's Spitfire IXs as replacement. Over the coming months it flew many bomber escort operations and offensive sweeps from its base at Manston.

## NO.322 SQUADRON

At the time that the first V-1s began to appear over Britain No.322 Squadron was based at Hartfordbridge, better known by its post-war name of Blackbushe, and was commanded by Major K.C. Kuhlmann DFC. The squadron had arrived in April to carry out defensive patrols to guard against *Luftwaffe* reconnaissance aircraft observing the build up to D-Day. A lack of action had left the Belgian pilots feeling rather disgruntled so the opportunity to fire their guns at aircraft that were incapable of firing back was to be welcomed. The first patrols were flown on 18 June and during the evening Flg Off L.M. Meljers and Flg Off R.F. Burgwal opened the score for the squadron by destroying one Diver each. Meljers saw a V-1 heading inland near Hastings at 1,000 ft and attacked from 600 yards, causing it to blow up in the air. Burgwal, who was to become 322 Squadron's top scorer with nineteen destroyed plus five shared, also fired at a V-1 near Hastings swinging round from a rear quarter attack to line astern. It eventually turned over and dived into the ground.

The next day nine sections of two aircraft flew anti-Diver patrols in the Hailsham – Hastings – Beachy Head area. Flg Off P.A. Cramerus was vectored onto a V-1 which he saw approaching on a course of 350 degrees. Diving down from 4,000 ft he was able to get into a good line astern firing position, two short bursts from 600 yards being sufficient to cause the starboard wing to disintegrate. Flg Off J.W. Dekker blasted another V-1 out of the sky and Flg Off G.F.J. Jongbloed did likewise, although as another Spitfire had cut in and fired, he could only claim a half share. Afterwards he had to make a hasty landing at Friston due to engine trouble brought about by debris from the V-1 puncturing a radiator. On 20 June 322 Squadron flew to West Malling where it joined forces with 91 Squadron. Shortly before this move was carried out, Flt Lt L.C.M. Van Eedenborg on a patrol near Beachy Head encountered one of the more intelligent V-1s as he later reported that it changed course by 10 degrees to pass through a gap in the balloon barrage. Such trickery was to no avail, however, as a long burst removed several pieces, including half of the starboard wing.

With V-1s being launched from the Pas de Calais at all hours, assuming that weather conditions were good, most pilots could look forward to firing their guns at some point during the day. Some were rather spoilt for choice and on 27 June F/Sgt J.H. Harms encountered three V-1s in quick succession. Two were flying very close together and one was being attacked by a Tempest which eventually broke away without having scored any hits. Harms then moved in and attacked the V-1 from 200 yards with half deflection, causing it to blow up. Not long after he saw another approaching Dungeness at 2,000 ft with a speed of approximately 340 mph. Although it was clearly desirable to hack down the V-1s well short of London, there was still considerable danger for those who lived under the flight path. On this occasion there was a lucky escape for some as the second flying bomb that Harms shot down impacted only fifty yards from a row of houses.

The busiest day of the campaign for 322 Squadron occurred on 29 June when sixty sorties were flown (thirty sections of two aircraft). The day got off to an early start when Flg Off F.W. Spietjens was vectored on to a Diver crossing the coast at Dungeness at 0635 hrs. He eventually intercepted it five miles north of Rye and in the course of three attacks the V-1 broke up and exploded south east of Lamberhurst. Not long after, Flg Off Jongbloed received warning of another V-1 coming in via Dungeness at 0712 hrs and he tracked it to the north west, finally bringing it down near Tenterden. Whilst patrolling between Newchurch and Tenterden at 0850 hrs, F/Sgt M.J. Jansson was told of a V-1 in the same area, following the usual track. His initial attack severely damaged it, cutting its speed to around 180 mph, and a further burst of fire removed the tail section causing it to crash south of Staplehurst.

The day was far from over and the next successful combat occurred at 1215 hrs when Flg Off Burgwal was patrolling between Rye and Hastings. He was vectored on to a V-1 as it crossed the coast and shot it down in a single attack from 200 yards. Fifteen minutes later Burgwal was in action again when he forced another V-1 down east of Halden. After a relatively quiet afternoon the next wave of flying bombs were reported just after 1700 hrs which brought Flg Off M.A. Muller into the action. Having been guided onto a V-1 he attacked from line astern at 200 yards and saw it dive into the ground near Salehurst. By way of a change Flt Lt J.L. Plesman was patrolling over the Channel at 1930 hrs when he was warned of an incoming V-1 and managed to bring it down before it had even crossed the coast. The next Diver to fall to the squadron's guns was claimed by Flg Off L.D. Wolters during a patrol to the north west of Hastings at 2047 hrs. An attack from dead astern crippled the V-1 and it was seen to crash between Battle and Netherfield.

Before darkness fell there were still opportunities for 322 Squadron's tally for the day to be increased. At 2120 hrs Flg Off F.J.H. Van Eljk was coming in to land at West Malling at the end of his patrol when he heard over his R/T that a Diver was in the vicinity. Having sought permission to intercept it, he overshot and soon picked up the V-1 which was being attacked by a Tempest. This aircraft then broke away and Van Eljk moved in to send the V-1 crashing to the ground just to the west of base. The last combat of the day occurred at 2210 hrs and involved F/Sgt W. De Vries who was advised that a V-1 was approaching to the south of Folkstone. Moving in from line astern at 200 yards range, his fire caused it to explode in the air between Ashford and Mersham, although during the course of the attack his Spitfire was hit in the engine cowling and fuselage by anti-aircraft fire. As the starboard aileron had also been shot off, De Vries carried out an emergency landing at the nearby ALG at Kingsnorth. This final victory brought the squadron's score for the day to ten V-1s destroyed.

Anti-Diver operations were to continue throughout July and on the 22nd 322 Squadron moved to Deanland to join up with 91 Squadron who had transferred the previous day. Before this, Flg Off Burgwal became the top scoring RAF pilot in a single day when he destroyed five V-1s on 8 July, the last being sent crashing to earth to the north west of Rye. By the end of the month the squadron score stood at 99 and there was considerable speculation as to who would have the honour of downing the 100th flying bomb. A bottle of Bols awaited the successful claimant and on 2 August F/Sgt R.L. Van Beers appeared to have won when he claimed two V-1s during the first patrol of the day. However, Group saw fit to halve these, one with 91 Squadron, and one with No.3

(Tempest) Squadron. As a complete victory would bring up the century mark, negotiations were immediately opened with 91 Squadron to see if they would be willing to give up their half share. In a sporting gesture, Flt Lt Nash agreed to do so and the Bols was duly presented to Van Beers. The total number of V-1s destroyed had risen to 108½ by 9 August when 'with much regret' 322 Squadron also changed their Spitfire XIVs for LF.IXs to carry out bomber escorts and armed reconnaissance missions over the Continent.

## No.41 Squadron

By the summer of 1944 No.41 Squadron was still flying the Spitfire XII and would continue to do so until eventually re-equipping with Spitfire XIVs in September. Immediately before the V-1 offensive the squadron was based at Bolt Head in Devon and was commanded by Sqn Ldr R.H. Chapman, however, the appearance of the first V-1s prompted a rapid move to West Malling on 19 June. Even though the Spitfire XII had been in service for over a year, it was still an able performer with a turn of speed at low levels that could easily cope with the cruise speeds of most V-1s or as the 41 Squadron ORB put it – 'The old XII was once more called upon for its speed to deal with the Huns' latest witticism.'

The squadron got off the mark straight away when Plt Off N.P. Gibbs shot down a V-1 north of Eastbourne on 20 June, with Flg Off K. Curtis soon adding a second. A steady stream of victories followed over the next few days including one to Flt Lt Terry Spencer who would become 41 Squadron's top scoring pilot with an eventual total of seven V-1s destroyed. His first was achieved on 23 June 10–15 miles NNE of Hastings when flying MB856. On 28 June the weather was operationally unfit all day and as a result the V-1s 'sailed through low cloud with sublime impunity', however, the squadron was at least able to move to Westhampnett to continue operations from there. This proved to be rather a waste of time and effort as an order was then received to move to Friston on 2 July together with 610 Squadron (Spitfire XIV), the two units between them being required to maintain two patrols during all daylight hours, with a further two sections at readiness and one at standby.

Although weather conditions were far from ideal on 3 July with cloud right down to ground level, Sqn Ldr Chapman managed to destroy a V-1, as did Flg Off M.A.L. Balasse on his first patrol. Throughout the rest of July No.41 Squadron added to its score on a regular basis with F/Sgt P.W. Chattin destroying a V-1 over the Thames Estuary on the 8th, although his aircraft was badly damaged when the flying bomb blew up directly in front of him, holing his radiator and blasting the mainplane, propeller and spinner. Despite the damage to his aircraft, Chattin managed to make at safe landing back at Friston. On 11 July the squadron was on the move again, this time to Lympne near Ashford, its fifth base in less than a month. Having led something of a nomadic existence, some stability would at last descend on the squadron as they were to remain at their new airfield until December. F/Sgt Chattin chalked up the unit's first victory from the Kent base on the 12th which was added to in succeeding days by Plt Off J.C.J. Payne and Flt Lt K.B. Thiele. On 16 July Flg Off D.P. Fisher dived on a V-1 from 11,000 ft over the Channel and intercepted it at 3,000 ft firing a burst which caused it to dive into the solid overcast below. It was later confirmed that it had exploded in the sea fifteen miles south of Beachy Head.

Towards the middle of July V-1 activity declined by day and although F/Sgt Stevenson managed to shoot one down on the 20th, more were to come over at night, the succession of explosions around Lympne testifying to the ever increasing efficiency of the anti-aircraft guns [the gun belt had been moved to the coast on 14 July from its previous position in central Kent and had begun to use proximity-fused shells]. After two days when operations were severely hampered by bad weather, an improvement on the 23rd brought further success when Plt Off Payne and Flg Off Balasse shot a V-1 into the sea ten miles south of Rye on the first patrol of the day. Flg Off P.B. Graham and W/O A.S. Appleton took off to relieve them and soon after reaching the patrol line were vectored onto another flying bomb which was intercepted with a high overtaking speed. The V-1 exploded in the air eight miles south of Bexhill after a short burst by Appleton who flew through the blast without damage to his aircraft.

Opportunities over the next few days were limited although Flg Off Balasse claimed his fourth V-1 on the 26th. As the Spitfires needed a height advantage of several thousands of feet to be able to dive onto their quarries with sufficient overtaking speed, good weather was essential and operations were frequently hampered by bands of cloud at varying heights. By now there was considerable competition from other forms of defence and although numerous chances still presented themselves, other fighters often got in first or the anti-aircraft guns took over to finish the job.

The answer appeared to be to extend the patrol line further towards the French coast and on 29 July Flg Off Payne (EN238) and Flg Off Balasse (EN609) took off in the evening for the Pas de Calais. They began a chase as soon as they got there and a V-1 was intercepted at 3,000 ft off Le Touquet. Balasse dived from 7,000 ft but misjudged his approach and narrowly avoided a collision as he passed under the V-1. Pulling up to come back for another attack, he saw the bomb going down into the sea where it exploded, the slipstream from his aircraft having done enough to send it out of control. Later in the day Balasse took an aircraft up for an air test and had only been airborne for five minutes when he saw a V-1 coming in over Romney Marshes. Diving to attack, his fire caused the V-1 to explode in the air about one mile south east of Woodchurch.

Low cloud was still causing considerable problems for pilots on many sorties and on the 30th some had to climb to 13,000 ft to find a clear area for their patrols. As the upper limit for the V-1s was around 3,000 ft, some were able to slip through unseen. The next success for the squadron occurred on 4 August when Flt Lt T.A.H. Slack destroyed a V-1 over the Isle of Oxley and the following day F/Sgt Stevenson tipped one up with his wing tip having run out of ammunition. On the 7th fifteen uneventful patrols were flown throughout the day, only for a wave of flying bombs to arrive shortly after dark, most of which were destroyed by anti-aircraft fire. Activity was, by now, becoming rather spasmodic and if nothing had been seen by 0700 hrs, there was little chance of any excitement during the rest of the day. In the early hours of 9 August Flt Lt Spencer got lucky when he shot a V-1 down just north of Wadham and another fell to the guns of Flg Off H. Cook, the flying bomb crashing into the sea eleven miles south of the coastal gun belt. The following day was just the opposite as twenty-one patrols, which were designed to catch V-1s coming in from the Somme – Dieppe area, failed to produce a chase or even a vector.

On 14 August the first patrol of the day involved Flg Off Graham and Flg Off R. Van Goens taking off at 0535 hrs. The first wave of V-1s was rather later than usual and the section was coming in to land when the flying bombs appeared near Lympne. Several got through the flak defences and the section split up to give chase but as they did not have height advantage, they found it impossible to close to gun-firing range. Graham then climbed to 12,000 ft and saw a V-1 heading towards London at 3,000 ft. Diving almost vertically, he came in behind it at what he thought was about 250 yards range but was actually a lot closer as his aircraft was promptly thrown onto its back by the tremendous slipstream coming from the bomb. After recovering, he attempted a burst of gunfire from astern but accuracy was impossible, so he dived and came up underneath it, firing a short burst before getting into slipstream once again. Graham then tried to close in to tip it up with his wing tip but by this time he had reached the balloon barrage and he was forced to break away. He had better luck on the 16th, however, when he shot the starboard wing off a V-1 near Wrotham and the following day he destroyed another between Ashford and Canterbury.

By 23 August the princely sum of £2 10s had been gathered to be presented to the pilot who shot down the squadron's 80th V-1 and this was won by Flt Lt Spencer. At 0820 hrs he was informed that a flying bomb was coming in east of Folkstone and having seen the flak defences open up, he dived from 9,000 ft to 2,000 ft, intercepting the bomb as it left the flak belt. He fired a two second burst and then overshot, but looking back saw the V-1 crash on a railway line about four miles south east of Ashford. As he was returning to Lympne he was told of another V-1 that was approaching his position and seeing flares, he dived from 10,000 ft to intercept and destroy it near Harrietsham. This turned out to be the 81st and last V-1 destroyed by the squadron as it reverted to bomber escort operations and armed recces shortly afterwards, the very last anti-Diver patrols being flown on 28 August.

## No.610 Squadron

Having introduced the Spitfire XIV to service in January 1944, 610 Squadron had latterly been operating from Harrowbeer on defensive patrols when the V-1 offensive began. A re-deployment to West Malling on 19 June saw the squadron carry out its first anti-Diver patrols the following day. The unit was commanded by Sqn Ldr R.A. 'Dickie' Newbury, a highly experienced fighter pilot who had previously been a flight commander with 118 Squadron at Coltishall in 1943. He had been joined by Flt Lt John Shepherd, who had also served with 118 at the same time, and the two would become the top scoring pilots for 610 Squadron during the V-1 campaign. Newbery would eventually claim eight destroyed with two shared, while Shepherd went on to shoot down five with another two shared.

Both pilots were to open their accounts during the first day of operations on 20 June. Sqn Ldr Newbery downed a V-1 near Tunbridge Wells at 1230 hrs and later in the day claimed a second which crashed to the north west of Bexhill. Flt Lt Shepherd despatched a V-1 at 2250 hrs eight miles north of Hastings and had to fly through the blast as it blew up, luckily without damage to his aircraft. To complete a successful evening, Plt Off R.C. Hussey claimed the squadron's fourth which dived into the ground near Wadhurst. After a blank day on the 21st, four more V-1s were shot down on 22 June, two by Sqn Ldr Newbery, one by W/O R. Roberts, with another shared between Flt Lt Shepherd and Flg Off G.M. McKinley.

Having been at West Malling for only a week, 610 Squadron moved to Westhampnett on 27 June to continue anti-Diver patrols, but this unfortunately sent the squadron rather too far to the west and very few V-1s were seen over the next few days. Naturally this did not go down too well with the pilots who therefore welcomed a further move to Friston near Eastbourne on 2 July. At first the number of Divers contacted increased once again and on 4 July F/Sgt G. Tate attacked a V-1 at 2015 hrs near Crowborough. After using up all of his ammunition with no result, Tate manoeuvred his aircraft alongside and tipped the V-1 up with his wing tip. On landing back at Friston he was congratulated by everyone except his airframe fitter who had to work overtime to straighten his Spitfire's port wing tip which had acquired a few degrees of anhedral as a result of the contact with the V-1's wing. This form of attack was also used by Plt Off B.R. Scawen on the same day when he also ran out of ammunition during an attack on a V-1 to the south of Tunbridge Wells.

The perils of attacking flying bombs were highlighted once again by Flt Lt H.D. Price on 8 July when he was vectored onto a Diver coming in near Bexhill. After opening fire at 600 yards, he had closed to an estimated 50 yards when the V-1 blew up directly in front of his aircraft. Price was fortunate to emerge on the other side with nothing more serious than a damaged radiator, small holes in the wings and tail and a chipped propeller. Four days later F/Sgt J.N. Philpott had a similar experience. When returning from a patrol he saw marker rockets being fired from the ground near Eastbourne to indicate the track of an incoming target. He soon saw a V-1 heading 340 degrees at 2,500 ft, flying at 320/330 mph and turned to deliver an attack from astern. His first burst was accurate and the V-1 blew up giving him no choice but to fly through the blast. When his Spitfire was inspected after landing it was declared Cat B with a scorched propeller and fuselage damage, including a longeron that had been punctured by debris.

Although 610 Squadron were to continue flying anti-Diver sorties longer than 91 and 322 Squadrons, their near neighbours at Deanland, the patrol areas allotted to the squadron did not produce many targets over the next few weeks. The progress made by the Allied armies eventually overran the V-1 launching sites in the Pas de Calais and on 3 September the squadron was informed that patrols were to end, an order which was greeted with joy all round. By this time the unit's total score had risen to 46½. Over the next three months 610 Squadron flew as withdrawal cover for bombers returning from targets in Germany and undertook occasional freelance sweeps. It eventually moved to the Continent on 4 December 1944, joining 127 Wing and then 125 Wing in 2nd Tactical Air Force.

## No.130 Squadron

As it did not convert to the Spitfire XIV until early August 1944, No.130 Squadron did not play a significant role in anti-Diver operations as the peak for V-1 launches had already passed by this time. Having previously flown Spitfire VBs from Merston/Tangmere, 130 Squadron moved to Lympne on 11 August and was able to claim its first victories on the 16th when three V-1s were shot down by Flg Off G. Jones, Plt Off D.G.E. Browne and Sgt P.E.H. Standish. The latter was to have considerable success in a relatively short amount of time and he dispatched two more V-1s before breakfast on 17 August with Flg Off K.M. Lowe and Plt Off F.C. Riley rounding off another good day for the squadron claiming one flying bomb each.

By now the number of V-1s being launched in daylight hours was considerably reduced, which meant that the busiest times for the squadrons involved in anti-Diver operations was just after daybreak and at dusk. On 19 August Flt Lt K.J. Matheson and Plt Off Martin shared in the destruction of a V-1 during an early morning patrol and Matheson claimed another four days later which exploded in the air near Ashford. Sgt Standish brought his total of flying bombs to four on the 23rd when he shot the wing off a V-1 near Dover and Plt Off W.P. Dobbs and F/Sgt G. Lord shared another during the last patrol of the day. The last claim submitted by 130 Squadron was by Plt Off J.R. Meadows who, together with the pilot of a Tempest, destroyed a V-1 on 24 August to bring the unit's final score to 11½. Thereafter, the squadron resumed operations over northern France for a time before joining 2nd Tactical Air Force on 30 September 1944 (see Chapter Thirteen).

## No.402 Squadron

Having taken over the Spitfire XIVs formerly flown by 91 Squadron on 9 August at Hawkinge, 402 Squadron spent just over two weeks on anti-Diver patrols during which it achieved some success. The first patrols were flown on 12 August in the Robertsbridge – Ashford area from 1005 hrs to 1740 hrs. The first victories were claimed by the squadron on the 16th when a total of three V-1s were shot down. During an early morning patrol Flg Off E.A.H. Vickers sighted a flying bomb at 2,000 ft four miles west of Cap Gris Nez and chased it to the gun belt at Folkstone. His fire had damaged the V-1 but unfortunately it headed straight for Hawkinge aerodrome and exploded very close to 402 Squadron's dispersal, breaking glass in the pilot's rest room. Luckily there were no casualties. During a patrol carried out by Flg Off H. Cowan and Flt Lt D. Sherk between 0805-0905 hrs, each pilot gave chase to a Diver and they both managed to destroy their respective targets over the sea.

The following day during a patrol of the Folkstone – Lympne area commencing at 0720 hrs, Flg Off D.W. Whittaker chased a V-1 that had been reported by control to be coasting in near Dymchurch, however, he inadvertently entered the flak belt and had to break off his attack. His aircraft was hit by ground fire and Whittaker received slight injuries, but he was able to land at Newchurch. After four days of uneventful patrols, on the 23rd F/Sgt W.G. Austin saw a V-1 eight miles east of Ashford and dived on it from 6,000 ft before firing a five second burst which caused it to lose height and crash. The final victories for 402 Squadron occurred on 24 August with Flg Off W.S. Harvey claiming a half share with a Tempest pilot and Flt Lt J.A. De Niverville destroying another east of Ashford at 1800 hrs. Two aircraft patrolled off Boulogne on the lookout for V-1s on 28 August and two were scrambled later in the day, but nothing was seen. Along with most other Spitfire XIV units, 402 Squadron moved on to bomber escorts, fighter sweeps and armed recces, and went on to join 2 TAF on 30 September 1944.

By early September the V-1 offensive was effectively over, although as already recorded, sporadic attacks were to continue for the rest of the war. By March 1945 the number of V-1s claimed as destroyed by the defences stood at 3,957, of which 1,979 had been brought down by fighters. With a total of 189 V-1s shot down, 91 Squadron was the third highest scoring RAF squadron behind Nos.3 and 486 Squadrons (both Tempest V) of the Newchurch Wing. No.322 Squadron were in fifth position with 108½ victories, followed by 41 Squadron in eighth with a total of eighty-one. No.610 Squadron destroyed 46½ V-1s, with 130 Squadron claiming 11½ and 402 Squadron 5½, to bring the total number of flying bombs shot down by Griffon-Spitfire squadrons to 442.

# CHAPTER THIRTEEN

# Spitfire XIV in 2nd Tactical Air Force

O ne of the lessons that came out of the ill-fated Dieppe Raid of 19 August 1942, the disastrous exploratory mission by elements of the 2nd Canadian Army, was that complete air supremacy and overwhelming firepower would be needed for any successful invasion of northern Europe. Further valuable experience was gained during the Desert campaign in North Africa, in particular the use of tactical air power operating in close co-operation with the ground forces. Techniques evolved in the desert became a basis for the air operations that were to be the key to success in Europe, the aims of 2nd Tactical Air Force being the attainment of air superiority to allow air-to-ground operations to be carried out and to have sufficient forces available at all times to assist the Army in achieving its objectives.

Although it was deployed in relatively small numbers in 2nd Tactical Air Force, the Spitfire XIV achieved great distinction during the last eight months of the war. Its main role was that of armed reconnaissance, however, there were still plenty of opportunities for aerial combat, its high performance being particularly useful when confronted with the latest versions of the Fw 190 and Bf 109. It was also one of the few Allied fighters that stood a chance on intercepting the jet-powered Me 262 and Arado 234, although it has to be said that most successful interceptions of these aircraft occurred when they were being flown near to their bases at reduced speed and were thus at their most vulnerable.

The first Spitfire XIVs assigned to 2nd Tactical Air Force where those of 91 Squadron at West Malling and 322 Squadron at Hartfordbridge which became part of 85 Group in April 1944. Their role was purely defensive as they were tasked with intercepting any *Luftwaffe* reconnaissance aircraft intent on monitoring the invasion preparations taking place at ports along the south coast. No contacts were made during this period and both squadrons were given permission to take part in occasional sweeps over northern France to maintain their offensive spirit. After D-Day on 6 June beachhead patrols were carried out until the 18th when both squadrons were transferred to Air Defence of Great Britain (ADGB) to participate in anti-Diver patrols (see Chapter Twelve). The next Spitfire XIV unit to be allocated to 2 TAF in the fighter role was 130 Squadron which, together with 402 Squadron, joined 125 Wing, 83 Group on 30 September 1944. To highlight the role of the Spitfire XIV in 2 TAF it is proposed to take a closer look at the activities of 130 Squadron which was to remain with 125 Wing until the end of the war.

Number 130 Squadron had been formed at Portreath on 20 June 1941, its initial equipment being the Spitfire IIA, however, these had been replaced by Mark VBs by the end of the year. After a relatively slow start, the squadron took part in its fair share of offensive sweeps and bomber escorts from various bases including Warmwell, Thorney Island and Perranporth. In November 1943 it was withdrawn to Scorton in North Yorkshire where it was disbanded on 13 February 1944, however, it was reformed again at Lympne on 5 April by re-numbering 186 Squadron, its equipment once again being the Spitfire VB. Spitfire XIVs arrived in August 1944 and after a short time flying anti-Diver patrols, the squadron moved to B.70 Antwerp/Deurne on 30 September.

The day after arriving on the Continent No.130 Squadron found itself having to move again, this time to B.82 Grave in Holland. Shortly after the squadron landed, the airfield was attacked by Me 262s which dropped a number of canister bombs, killing one person and injuring several others. The first patrols carried out by the squadron took place on 2 October over the Arnhem area. These were mostly uneventful, an Me 262 was seen near Nijmegen in the afternoon but on being chased by a section of Spitfires it broke away in a fast climbing turn and was soon lost to view. The first of many armed reconnaissance missions was flown on 5 October, six MET (mechanised enemy transport) and a staff car being left burning in the Munster/Enschede area. In the early evening a similar operation was completed around Apeldoorn, but heavy flak was experienced which accounted for Wg Cdr Geoffrey Page DFC (125 Wing Leader) who was flying at the head of 130 Squadron in RM763. He was forced to crash land and was injured in the process.

The good weather conditions experienced in the first week of October held out until the 7th, an early morning armed recce on that date to Zwolle/Emmerich producing excellent results. A fast moving train was attacked at Zutphen and was left halted with the locomotive enveloped in steam, and around thirty barges were shot up on the river Ijssel near

Arnhem. Intense flak from the train, however, hit the aircraft flown by 130 Squadron's C.O. Sqn Ldr P.V.K. Tripe DFC (RM808) and he was forced to return to base. Bad weather conditions over the next few days turned the strip at Grave into a mass of mud and it was not until the 11th that unrestricted operations could be carried out again. Anti-jet patrols were flown throughout the day (36 sorties) and Me 262s were seen on two occasions. A section of four aircraft led by Flt Lt K.J. Matheson fired at one of these aircraft from 500 yards but no strikes were seen and it was soon lost in cloud. The German jets were seen again the following day, one 262 being forced to jettison its bombs when the squadron attempted to engage.

By way of a change eleven aircraft took off at 1335 hrs on 13 October for an armed recce of the Zuider Zee area. A convoy of trucks was attacked, seven being left on fire, and two more trucks and an AFV (armoured fighting vehicle) were damaged. In the afternoon Grave was hit by Me 262s once again, two bombs falling only 200 yards from 130 Squadron's dispersal, close enough for shrapnel to damage Sqn Ldr Tripe's aircraft. The next few days brought more patrols over Arnhem/Nijmegen and on the 14th and 15th vapour trails were seen rising vertically as V-2 rockets were fired.

Heavy rainfall and constant operations, which tended to cut up the soft ground, meant that by the middle of October the airfield at Grave was in a very poor state and from the 18–23rd it was declared unserviceable. Operations were resumed on the 24th with an armed recce to Zutphen. Results were disappointing with just one troop carrier bus being damaged. The driver of the bus was not one to run away and showed his annoyance by firing his revolver at the attacking Spitfires, hitting Sqn Ldr Tripe's hood, luckily without causing injury. On the 28th the squadron was scrambled in the late afternoon to intercept enemy aircraft that had been reported in the local area, however, a conflicting series of vectors hinted that Control was not quite living up to its name on this occasion and they only succeeded in directing the Spitfires over a nest of anti-aircraft guns hidden in the Reichswald Forest. From the resultant shambles, three aircraft emerged with flak damage and although all aircraft returned safely, the pilots were much shaken by the experience.

With the strip at Grave showing signs of deteriorating even further, it was announced that 130 Squadron would be moving to B.64 Diest/Schaffen and this was completed on 1 November. Unfortunately the pilots soon discovered that the new strip was little better than the previous one as it had an extremely tricky surface, with strange contours to trap the unwary. On the upside they were happy enough with their billets as these were located in a local hostelry; to actually live in a pub being the fulfilment of a lifelong ambition for some! The first armed recce from the new base was carried out on 7 November, the only event of note being an unproductive chase after a V-1 flying bomb as far as the Brussels gun belt. Bad weather throughout the rest of November and the poor condition of the runway meant that very few operations could be carried out. In an attempt to provide an all-weather surface, Sommerfeld wire-mesh tracking was laid at Diest over a two week period commencing 21 November. During this time 130 Squadron did no flying at all which meant that total operational flying for the whole of the month was a dismal 48 hours in 54 sorties.

The strip was declared operational again on 3 December and on the 8th 130 Squadron had its most successful day of the war to date. In the afternoon ten aircraft took off (including Wg Cdr George Keefer DSO DFC, the new 125 Wing Leader) for an armed recce of Dulmen, Hamm and Munster. An attack was already under way against a locomotive and its attendant trucks when a large gaggle of Fw 190s and Bf 109s appeared. One of the pilots involved was Flt Lt Harry Walmsley who recorded the day's events in his combat report

'I was Yellow 3 and at about 1535 hrs we were approaching Burgstein. Red and Blue sections went to one side of the town and my section went to the other. We saw a locomotive with about ten trucks. We had made one attack on the loco, two on the trucks and were preparing to make another when about a dozen aircraft appeared from the east. They dived straight past us as if they were joining in the attack on the train. These aircraft had cigar-shaped drop tanks slung under the centre of the fuselage and I thought at first that they were American. I then saw the crosses on the wings and I could see they were Me 109s and Fw 190s. A dogfight started with everyone milling around. After about five minutes I found myself alone. I saw another train pulled up in a station so I went down and had one squirt at it, seeing strikes on the loco.

When I pulled up I saw a Spitfire in trouble. It was smoking and the undercarriage was partly down. I joined up with it to protect it, together with five other Spitfires. I do not know what happened to the damaged Spitfire for suddenly six enemy aircraft, probably some of the ones I had first seen, came diving down through cloud. They had obviously climbed and reformed after the first initial surprise attack. This second attack made from 10/10 cloud at 1,500 ft was obviously directed against the damaged Spitfire. Some of the others in the squadron chased them off. I went for two which were making an attack. I made a quarter attack on one of them, an Me 109, closing to 300 yards and giving a two second burst with all guns. I saw strikes behind the cockpit and the enemy aircraft went straight into the ground. I found I was being fired at by two other aircraft so I used full evasive tactics for about five minutes and finally got away in cloud. The Spitfire XIV is definitely better then the 109 as I could do a better climbing turn even with my tank on. With my tank on the 109 could almost follow me but he could not get a deflection shot at me.'

F/Sgt G.W. Hudson, who was flying as Yellow 2, was also heavily involved in the action

'I was last to attack the train and as I flew through the smoke my windscreen became badly covered. I flew round for a while and then I saw some aircraft coming from the south east at about 500 ft, diving towards the train. I could not see very well and at first I thought they were Mustangs as they looked as if they were camouflaged silver-grey, but then someone called up and said they were Huns. I looked around and found that one of them was on my tail firing at me. I did a steep climbing turn to the right and evaded by getting into cloud. I flew above cloud for a minute or two and then came down again but could see nothing of the enemy aircraft. I then heard someone call saying "There are Huns up there", but when I went up again I saw nothing.

By this time my windscreen had cleared so I came down again and then saw a dogfight going on about two miles away behind me on my port side. I saw two Me 109s going away on the deck. They had black spinners and what appeared to be a black ring behind the propeller. I went after them and attacked what appeared to be the No.1 of the section. I came in from the starboard side and fired from about 300 yards but my first burst was behind. My angle of deflection had been about 35 degrees. I pulled the stick back hard and my next burst of about 1½ seconds from 200–250 yards at an angle off of 25–30 degrees hit him. I saw strikes all over the wings and the fuselage. The enemy aircraft broke left and the other broke right. The one I had attacked was wobbling very badly and I very nearly overshot him. The pilot had the hood open, there was smoke coming from the starboard side and I could see the holes in the wings where I had hit him. I broke away to the left and climbed into cloud as the No.2 was now beginning to attack me from behind. I could not get rid of my tank at first but I found that even with the tank on I could turn inside the enemy aircraft.'

There were further successes for Plt Off F.C. Riley (Red 2) who destroyed a Bf 109 and Flg Off K.M. Lowe (Blue 1) who shot down an

Fw 190 which was seen to dive into the ground on fire. W/O J.W. Turnbull also claimed a Bf 109 as probably destroyed (plus another damaged). The Spitfire that Harry Walmsley had seen in trouble was RM749, flown by Flt Lt D.J. Wilson who was killed when his aircraft crash landed.

The rest of the month of December was something of an anti-climax for 130 Squadron. Bad weather curtailed flying on a number of days and problems were still being experienced with the state of the landing strip. When operations were possible further high level patrols were flown over Nijmegen together with another armed recce of Dulmen. On 22 December the squadron set out for a sweep in support of the American ground forces in the Ardennes but several aircraft were hit by flak. Both Flt Lt Walmsley and Fg Off Heale were hit, Heale managing to reach base, but Walmsley was unable to make it as he recalls

'This was the first day that the weather was good enough to attempt to intervene on behalf of the beleaguered American troops in the Ardennes following the surprise German attack on 16 December. We were making an armed reconnaissance in the St Vith area below 8/8 cloud between about 1,000 and 3,000 ft when we were suddenly attacked by ground fire which could have been German or American. With my cockpit full of smoke and the smell of burning oil, I just managed to reach the top of the cloud layer when the engine seized and I bailed out. I ended up in a pine tree and dropped into the snow to be met by two Belgian timberjacks who had been attracted by the explosion of ammunition from my aircraft which had crashed 200 yards away. Having ascertained that there were no Germans nearby, they kindly led me to the nearest American forces and I was back with the squadron by the evening.'

Plt Off Riley (RM711) was also hit by flak and was injured in the subsequent force landing inside Allied lines. After patrols of Nijmegen on the 31st, 130 Squadron's Spitfires landed at a new airfield, Y.32 Ophoven, an American strip in eastern Belgium. Initial impressions were good as the runway appeared to be in much better condition than the landing strips they had become accustomed to. Personnel changes during the month included the departures of Flt Lt D.G.E. Brown and Flt Lt J. McConnell, both tour expired, with Flt Lt Walmsley taking over 'B' Flight.

In the early morning of New Year's Day the *Luftwaffe* launched Operation *Bodenplatte*, a last desperate attempt to inflict serious damage on the Allied tactical air forces. Co-ordinated attacks were carried out on many fighter airfields and although large numbers of RAF and USAAF aircraft were destroyed on the ground, the losses incurred on the German side, in particular the loss of experienced pilots, was proportionally much greater. Ophoven was mistakenly attacked by elements of *Jagdgeschwader* 11 led by Major Gunther Specht who had been given nearby Asch, the home of the Mustang-equipped 352nd Fighter Group, as a target. The RAF dispersals at Ophoven were strafed by Fw 190s and Bf 109s and although a number of Spitfires of 41, 350 and 610 Squadrons were destroyed or damaged, 130 Squadron got off relatively lightly with only three aircraft damaged. One member of the ground crew was seriously wounded by an exploding cannon shell and but for the prompt action of two 130 Squadron pilots, F/Sgt P.E.H. Standish and F/Sgt P.H.T. Clay, he would have died. At great personal risk Clay also taxied two aircraft that were threatened by fire to a place of safety while the attack was still in progress. He then directed fire crews towards a fuel bowser which was in danger of exploding. For these actions he was later awarded the British Empire Medal. Later in the day patrols were flown in the Malmedy area and during one of these Plt Off C.A. Joseph was hit by friendly fire. His aircraft (RM760) spun in north of Malmedy and his body was recovered and buried by the US Army.

Although the landing strip at Ophoven was a big improvement, the accommodation left a lot to be desired as there were minimal facilities, however, a brief respite was arranged by the local Belgians as Flt Lt Ian Ponsford, a recent arrival from 83 GSU, recalls

'The Americans had built the strip using Sommerfeld tracking and we were billeted in a disused nunnery which was pretty austere and totally unheated. It was a very cold winter so we had to more or less live in our clothes. As it turned out we were located very near a number of coal mines that the Belgians had in that area and this turned out to be very good news for us. We were invited by the local authority to inspect one of these mine shafts and when we got down to the bottom we discovered the most marvellous boiling hot showers that the miners used to use. Of course we all stripped off and had a hot shower, for many of the pilots it was their first one for a long time!'

Bad weather with heavy falls of snow disrupted activities during the early part of January, although occasional breaks allowed the squadron to fly three Ramrod operations, providing escort to Mitchell medium bombers attacking targets near St Vith. Even this type of operation could be fraught with danger as the German flak defences could be formidable as Flt Lt Ian Ponsford recalls

'The only time during my tour that I was actually hit was by flak. It was quite frightening on occasions as it could be very intense. I remember coming back from a sortie at high level after we had been escorting Mitchells and the German gunners started firing at us with their 88 mm guns. They were incredibly accurate in terms of altitude and I remember looking behind me and seeing a whole series of black puffs at exactly the same altitude as I was flying at but about 200 yards behind so they had got the range right, but not the deflection. It was amazing that they could get up to 20,000 ft and get the shells to explode with that level of accuracy. The 40 mm anti-aircraft fire, the stuff that looked like golf balls, was also very accurate and intense as the rate of fire was extremely rapid. Of course our own RAF Regiment gunners with their Bofors were very good as well and I recall that later when we were at Twenthe we had these chaps defending the airfield. One evening a Junkers Ju 188 came over to do a bit of harassing. We had just moved into the place but they picked him off with no trouble at all and it came down more or less in the circuit which was a cause for celebration.'

On the 16 January ten aircraft took off at 1315 hrs for an armed recce around Malmedy. The total score for the day was five MET destroyed plus two damaged but Flg Off G. Jones (RM655) and Flg Off K.M. Lowe (RM815) were both hit by enemy flak and had to force land inside Allied lines, Lowe suffering head injuries which required hospitalisation. The Spitfire flown by Sqn Ldr Tripe (RM762) was also hit, but he managed to return to base where he was forced to abandon his, by now, blazing aircraft. This was to be his last sortie with the unit as he relinquished his command of 130 Squadron to be replaced by Flt Lt M.R.D. Hume who was promoted to Squadron Leader. At the same time Flt Lt C.J. Samouelle DFC was posted in from 41 Squadron to take over command of 'A' Flight.

Over the next few days a number of armed recces were made to the area around Munster and on the 23rd a total of fifty MET, two AFV and sixteen half-tracks were damaged. Intense flak hit the aircraft flown by Flg Off W. Dobbs (RM756) which was written off in a crash landing at Ophoven. A similar operation the following day left twenty-one half-tracks and six rail trucks destroyed, the latter containing petrol, the smoke from which could be seen twenty miles away. No flying was possible over the next two days and on the 27th the squadron was on the move again, this time to B.78 Eindhoven. Bad weather again prevented flying until 3 February when 130 Squadron flew to No.17 Armament Practice Camp (APC) at Warmwell for a two week course in gunnery and bombing. The appalling winter weather that had been experienced in recent weeks unfortunately extended as far as Dorset and several days flying were lost, the squadron diarist at least conceding that the pilots had been able to have a good rest.

The return to Eindhoven was made on 21 February, all aircraft arriving safely except for two which were forced to divert to Manston with engine trouble. Readiness was maintained from 0630 hrs the following day but the first operation, a sweep of Lingen and Osnabruck did not take place until 0930 hrs. Two similar missions were flown later in the day but there was no enemy activity and all pilots returned feeling a little frustrated. Better results were achieved on the 24th when three armed recces to Rheine produced a score of four MET destroyed (plus twenty-five damaged) with two locos and fourteen trucks damaged. Two aircraft also flew a Ranger in the same area and blew up what appeared to be a V-2 trailer.

In addition to the usual armed reconnaissance missions, 130 Squadron also provided cover to Mitchell bombers on two occasions on the 25th, however, the intensive flying of the last four days led to concern over the serviceability state of the unit's Spitfires and operations had to be cut back for a short time while sufficient aircraft were brought back on line. Normal service was resumed on 27 February when eight aircraft took off in the morning to provide cover for Mitchells, and on completion of their escort duties the Spitfires went down through cloud to carry out an armed recce. Heavy flak was experienced near Dulmen which set fire to RM865 flown by Flg Off W. Dobbs who, in abandoning his aircraft, badly bruised his arm. He was picked up by British troops near Venlo and taken to hospital in Eindhoven. Ian Ponsford was flying alongside Dobbs at the time that he was hit

> 'I vividly recall the shooting down of Bill Dobbs. We were letting down in cloud and I was in close formation with Bill when all hell was let loose in the form of medium flak. I would guess that we were at about 4,000 ft and I saw strikes on Bill's aircraft which caught fire. He was lucky to get out without being burnt or badly injured. I visited him in hospital that evening where he looked badly shaken up with his arm in a sling. I never saw him again as he returned to Canada after he had recovered.'

Total operational flying for 130 Squadron during February amounted to 150 hours in 115 sorties.

Despite the fact that the Spitfire XIV had been developed to out-perform the Fw 190D and Bf 109G at high level, in 2 TAF service it was spending much of its time at low level on armed reconnaissance sorties although it was equally effective in this height band as Ian Ponsford recalls

'The Spitfire XIV was the most marvellous aeroplane at that time and I consider it to have been the best operational fighter of them all as it could out-climb virtually anything. The earlier Merlin-Spitfire may have had a slight edge when it came to turning performance but the Mark XIV was certainly better in this respect than the opposition we were faced with. The only thing it couldn't do was to keep up with an Fw 190D in a dive. It could be a bit tricky on take off if one opened the throttle too quickly as you just couldn't hold it straight because the torque was so great from the enormous power developed by the Griffon engine. One big advantage that we had over the Germans was that we ran our aircraft on advanced fuels which gave us more power. The 150 octane fuel that we used was strange looking stuff as it was bright green and had an awful smell – it had to be heavily leaded to cope with the extra compression of the engine.'

Although 130 Squadron had not encountered *Luftwaffe* fighters for some time, this was all set to change on 2 March during an early morning sweep of the area around Rheine with 350 Squadron. The Bf 109s of JG 27 were in the vicinity protecting Me 262s taking off and seventeen Fw 190Ds of III/JG 26 were also nearby. With 350 Squadron taking on the 109s, 130 Squadron waded into the Fw 190s and a sharp dogfight ensued. F/Sgt Clay (Red 4) spotted a single 190 but the pilot saw him coming and immediately dived away after rolling on to his back. Clay was able to turn inside his adversary, however, and opened fire from 300 yards, seeing several cannon strikes and what appeared to be the cowling or the canopy fly off. The 190 then pitched into a spin which was maintained until it hit the ground [this was most likely the aircraft of Uffz Walter Hahnel of 10./JG 26]. The fight was not without loss for 130 Squadron as Flt Lt G.G. Earp (RM750) and Flg Off N.W. Heale (RM914) did not return. Earp was heard to say over the R/T – "I am very low and I do not think I shall be able to make it. Cheerio chaps." He also claimed to have shot down an Fw 190 but JG 26 only suffered one loss on this day. Happily, it was later confirmed that both Earp and Heale had survived and were PoWs.

In the morning of 3 March an area cover to Mitchells bombing The Hague was completed uneventfully and later in the day the squadron had the honour of providing two aircraft to escort Winston Churchill who was arriving on a tour of front line units. A period of bad weather over the next few days restricted operations and it was not until the 13th that enemy forces were encountered again. On this day an uneventful bomber escort was followed by a sweep comprising ten aircraft to Rheine which produced another hectic encounter with the Fw 190D-9s of JG 26. Although three pilots each claimed a Focke-Wulf as destroyed (Flt Lt Walmsley, Flt Lt Ponsford and F/Sgt Clay) it appears from German records that only one was shot down, that flown by Uffz Heinz Meiss of the 7th Staffel. F/Sgt Clay's aircraft was hit by a cannon shell but he was able to return safely to base.

Six days later 130 Squadron was back over Rheine/Osnabruck on the lookout for suitable targets. They did not have long to wait as W/O Edwards sighted 12+ Bf 109s in the circuit at Rheine airfield and in spite of vigorous opposition from the ground defences, two 109s were shot down by Flg Off G. Lord and F/Sgt G.W. Hudson, with a further seven being claimed as damaged. No losses were incurred, although F/Sgt Hudson's aircraft was damaged by flak. On 23 March the pilots of 125 Wing were briefed by the O.C., Gp Capt David Scott-Malden DSO DFC, on the Wing's sphere of operations for the Rhine crossing which was scheduled for the 24th. No.130 Squadron carried out four freelance patrols in the Dulmen area on the day but the *Luftwaffe* did not put in an appearance. The following day was one of intensive flying with five armed recces to the area around Rheine/Munster/Hamm, each of eight aircraft. The first was airborne at 0550 hrs with the last returning at 1915 hrs. During the course of the day five MET were claimed destroyed, together with twenty-eight damaged, two locos were shot up and a total of sixty rail trucks were either destroyed or damaged.

One of the most successful operations carried out by 130 Squadron occurred on 28 March when an armed recce by eight aircraft to the Gutersloh area encountered a formation of a dozen or so Fw 190Ds of IV/JG 26. The cloud base was around 4,000 ft and as soon as the RAF aircraft were seen the 190s climbed towards the overcast with the Spitfires in pursuit. A running battle then took place in and out of cloud. F/Sgt Clay (Red 3) recorded his observations in his combat report

'Red 1 called up and said, "Watch these" and we broke round after the aircraft which were Fw 190s of the long-nosed variety. I closed on one and he started to turn, going down, and I went through cloud after him right down to about 200 ft. I got in behind him and opened fire and I saw strikes on the engine. I closed right into him, firing all the time. I broke away to one side and then I saw the pilot jettison the hood. He climbed to about 500 ft and then he rolled over on his back and he baled out, but his parachute did not open. The aircraft went straight into the ground and I took a photograph of it as it was burning.

After this I climbed above the cloud and found a number of Spitfires circling there. I saw one Fw 190 on his own so I chased after him and caught him easily. I opened fire from dead astern at 300 yards and I saw strikes on the port side of the fuselage and on the engine. The aircraft flicked over and went down through cloud. I claim this aircraft as damaged.'

Flt Lt P.E. Sibeth (Red 2) also claimed one of the Focke-Wulfs in what was to be his first encounter with enemy aircraft

'I fired at three 190s but saw no strikes. I was coming down when I saw another 190 and this one was trying to get a beam shot at me. I turned and got on his tail and he went up through cloud. He came down again and was just to the left of me. I slipped in behind him and from almost dead astern opened fire from about 250 yards. We were then at about 900 ft. I gave him a long burst and saw strikes where the port wing joins the fuselage. The enemy aircraft immediately flicked over on its back and crashed straight into a small wood where it caught fire.'

F/Sgt B.W. Woodman also broke his duck during this particular combat

'Yellow 1 and 2 had returned so W/O Boulton (Yellow 3) and myself comprised Yellow section. We broke round into the 190s and I found there were three of them in front of me. I picked on the last one of the three and climbed after him. I opened fire from about 800 yards and saw strikes on the wing. The enemy aircraft rolled away and I claim it as damaged.

I then got onto the second one and from about 30 degrees angle off opened fire again from about 800 yards. I closed in to about 400 yards and fired again from dead astern while climbing. I saw strikes on the wing roots on the port side. There was a burst of yellow flame from where I had seen the strikes. The aircraft went over on to its back and it went down out of control. I saw a trail of smoke right down until it hit the ground.'

This combat was witnessed by W/O Boulton who also claimed an Fw 190 as destroyed. In all, 130 Squadron claimed seven Fw 190s shot down with one probable and two damaged, the other claimants being Flt Lt Walmsley, Sgt G. Warren, and one shared by Flg Off D.A. Stott and W/O R.E. Coverdale. In his combat report Flt Lt Sibeth mentioned that he saw four aircraft burning on the ground in the combat area and this may have been a more accurate assessment of the German losses as JG 26 admitted that four of its aircraft were shot down at this time. There were no survivors on the German side, Uffz Reinhard Flakowski, Uffz Harry Kaps and Ofhr Hans-Jurgen Hansen were all killed and Uffz Otto

Weigl died when his aircraft hit trees as he was attempting to escape at low level.

On 30 March patrols were carried out all day along the line Burgsteinfurt to Munster. A total of thirty-eight sorties produced eight MET destroyed with another fourteen damaged. Whilst attacking a truck near Munster, however, Flg Off Trevorrow's Spitfire (RM713) hit a tree and he was forced to bale out shortly afterwards. Fortuitously he came down on the Allied side of the front line and was able to return to the squadron in the evening. The last day of March was relatively quiet with just two armed recces to Enschede/Bremen, both of which were unproductive. Thanks to better weather in March and longer daylight hours, total operational flying time for the month was 665 hours in 486 sorties.

Despite the fact that the war was close to being won the Allied tactical air force squadrons were still operating at maximum intensity, although a lack of suitable targets was becoming evident on occasions. On 1 April two sections of four aircraft patrolled the area around Rheine without encountering anything of note although a flak battery hit RN196 flown by W/O A.D. Miller who had to force land eight miles inside enemy held territory. Fortunately for him, he managed to evade capture and was picked up by Allied ground forces in the evening. The following day three armed recces were made to Lingen/Quackenbruck which left ten MET destroyed and fifteen damaged. Over the next few days similar operations were carried out during which Flg Off H.C. Finbow had to crash land near Ahaus in SM818 after being hit by flak. He was admitted to hospital with slight wounds.

No operational flying was carried out on 6–7 April as the squadron was in the process of moving to B.106 Enschede/Twente which had recently been vacated by the *Luftwaffe*. Ian Ponsford had been given the resposibility of checking the airfield to see if it was suitable for operations

'I flew there with Geoff Lord to see whether it was fit to receive the Spitfires from Eindhoven as it had been heavily bombed by the Americans. The runways appeared to be repaired (presumably by the Germans who had just departed) and we reckoned it was safe to move in. On attempting to restart my aircraft for the return to Eindhoven I found that my battery was flat (I had probably failed to isolate the electrics on landing) and I was obliged to spend the night at Twenthe whilst the Army, who had taken the airfield, looked for a spare. There was nowhere to sleep so I spent the night – or most of it – in the cockpit! Much to my relief some RAF Regiment types turned up next morning and I was able to start up and return to Eindhoven. We moved the squadron to Twenthe without delay and were housed in the former German barracks. Every building appeared to be wired up to be demolished, but the Germans had insufficient time to detonate the bombs planted in each building. My first night in the Block assigned to 130 Squadron was spent sleeping soundly over a 500-kg bomb (unconnected to the fuse wires) which fitted neatly under my bed. Next day the Army Sappers arrived to remove the bomb and I was astonished to see them roll 'my' bomb down the concrete steps to be collected and driven away to be disposed of.'

On the 8 April patrols of four aircraft flew as part of the cover operation to the Allied bridgehead over the River Weser, the squadron's patrols taking in Nienburg and Verden. Most of these were uneventful, however, Sgt Warren's Spitfire (RM808) was hit by flak as he was attacking motor transport near Verden but he emerged safely from the subsequent forced landing. Two days later four patrols, each of six aircraft, were made around Dummersee but only one loco was claimed as damaged. A freelance patrol in the evening led by Sqn Ldr Hume was rather more productive as a Ju 188 was spotted landing at Stade airfield. Hume dived down to attack from 7,000 ft and shot the Junkers down with a single burst. This proved to be a fitting end to his command of the squadron as the operation marked the end of his tour, a DFC being gazetted the following month. His place was taken by Sqn Ldr F.G. Woolley DFC who relinquished his brief command of 350 Squadron when that unit's C.O., Sqn Ldr Terry Spencer, returned after escaping from captivity. Spencer had been shot down and captured on 26 February 1945 but taking advantage of German inattention, later walked out of his PoW camp unchallenged to make his way back to Allied lines.

Sqn Ldr Woolley's first day in charge was a busy one and commenced with six aircraft flying a freelance patrol of Hamburg/Saltau during which four MET were destroyed (plus six damaged) and two locos were shot up. A patrol line between Bremen and Nienburg was then flown for the remainder of the day, a total of twenty-nine sorties being made. Most of these produced little of note although during the second patrol eight rail trucks were destroyed with another thirty damaged. Some of the trucks contained ammunition and when they blew up Flt Lt Sibeth's aircraft (RN212) was hit by debris even though he was flying at 500 ft at the time. Ian Ponsford had a clear view of what happened

'I had already made my attack and saw some trucks ablaze when the train blew up. Phil Sibbeth was making his attack at the time and flew right through the debris which had been propelled up to about 800 ft (my altitude). I was amazed to see two wheels joined by a spoke, from one of the trucks, rising end over end up to my altitude, before subsiding into the conflagration below. It was an awe inspiring sight and a miracle that Phil and his aircraft survived. We set course for base but before long it became clear that Phil was in trouble and I saw smoke and flames coming from his engine. He called up and said that he was bailing out, which he appeared to do in an almost leisurely fashion. He slid along the fuselage of his Spitfire and was flipped over by the tailplane. His parachute opened quickly at about 1,000 ft and he descended into an orchard, where we saw him being collected by chaps in red berets – the Airborne Division. His Spitfire went vertically into the ground nearby and made a sizeable hole. Phil was flown back to base by an American light aircraft, apparently unharmed. He had an unflappable character and made little of his experience.'

On 12 April several patrols were flown, some of which were uneventful, although five aircraft which carried out an armed recce to Rotenburg/ Soltau/Celle came back with a useful score of three locos and five rail trucks damaged. A similar operation in the afternoon by a section of four Spitfires discovered various MET near Luneberg and left two destroyed and ten damaged. Although all aircraft returned safely, Ian Ponsford had a lucky escape

'On landing back at Twenthe after an armed recce in which we had experienced intense light flak, my right tyre burst and my aircraft swung to the right off the runway and straight into a bomb crater. I put my hands up to prevent my face hitting the gun sight when the hood crashed forward (it had not securely locked back before landing) and cracked some of my fingers very painfully! I was otherwise unscathed, but my aircraft (AP-T) was badly bent. I was rather upset by the Engineering Officer who insisted on my filling in a Form 765C accident report, when I reckoned the accident was operational, for which no such report was necessary.'

After a short stay at Twente, 130 Squadron moved into Germany on 17 April when they took up residence at B.118 Celle, a location that provided rather better accommodation than had been available at their previous airfield. The first two operations from Celle were armed recces to Hamburg in which several MET and locos were damaged. At 1250 hrs Flt Lt Walmsley led a section of six aircraft to Wittenburg/ Rheinburg. After attacking ground transport, a Ju 52 was seen at low level and Walmsley attacked immediately causing it to crash in flames. Three more armed recces were flown later in the day producing a total of one barge destroyed (plus four damaged), two MET, three locos and twelve rail trucks damaged.

The following day was equally eventful and commenced with three aircraft taking off for an armed recce to Bremen/Hamburg at 1135 hrs. A further operation to the same area and one to Kremmen/Rheinsburg produced an increasing tally of MET destroyed and damaged. During the operation to Kremmen five Fieseler Storch aircraft were seen on a temporary landing ground. These were shot up and all but one destroyed, two being claimed by Flt Lt Walmsley, with one each to Flt Lt Sibeth and Flt Lt Samouelle. On the last show of the day eleven Bf 109s were seen preparing to take off at Parchim airfield and six of these were destroyed (all flamers) by Flg Off Trevorrow who pressed home his attack so closely that his aircraft was hit by flying debris. On this occasion, however, he was able to return safely.

On 19 April the first armed recce was airborne at 0825 hrs for Salzwedel/Lubeck, the first of six operations of this nature throughout the day. Flg Off W.H. Carter experienced engine trouble in SM827 during the first mission and was obliged to force land near British troops during which he suffered slight injuries. A mounting total of motor and rail transport throughout the day was offset in the evening by the loss of two more aircraft. Flt Lt Walmsley led a section of four to reconnoitre the line from Salzwedel to Hamburg but had to return early with another case of engine trouble. The remaining three aircraft ran into a gaggle of around twenty Fw 190s and in the ensuing dogfight Flg Off V Murphy (RN203) and W/O Clay (RM766) were shot down. The remaining member of the section, Flt Lt Ian Ponsford, claimed one of the 190s destroyed before returning to Celle alone. Sixty years on he still has clear memories of the encounter

'We were flying in a north-easterly direction and ran into a large gaggle of Fw 190s heading south-west. They were about 1,000 ft above us and were also up-sun of us so the advantage was entirely with them. Unfortunately Phil Clay, who was my No.2, was the architect of his own misfortune as he was out on my starboard side and turned straight into them, which was a ridiculous thing to do as he became a sitting duck. I called to say that we must climb up and get behind them but he didn't take any notice, went sailing in, as did Murphy, and of course they were both clobbered. It was all a bit silly as it was completely unnecessary and it would have been better not to have engaged them at all. After Clay and Murphy had been shot down I was fully occupied avoiding a similar fate and thanks to the Spitfire XIV's remarkable climb and turning performance was able to avoid being hit by the opposition, who were anxious to add me to their score. Eventually

I found myself turning with one remaining 190. He realised that he could not get enough deflection on me so he rolled over and dived away at a steep angle. I took a quick look around, could see no other aircraft and followed him down. As the ground approached, the 190 started to level out and I was able to gain on him by cutting off the angle. He was about 600 yards ahead of me and I think the only reason I caught him was because he either hit or narrowly missed a tree. He presumably thought it was a good idea to lead me towards some trees but he probably hit one as he definitely seemed to slow up a bit and that was when I was able to get him. The 190 suddenly turned sharply left and plunged straight into the ground and exploded in what appeared to be a farmyard.'

Despite the losses incurred the previous day it was business as usual on the 20th when six aircraft took off at 1025 hrs for an armed recce to Wismar/Muritzsee during which three locos were damaged. A similar mission to Pritzwalk saw eight oil tankers destroyed but a third recce to the same area was even more productive. A section of four aircraft came across eight Fw 190s near Kremmen and in the fight that followed two were shot down by Harry Walmsley and Ian Ponsford, the latter also claiming a probable with another damaged

'Initially there were four of us, Harry Walmsley and myself and our respective wingmen but when we engaged the Fw 190s our No.2's for some mysterious reason just disappeared. They were both newly arrived NCO's and did not seem to want to get involved! Two of the 190's broke upwards and the others went down, so I went for the ones above while Harry dived after the others. After I had disposed of the first one I called Harry to enquire as to his whereabouts and saw him about 2,000 ft below in a circle with two 190's. He said he was unable to jettison his slipper tank and could not get inside the Huns to obtain enough deflection to fire. I had been able to get rid of my ventral tank and having joined the circle, I had no problem in turning inside the 190's. The nearest 190 to me was turning pretty tightly, and was firing. He passed very close to me and slightly below and I was able to look down into his cockpit. He can't have been more than a few feet below me, still firing, and I clearly saw the pilot, with his black helmet, looking up at me! I think he must have stalled his aircraft as he fell away and I had no difficulty in getting on to his tail and firing with cannon and machine-gun. His aircraft was well peppered with strikes and he dived away at a steep angle with smoke pouring out. He just kept going down but I decided to stay up with Harry and the remaining 190 which were still orbiting.

I joined the circle once more and the third 190 broke down and headed off in an easterly direction. I followed but was frustrated to find that I had exhausted all my 20 mm cannon ammunition. However, I chased the 190 for a few minutes and managed to hit him with some machine-gun rounds. We were heading, flat out, at about 800 ft and a largish town seemed to be coming up. It was very murky, with poor visibility, when I saw some barrage balloons and decided to give up the chase. I broke off and headed home to Celle, rather short of fuel. Harry had returned before me, together with the No.2's, who said that they had lost us (their No.1's) when we went after the 190's!' [for further details of this combat see Chapter Fourteen].

In the evening there was further success for the squadron when Flt Lt Samouelle shot down one of two Bf 109s encountered near Wittstock.

The next big day for 130 Squadron took place on 24 April. The first armed recce was under way at 0625 hrs with Flt Lt Samouelle leading six aircraft to Pritzwalk/Neustadt. During the mission an Fw 190 was seen flying right to left just above the section and this aircraft was chased to Neustadt airfield where other 190s were orbiting. With the element of surprise in their favour the Spitfires shot down three, one each being claimed by Flt Lt Samouelle, Flt Lt Bruce and F/Sgt Woodman without loss. On the way back to base four MET were damaged just for good measure. Meanwhile Sqn Ldr Woolley was leading another section of six Spitfires which spotted a Bf 108 at zero feet near Wismar and this was coolly shot down by the C.O. Later a lone Fw 190 was encountered near Haginow and this was despatched by W/O Coverdale. The *Luftwaffe* was unusually active on this day and further combats took place during an evening sweep of Kyritz/Malchow. A single Bf 109 was shot down by Flt Lt W.N. Stowe and Flt Lt Bruce and not long after a number of Fw 190s were seen in the circuit at Rechlin aerodrome. These were attacked with good effect and two were shot down by Flt Lt Stowe and Flt Lt Sibeth. During what was an extremely busy day it was announced that Flt Lt Walmsley would be taking over the command of 350 Squadron and that Flt Lt Stowe (recently arrived from 41 Squadron) would take over from Walmsley as 'B' Flight commander.

The hectic pace of the last few days was maintained on 25 April and again there was good fortune for the squadron. The first recce of the day was to the Pritzwalk area and again Bf 109s were active at Rechlin. Flt Lt Ponsford (together with his No.2 W/O Coverdale) dived on a 109 which had its wheels down. Ponsford was able to get in close to about 50 yards range and his fire caused the 109 to roll slowly over onto its back before crashing into woods. After the section had reformed Ponsford saw an Fw 190 about 3,000 ft above and immediately climbed to attack. The German pilot was aware of danger, however, and he rolled over and spiralled down to about 1,000 ft. Ponsford followed and closed to 100 yards before opening fire with a deflection shot, achieving a number of strikes on the side of the fuselage. This prompted another spiral dive by the German down to ground level, but in the event it could only be claimed as damaged as it was seen to pull out at very low level after which it was fired upon by light flak from its own defences. At the same time a further six aircraft led by Flt Lt Stowe saw a Ju 87 taking off from Schwerin and this was attacked and forced down by W/O Boulton. It was subsequently strafed on the ground but as it was not seen to burn, it could only be claimed as a probable. A Messerschmitt Me 262 was also attacked by Flt Lt Stowe and W/O Ockenden as it was landing at an airfield near Lubeck, the pilot 'baling out' when the aircraft was halfway down the runway.

A further section of four aircraft took off at midday for Rostock/Gustrow. Three MET had already been destroyed in this area when sixteen Fw 190s were seen taking off from Pritzwalk. The resulting melee at least showed that the *Luftwaffe* could still mount effective localised opposition, but in the dogfight that followed one of the 190s was shot down by Plt Off Freddie Edwards without loss. Another recce to the same location in the afternoon saw a twin-engined Siebel Si 204 shot down in flames by Sqn Ldr Frank Woolley although it could easily have been two. Ian Ponsford was also flying on this mission and he too saw a Siebel at low level. He immediately got on the radio to tell Woolley that he was going after it but the latter said, 'Don't worry, I'm right behind it and I'm going to get him.' Unfortunately he was referring to a completely different Si 204, a type which was now being seen quite frequently, and in the confusion the other one managed to get away. The last operation of the day commenced at 1630 hrs, although Flt Lt Bill Bruce had to return early when his aircraft began to burn as a result of a mechanical fault. The remaining aircraft flew to Gustrow where they destroyed seven MET and damaged another eleven. Two locos and four rail trucks were also attacked and damaged.

A total of five armed recces were flown on the 26th but these proved to be something of an anti-climax as there was little or no movement on the roads and no enemy aircraft were seen. Four missions were flown the following day, the first by four aircraft to Ludwigslust which attacked a convoy leaving seven MET destroyed and three damaged. Another section operating to Parchim and Wismar chanced upon a Ju 188 which was attacked by W/O Miller. Although he damaged the Junkers, return fire from the rear gunner hit Miller's aircraft (NH691) which was seen to crash and blow up, killing its pilot instantly. Bad weather over the next two days severely restricted operations allowing only one successful recce to be made to Lubeck.

This brief respite was more than made up for on 30 April when 130 Squadron had its best day of the war claiming ten enemy aircraft destroyed without loss. The patrol area for the day was the Wittenburg/Ludwigslust sector and thirty sorties were flown between 0700 and 1800 hrs. A section of four Spitfires led by Flt Lt Stowe were the first away and saw nine Fw 190s flying at zero feet near Banzkow. Three were shot down, one each being claimed by Flt Lt Stowe and Flg Off Lord, with a third shared by Stowe and Flg Off Trevorrow. Later, another section of four led by Flt Lt Ponsford decimated a much larger formation of Fw 190s near Schwerin. Ian Ponsford's combat report describes some of the action

'I was leading Yellow section and we were out on patrol in the Wittenburg area. At about 1130 hrs when we were at 4,000 ft about a dozen short-nosed Fw 190s were sighted in the circuit of a landing ground at Banzkow to the south of the lake at Schwerin. I had seen Yellow 3 (Plt Off Edwards) go in to attack and one Fw 190 went down into a wood and exploded. I went after another of the enemy aircraft and he immediately went down to the deck. I followed him down and opened fire at 100 yards astern. I saw strikes on the wings and the cockpit. He pulled up sharply and I came up behind him, closing to about 30 yards. At this point the belly tank exploded and the aircraft burst into flames. The pilot baled out but his parachute did not open.

By this time I was at about 500 ft and looking down I saw two more enemy aircraft. I went down and got on the tail of one of them and closed in very rapidly, firing from about 100 yards down to 50 yards. I saw strikes on the fuselage and the aircraft immediately caught fire in the air. I broke hard left and I watched him going down. The Fw 190 crashed and exploded on the ground – the pilot did not get out.'

In addition to their individual claims, Ponsford and Edwards also shared in the destruction of two more of the 190s. Sqn Ldr Woolley shot down a short-nosed Fw 190 during an evening sweep and the last patrol of the day was also eventful as F/Sgt Woodman attacked a Siebel Si 204 which was seen to dive into the lake at Schwerin where it exploded. The amount of operational flying carried out by 130 Squadron in April showed another significant improvement to 964 hours in 557 sorties. In fact Ian Ponsford recalls that the operatonal flying carried out during the month had been of such intensity that the Spitfire XIV Wing at Celle actually ran out of fuel on one occasion. This caused a major panic and resulted in the Wing being declared non-operational for half a day until a fleet of fifty Dakotas suddenly appeared loaded with Jerry cans full of 150-octane fuel!

On 1 May six Spitfire XIVs of 130 Squadron formed part of the escort for medium bombers attacking Lubeck and after lunch another section of six aircraft carried out an armed recce to Schwerinsee/Sternberg damaging a total of twenty MET. A similar operation in the late afternoon had destroyed three MET and damaged another thirteen before a Bf 109 was seen near Schwerin. This was attacked by Flg Off Lord who saw it crash near Holzendorf. In the evening two more patrols were made, this time to Wittenburg/Ludwigslust and during the first of these operations F/Sgt Woodman attacked and damaged a Heinkel He 111 near Lubeck despite intensive flak from ground defences.

Operations the next day began early with five aircraft taking off for Wittenburg at 0545 hrs. Not long after a very one sided combat took place between 130 Squadron's Spitfires and five Bu 131 Jungmann trainers that were seen flying at low level near Schwerin. This was an unusual type of aircraft to meet in a combat area but it emphasized the desperate situation that the Germans found themselves in and the fact that for some time now Allied fighter-bombers had been able to operate over all German-held territory, an area that was shrinking day by day. Two of the biplanes were shot down by Flg Off Lord and one by F/Sgt Woodman, another being shared. A further section of four took off at 0755 hrs looking for enemy activity and chanced upon a single Bf 109 which was shot down when in the circuit at Schwerin by Flg Off C.E. Mertens and Plt Off Edwards.

The next three patrols (each of four aircraft) produced a total of five MET destroyed and fifty-six damaged with one loco and ten rail trucks also damaged. Near Schwerin a Fieseler Storch was shot up by W/O Coverdale who had to abandon his attack due to heavy anti-aircraft fire from the ground. During an armed recce to Oldenburg in the late afternoon Flt Lt Stowe's Spitfire (SM833) was hit by debris and he had to force land inside friendly territory. Although his aircraft was written off, Stowe was unhurt and returned to the squadron later. The final operation of the day was an uneventful sweep to Lubeck between 1935–2100 hrs.

On 3 May the first mission was an armed recce to the Kiel area in which a Ju 188 was seen flying at tree top height. Flg Off Trevorrow and Plt Off Edwards dived from 4,000 ft and attacked the Junkers, setting fire to its starboard engine which caused it to crash near Grossenbrode. The rest of the day's flying consisted of twenty-three sorties covering armed recces and patrols in the area between Lubeck and the River Weser, however, these produced little of note due to bad weather and hardly any road movement. For 130 Squadron the highlight of the day was the return of Flg Off Murphy and W/O Clay who had been shot down on 19 April. Both had been captured and had only just been liberated by the advancing US Army. It transpired that the squadron's score of enemy aircraft destroyed was actually one less than it should have been as W/O Clay had accounted for an Fw 190 before being shot down himself. Clay was to remain with the squadron for the immediate future, but Murphy began to prepare for demobilisation and a return to his home in Australia.

Four patrols were flown on 4 May to the Hamburg area but all were uneventful. The next day saw the very last operation of the war for 130 Squadron when a section of three aircraft carried out an early morning patrol to Hamburg. At 0630 hrs they were vectored on to a Siebel Si 204 which began to take evasive action when sighted. Flt Lt Gibbins and W/O Seymour went in to attack and after catching fire, the German aircraft crashed to the west of Hamburg. With the conclusion of the Second World War, the 130 Squadron diarist tried to put into context the unit's achievements since its arrival in Europe

'. . . so ended the war. The Hun has suffered a crushing defeat – a defeat which is reflected in this squadron's own score in the past few months. Since 8 December 1944, when the first enemy aircraft was destroyed by the squadron since joining 2nd Tactical Air Force, no fewer than ninety-eight enemy aircraft have been destroyed, probably destroyed or damaged. In addition the enemy's road, rail and river transport have suffered enormously at the hands of our pilots – nearly 1,000 trucks, cars, locos, rail trucks and barges were destroyed or damaged during this period. All this was achieved with relatively little loss – three pilots killed in action.'

Following the end of hostilities, events moved quickly and 130 Squadron moved to B.152 Fassberg on 7 May where the unit's Spitfire XIVs had to be given up in favour of Spitfire IXBs formerly flown by 411 Squadron. After a four month tour of duty in Norway, 130 Squadron returned to the UK and for a short period flew the Vampire F.1 before being disbanded in January 1947 when it was re-numbered 72 Squadron. It was reformed on 1 August 1953 at Bruggen with Vampire FB.5s and later flew the Sabre F.1/F.4. As part of a series of defence cuts, 130 Squadron was disbanded for good on 30 April 1957.

At the end of the war the Spitfire XIV was operational with 2nd Tactical Air Force's 125 Wing (41, 130 and 350 Squadrons) at B.118 Celle, 126 Wing's 402 Squadron at B.116 Wunstorf and with two of the RCAF squadrons that comprised No.39 (Recce) Wing at B.154 Schneverdingen (Nos. 414 and 430). It also formed the equipment of No.2 Squadron of

35 (Recce) Wing at B.106 Twente. Most of these units had disposed of their Spitfire XIVs by the end of the year. The Mark XIV was also flown by a number of Auxiliary squadrons in the UK in the immediate post-war period, however, these were quickly withdrawn and replaced by the Spitfire F.22/F.24.

# CHAPTER FOURTEEN

# Top Scorers

In marked contrast to the early war period, pilots of Griffon-engined Spitfires had much less opportunity to accumulate high scores in aerial combat. The large-scale defensive battles that had taken place over south-east England in 1940 and over Malta in 1942 would not be repeated and the gradual decline of the *Luftwaffe* meant that very few pilots commencing their operational careers after 1943 managed to get into double figures. Although it was much more difficult to become an 'ace' towards the end of the war, a number of pilots had considerable combat success whilst flying the Spitfire XII and XIV and this chapter looks at their achievements.

The top scoring pilot on the Spitfire XII was Squadron Leader (later Wing Commander) Ray Harries DSO DFC. A former medical student at Guys Hospital in London, Harries had already completed a tour of operations as a flight commander with 131 Squadron during which time he put in several claims including an Fw 190 shot down during the Dieppe Raid on 19 August 1942. In December 1942 he was given command of 91 Squadron which, together with 41 Squadron, introduced the Spitfire XII to RAF service in the spring of 1943. The squadron achieved operational status in May and victories soon followed, his first success coming on 25 May when he shot down two Fw 190s flying EN625. The Spitfire XII was one of the few aircraft in Fighter Command's inventory that was capable of catching Fw 190 *Jabos* which were carrying out hit-and-run raids along the south coast and Harries' combat report describes what happened. The action took place in the late evening in conditions of 8/10 heavy cloud at 3,000 ft with a visibility of five miles.

'I was leading Blue section comprising four aircraft of 91 Squadron on a defensive patrol. I had just returned to base and with my No.2 had just landed when the scramble signal was given from the watch office. We both immediately took off again and saw enemy aircraft approaching Folkstone. I dived towards the sea, the enemy aircraft turning back and jettisoning their bombs as soon as they saw us. Going over Folkstone I experienced very heavy flak, luckily inaccurate, from our ground defences. I sighted one lone Fw 190 at sea level returning to France. I came in from his starboard side, delivering a three second burst at 250 yards. The 190 hit the sea tail first, split in two and sank immediately.

I then spotted another Fw 190 to starboard. I flew straight over the top of it in order to identify it in the failing light and he pulled up his nose and gave me a quick squirt as I did so. I pulled straight up to about 1,000 ft and turning to port dived right onto his tail, opening fire from 300 yards and closing to 150 yards. I fired a four second burst, seeing strikes and flashes all over the enemy aircraft. It then lost height very gradually with smoke and flames coming from it, skimmed for some distance along the surface of the water and then sank. This was confirmed by F/L Matthew and F/L Kynaston. I orbited around taking cine gun snaps of the oil patch and pieces of wreckage visible.'

Ray Harries had his most successful day on 18 July 1943 when he accounted for three Bf 109s when flying MB831. In all, Harries claimed fifteen enemy aircraft destroyed plus three shared, of which ten plus one shared were shot down during his time on Spitfire XIIs. He remained in the RAF after the war and was given command of 92 Squadron in November 1949 but was killed on 14 May 1950 when attempting to bale out of a Meteor F.4 (VW267) near Worksop having run out of fuel in bad weather.

The second top-scoring pilot on Griffon-Spitfires was Squadron Leader Harry Walmsley DFC. Having been taught to fly in Rhodesia, Walmsley had his first taste of operational flying with 611 Squadron in September 1942 and subsequently served with 132 Squadron as a flight commander. After a spell as an instructor at 57 OTU, Eshott, he was posted to 130 Squadron on Spitfire XIVs in late September 1944, shortly before the unit moved to Antwerp/Duerne (B.70) as part of 2nd Tactical Air Force. His first combat success occurred on 8 December when he shot down a Bf 109 near Burgstein but then had to wait until the following March to increase his score.

In the space of six weeks, Walmsley shot down eight more aircraft plus one shared, commencing with an Fw 190D that was dispatched ten miles east of Hamm on 13 March 1945. His subsequent report recalls the action

'I was flying as Spinner Blue 1. We had passed south of Munster heading east at 11,000 ft when I saw eight plus aircraft flying south at 2,500 ft. I called up and went down after them, intercepting over Hamm, and, finding that they were long-nosed Fw 190s, engaged the one on the extreme left. He broke downwards to proceed due east at 200 ft. After chasing him for ten miles, firing occasional short bursts, I hit him around the cockpit with several cannon shells and quite a bit of debris came away. The range was 200–250 yards, angle off 5 degrees. He pulled up steeply to port and the pilot baled out at 1,500 ft, the aircraft crashing close to where the pilot landed and lay on the ground without releasing his parachute. Both the enemy aircraft and I had long-range tanks, neither of which were dropped and at no time did I have to go "through the gate" in order to stay on his tail.'

After the war Harry Walmsley became Squadron Leader Operations at No.84 Group before taking command of 80 Squadron flying the Tempest V in 1946/7. By coincidence he was posted as Training Officer and then Adjutant to 611 Squadron in 1948 in which squadron he had begun operations at Redhill in Surrey and subsequently at Biggin Hill during 1942. In April 1955 Walmsley was given the command of 67 Squadron at Wildenrath on Sabres, the unit converting to the Hunter F.4 shortly after. He was then made Wing Commander Flying at Tangmere and after promotion to Group Captain he commanded RAF Boulmer in Northumberland. After retirement from the RAF in 1971, he worked as Deputy Director of the British Defence Consortium in Saudi Arabia and then as General Manager for Airwork in Oman. At the time of writing he is retired and lives in Suffolk.

Flight Lieutenant Ian Ponsford DFC had a distinguished operational career on Spitfire XIVs despite the fact that he did not join a front line squadron until early January 1945. He had, in fact, learned to fly three years previously but had undertaken further training in the USA where he had been retained as an instructor at Yuma, Arizona. After returning to the UK he undertook a refresher flying course at 53 OTU, Kirton in Lindsay, before joining 130 Squadron at Y.32 Ophoven. His first combat success was secured on 13 March when he shot down an Fw 190 and damaged another during an offensive sweep of the area around Munster. In the last few weeks of the war, with the retreating German forces being compressed into a relatively small area, targets were plentiful and 130 Squadron encountered opposition on a number of occasions during this period. Ian Ponsford had a particularly successful day on 20 April during an armed reconnaissance of the area around Oranienberg

'I was Blue 3 in a section of four aircraft on an armed recce to the Kremmen area and at 1510 hrs, when at 5,500 ft, I saw approximately eight aircraft above approaching on our starboard side. They were Fw 190s of the long-nosed variety. We broke round on to them and two of the enemy aircraft broke upwards and started to turn together. I got in shots at one of them from 100 yards at about 20 degrees angle off and I saw strikes around the wing roots and cockpit. The aircraft caught fire and the pilot baled out.

Afterwards I called Blue 1 (F/L Walmsley) and asked him where he was and he said he was down below with two of them. I dived down and started to turn with them. I got behind the second one and gave him a short burst from about 75 yards from 20 degrees off. I saw strikes around the cockpit. We were then at 3,000 ft and the enemy aircraft dived down at an angle of about 40 degrees with smoke pouring out. It was still diving when I last saw it at 1,000 ft and I claim this aircraft as probably destroyed.

I did not follow this aircraft down any further because I wanted to get the other one which was still turning with Blue 1. When the pilot of this aircraft saw me coming up behind he broke downwards. I fired at him as he was going down and I saw strikes on his starboard wing. My cannon ammunition had run out by this time but I chased the enemy aircraft for about ten miles firing with my machine guns only. I saw more strikes on the fuselage and then my 0.303 in ammunition ran out. I followed for another five miles and then gave up the chase. I claim this aircraft damaged.'

Although the war had just a few days to run, Ian Ponsford was credited with destroying three further Fw 190s and a Bf 109 in that time which left him with a total of six destroyed plus two shared, one probable and three damaged. He came out of the RAF in July 1946 and subsequently trained in law. After qualifying as a solicitor, he joined the Royal Auxiliary Air Force and flew with 604 (County of Middlesex) Squadron from North Weald. Now retired, he lives in Berkshire.

Squadron Leader John Shepherd DFC of 41 Squadron also saw considerable action towards the end of the war, however, his operational career had begun during the Battle of Britain when he joined 234 Squadron at Middle Wallop in September 1940. He later flew Spitfire VBs as a flight commander with 118 Squadron before being posted to 610 Squadron in June 1944 where he achieved considerable success against V-1 flying bombs flying Spitfire XIVs. In April 1945 he was given command of 41 Squadron, his first victory on Griffon-Spitfires occurring on 14 April when he accounted for a Bf 110 and the Me 163B rocket-powered fighter that it was towing at the time. This unusual combination was encountered near Norenholz airfield during an evening sweep. In fact this method was often used to move Me 163's from one base to another and could also be used operationally as a towed take off followed by ignition of the rocket motor at altitude was slightly less hazardous than a powered take off and also saved fuel. This method of launch could only be contemplated, however, if warning of a raid was received sufficiently early and there was little chance of being intercepted by marauding fighters, a rather forlorn hope in the skies over Germany in early 1945. On this occasion, Shepherd, who was flying SM826, dived to attack the Bf 110 and closed very rapidly, obtaining strikes on the port engine and cockpit. The 110 went into a left-hand diving turn which was not corrected and it eventually turned over on its back, crashing in a field near the airfield and bursting into flames. The Me 163 appeared to break away from the 110 and was seen to perform a wide left-hand turn before diving straight into the ground not too far from where the 110 was burning.

During the last three weeks of the war Shepherd extended his score shooting down an Fw 190 in the vicinity of Hagenow on 16 April. He followed this with another 190 (plus one shared) on the 20th near Oranienburg and an Fw 190 and a Bf 109G shot down on the 30th during a sweep to the north of Ratzenburg Lake. His final combat claim was a half share in an Fw 190D on 1 May to the east of Schwerin Lake to bring his total score to eight destroyed with another five shared, of which six plus two shared were during his brief spell on Spitfire XIVs. Sadly, Shepherd did not live long after the end of the war as he was killed in a flying accident in Germany on 22 January 1946.

Pilot Officer Pat Coleman also flew with 41 Squadron and, like John Shepherd, was to have considerable success in the last few weeks of the war. From Southend-on-Sea, he had been trained in the USA and joined 41 Squadron (then still flying Spitfire XIIs) on 7 June 1944. In the early afternoon of 3 September, flying EN229, Coleman took part in a sweep over Belgium when three Fw 190s of II/JG 26 were encountered near Tirlement. In the ensuing combat Warrant Officer P.W. Chattin was shot down and killed in EN622 but Coleman latched onto Leutnant Alfred Gross, a 51-kill ace from the Eastern Front, and forced the German to bale out.

After this initial victory, Coleman had to wait until 20 April 1945 for his next 'kill' when he shot down an Fw 190 near Neuruppin. A half share in a Ju 88 on 25 April and a quarter share in an He 111 three days later were followed by his most successful combat which occurred on 1 May despite the fact that he had become detached from the rest of the squadron

'I was flying as Kudos Red 4 but became separated from my section whilst identifying an aircraft. I decided to scout around Schwerin airfield before returning to base. I climbed to 24,000 ft and worked round to the east along the Baltic coast, turning south at Rostock and finally descending to below the 7,000 ft cloud base and approaching Schwerin from the east after jettisoning my 45-gallon tank. There was a 1,000 ft blanket of thick, dark cloud over the lake area. Flying at 6,000 ft, I observed nine plus Fw 190s in no orderly formation, nipping in and out of the cloud above. I climbed to attack the rearmost of the gaggle but found the two leaders on my tail firing at me. I evaded the foremost in a climbing turn through the cloud, then swiftly descended again and found only one Fw in view.

I attacked this one using the gyro sight, he climbed and my sight disappeared below my vision, however, I continued to pull my nose straight through him whilst firing and observed strikes about the cockpit. The enemy aircraft went into a tight spiral towards the ground but I did not attempt to follow up my attack until I saw it straighten out on an easterly course. I then pursued, closing rapidly, saw him jettison his hood, losing height all the time and finally bale out. I used the independent camera switch and took film of the enemy aircraft on the dive and also burning on the ground south west of Plau.

I climbed up above the cloud once again making towards Schwerin. Flying at about 200 ft above the layer I was attacked from astern by an Fw 190 which I presume had been lurking just below the top of the cloud. I evaded by diving down through the cloud, the enemy aircraft did not follow. Whilst still diving I found myself over Schweriner lake and observed two aircraft below flying north in close line abreast, low over the water. I continued my dive towards them and recognised them as Fw 190s. Preparing to fire at them from 800 yards I saw the left-hand aircraft turn sharply into the other. The two enemy aircraft interlocked and plunged into the northerly waters of the lake, the cause, presumably, panic. I had informed Kenway control and also my C.O. (S/L J.B. Shepherd) leading another Kudos section of the Huns' position.'

Finishing one place below Coleman in the list of Griffon-Spitfire aces was Flying Officer Geoff Lord who had joined the RAF in 1940 as an electrician before re-training as a pilot in 1942. He eventually joined 130 Squadron as a Sergeant pilot in October 1943 flying Spitfire VBs and continued to serve with this unit until the end of the war. Shortly after D-Day Lord was forced to crash land behind German lines in northern France on 19 June but returned home after passing unseen through the front line and linking up with Allied forces. His first victory (apart from a half share in a V-1) came on 19 March 1945 when he claimed a Bf 109 destroyed, with another damaged, during a squadron sweep of Rheine and Osnabruck. He shot down an Fw 190 near Salstorf on 30 April and the following day he dispatched a Bf 109 near Holzendorf. His final victories consisted of two Bucker Bu 131 Jungmann training aircraft (plus a third shared) shot down near Schwerin Lake on 2 May. Even though the war was soon finished, Geoff Lord's troubles were far from over as he was shot down on 6 July by ground fire from German troops who were supposedly surrendering. By this time the squadron was operating from Norway and Lord spent an uncomfortable forty-five minutes in the sea before he was rescued. After demobilisation Lord returned to civilian life in his home town of Hebden Bridge in West Yorkshire.

The top-scoring Australian pilot to fly Griffon-powered Spitfires was Squadron Leader Tony Gaze DFC from Melbourne whose first operational tour was with 610 Squadron commencing in March 1941. The following year he became a flight commander on 616 Squadron flying the Spitfire VI and later flew with 64, 129 and 66 Squadrons. During his time with 66 Squadron he was shot down over northern France but was able to evade capture and returned to the UK via Spain and Gibraltar. After a spell with the Air Fighting Development Unit at Wittering, Gaze returned to operations with 610 Squadron in July 1944 taking part in anti-Diver operations over southern England. His first air combat victory on the Spitfire XIV occurred on 1 January 1945 when he shot down an Fw 190 near Ophoven airfield (Y.32).

Further success followed on 14 February during a late afternoon sweep of the area around Nijmegan and Cleve as recorded in his combat report

'I was leading Wavey Black section of two aircraft on a standing patrol over Nijmegan. At about 1630 hrs I sighted an Arado 234 pulling up from attacking the Cleve area. I dropped my tank and attempted to intercept but despite the fact that I cut the corner it pulled away easily at 7,000 ft. After this we continually chased Arados over the area. I fired at two without result. At about 1700 hrs when it was apparent that the jets were diving through the cloud which was at 9–11,000 ft, I climbed up through it, leaving Black 2 (Flight Lieutenant A.W. Jolly) below, hoping to warn him when they dived. I then did an orbit at 13,000 ft to clear off the ice on the windscreen and sighted three Me 262s in vic formation passing below me at cloud top level. I dived down behind them and closed in, crossing behind the formation and attacking the port aircraft which was lagging slightly. I could not see my sight properly as we were flying straight into the sun, but fired from dead astern at a range of 350 yards hitting it in the starboard jet with the second burst at which point the other two aircraft immediately dived into cloud. I pulled up slowly and turned to starboard and fired again obtaining more strikes on the fuselage and jet which caught fire. The enemy aircraft rolled over onto its back and dived through cloud. I turned 180 degrees and dived after it calling on the RT to warn my No.2. On breaking cloud I saw an aircraft hit the ground and explode about a mile ahead of me.'

Flight Lieutenant Jolly's view of this action was as follows

'At about 1630 hrs I saw a lot of flak over Cleve and an Arado 234 at 8,000 ft going east. My No.1 and I chased it but it pulled away from us. My speed was 340 mph indicated and I estimate that the enemy aircraft was 50 mph faster. We turned round and saw another 234 diving down on Cleve which we closed unsuc- cessfully. We both fired at another one which passed over the top of us, but the angle off was too great – almost 90 degrees. There were five of these Arados and in my opinion they were dropping armour piercing bombs on our troops. They were diving down, dropping their bombs and then pulling up to just below cloud, then heading east for Germany. We could not do anything about the others as they were out of range. Black 1 went above cloud and I stayed below at about 5,000 ft. Suddenly I saw an explosion on the ground below me, east of Cleve. I am of the opinion that this explosion was caused by the aircraft shot down by Black 1.'

Having dispatched a Junkers Ju 52 on 11 April, Tony Gaze finally succeeded in shooting down an Arado 234 (albeit a half share) the following day during a combat that took place near Bremen. His final victories were a half share in an Fw 190D on 28 April and another long- nose 190D which he destroyed two days later near the Elbe bridgehead. After his wartime service he eventually returned to Australia to take up farming. He went on to represent his country in the World Gliding Championships at Cologne in 1960.

Although vastly superior in terms of outright speed, the Arado 234 was vulnerable if its pilot was caught unawares. Flight Lieutenant Derek Rake of 41 Squadron was in such a fortunate position towards the end of the war and recalls how easy it could be

'Some of our Spitfire XIVs had gyro gunsights. I was flying one of these near Delmenhorst and Verden on 12 April 1945 when we spotted an Arado 234 which the *Luftwaffe* used for reconnaissance. I managed to get all the diamonds on the gunsight nicely enclosing his aircraft during a quarter attack and, somewhat to my surprise, he went on fire. Had he seen me first there is little doubt that he could have got away.

A few days before the end of the war in Europe I destroyed a Junkers Ju 188 which turned out to be the 200th wartime victim of 41 Squadron. I hit him in one engine and he dived to ground level and flew so low that I could not get a proper sighting until he pulled up over an obstacle. It was an exciting chase largely because of the very low flying involved.'

In addition to being one of the top scoring pilots in the defensive actions against V-1 flying bombs, Squadron Leader Norman Kynaston DFC also had success during offensive operations over northern France flying the Spitfire XII. He joined 91 Squadron at Lympne as a flight commander in November 1942, but after the unit converted from Spitfire VBs to the Mark XII in April 1943 he was credited with the destruction of four enemy aircraft with another shared, all Fw 190s. His mount during this period was MB803, his first success being recorded near Le Touquet on 4 September 1943. By this time Kynaston had been given the command of 91 Squadron and he was to continue in this role for almost exactly a year. During this period the squadron was kept busy flying escort missions over occupied Europe during which it encountered opposition on a number of occasions.

In the late afternoon of 23 September escort cover was provided for an operation to Beauvais. A formation of nine Fw 190s were spotted below and to port so Kynaston led his section down, at which point most of the German aircraft broke away and climbed. One aircraft, however, dived down and went inland, prompting Kynaston to chase after it and open fire with two bursts at 300 yards from dead astern. The 190 then pulled up into the sun, thus forcing his adversary to pull to one side to keep it in view, but the attack was then taken up by Kynaston's No.2 (Flight Sergeant R.A.B. Blumer) who observed strikes and saw pieces flying off the German aircraft. After Blumer broke away, Kynaston moved in once again and fired a two second burst at the 190 which seemed to stagger in the air and then burst into flames. The pilot quickly baled out and the aircraft fell away to crash in open country near Grand Villiers.

The following day was a virtual repeat performance with 91 Squadron (call-sign Bumper) acting as part of the escort cover for Ramrod 242, another attack on Beauvais. When in the target area, a force estimated at fifteen Bf 109s dived down on to the squadron. Kynaston called the break and then dived down after one but gave up the chase after it was seen to be heading straight towards Beauvais aerodrome. Climbing back up again, he saw two pairs of Fw 190s passing underneath him so dived once again and selected the right-hand 190 of the nearest pair. After closing to about 250 yards, he fired a three second burst and saw numerous strikes on the engine and cockpit. Not long after the 190 began to break up and eventually flew into the ground where it exploded. In August 1943 No.91 Squadron swapped its Spitfire XIIs for Mark IXBs but on the 15th Kynaston was shot down by flak near St Trond during an evening sweep. Although he was seen to bale out off the French coast, no further news was received and his body was never found.

The final Griffon-Spitfire 'ace' of the war was New Zealander Pilot Officer B.W. Woodman of 130 Squadron. Woodman had completed his training in Canada and arrived in the UK in June 1944, passing through 57 OTU at Eshott prior to his operational posting. Like several others in 130 Squadron, Woodman found plenty of shooting practice in the last few weeks of the war, his first victory coming on 28 March when he shot down an Fw 190D near Warendorf, one of seven claimed by the squadron. Another 190 fell to his guns on 24 April near Neustadt airfield as it was approaching to land. His final victories consisted of a Siebel Si 204 shot down near Schweriner Lake on 30 April and one Bucker Bu 131, plus another shared with Geoff Lord, at the same location on 2 May. After the war Woodman returned to New Zealand and was involved in farming until his untimely death from cancer in December 1975.

Many other pilots were credited with 1–4 combat victories when flying Griffon-Spitfires including several wing and squadron commanders, notably Wing Commander George Keefer DSO DFC, the leader of 125 Wing, Squadron Leader Frank Woolley DFC who led both 350 and 130 Squadrons and Squadron Leader Douglas Benham DFC of 41 Squadron. Although born in New York, Keefer was a Canadian who joined the RAF in 1941, initially serving in the Middle East. By the summer of 1943 he was a flight commander with 412 Squadron and was given command of 126 Wing flying Spitfire IXBs the following year. After a short rest period he took over the leadership of 125 Wing in November 1944 and shot down another four enemy aircraft whilst flying Spitfire XIVs to bring his overall total to twelve.

By the time that Frank Woolley came to fly Spitfire XIVs he already had nearly four years combat experience, commencing with antiquated Vickers Vincents in Iraq in 1941. After serving with 132 and 602 Squadrons on Spitfire VBs and IXBs he was posted to the Fighter Leaders' School prior to joining the Central Fighter Establishment. His final operational posting was as C.O. of 350 Squadron as replacement for Squadron Leader Terry Spencer who had been shot down on 26 February 1945. Woolley's first confirmed 'kill' was an Fw 190D shot down near Hamm on 13 March, but after Spencer returned to resume his command, Woolley was then given command of 130 Squadron. He saw considerable action towards the end of the war with this unit claiming three more aircraft as destroyed, finishing with an Fw 190A shot down on 30 April.

Douglas Benham led 41 Squadron from August 1944 until April 1945 and achieved distinction on 23 January when, flying Spitfire XIV RM791, he was able to claim two Fw 190s as destroyed, despite the fact that he had only fired at one. His combat report explains how he did it

'I was leading Red and Blue sections when flying along a railway to Munster on an armed reconnaissance after shooting up locos and MET when twelve Fw 190s carrying 2 x 250 lb bombs appeared on the deck flying south west from Munster. The aircraft made for the Dettein and Waldrop balloons in a gentle curve to their right at 360 mph. We followed and just overhauled them with 18 lbs boost, having previously dropped tanks. I closed on an Fw 190 to 200 yards on a slight turn to port and opened fire with a half ring of deflection. The Fw 190 struck some trees, crashed and blew up at A9543. Seeing other of our aircraft chasing an enemy aircraft I looked in the mirror and saw another firing at me causing one hit on my starboard wing. I pulled back and climbed vertically, turning to starboard. My No.2 (F/O Hegarty) saw the Fw 190 try to follow my manoeuvre but it flicked over and after stalling on its back, during which time the pilot baled out, the Fw 190 spun in from 500 ft at A9038.'

Although the Spitfire XII was only really effective at low to medium levels due to its single-stage blower, several pilots had considerable combat success with this variant including Flight Lieutenant Chris Doll of 91 Squadron who shot down three Fw 190s in a single week in September 1943. His first victory came on the 19th when he was flying MB851 as part of a sweep over northern France. Doll was rather fortunate in that having become detached from the rest of his squadron at 9,000 ft over Lille he was able to catch up with a section of Spitfires just before a mixed force of Bf 109s and Fw 190s were able to launch an attack. A general dogfight soon developed during which Doll damaged an Fw 190 which was attacking another Spitfire. He then saw another 190 pulling up to rejoin the fight and managed to get in several short bursts down to 300 yards range. The 190 suddenly flicked over and did a gentle gliding turn down to 5,000 ft at which point Doll saw an object leave the aircraft. It then went into a spin which was not recovered before it hit the ground.

On 23 September Doll was flying as Yellow 4 during an escort operation to the airfield at Beauvais. The attacking force comprised seventy-two B-26 Marauders and very soon a formation of Fw 190s was seen diving towards the bombers. In the melee that followed one of the 190s carried out a determined attack on Yellow 3, following the Spitfire and firing hard during a steep climbing turn to port. Doll was able to close to 300 yards range and fired a short burst but with too little deflection. A second burst from 150 yards, however, hit the 190 on the wings, fuselage and cockpit. Various pieces were seen to fall off the aircraft and it poured flames from the front of the cockpit. It then turned over on to its back and went down in a spin before impacting with the ground around fifteen miles north east of Rouen. Doll was in action again the following day during a return trip to Beauvais

'I was flying Red 2 to the C.O. (S/L N.A. Kynaston) at about 15,000 ft when suddenly about ten Me 109s in line abreast dived vertically down in front of us. Red 1 turned over on his back to follow one and I rolled with him. He did an aileron turn to port, myself still following, when I saw flashes near my port wing and one very bright flash about two yards to the left of my cockpit. I looked round and saw another Me 109 about 800 yards behind me. My No.1 disappeared from view so I did a half roll, now at about 9,000 ft, and went straight down to the deck.

When at about 3,000 ft I saw many Spitfires, Fw 190s and Me 109s at varying heights between 4,000 ft and the ground. I saw two Fw 190s at 500 ft, line abreast 50 yards apart, about four miles away travelling south. I continued down to about 200 ft and gave chase, apparently unnoticed as they both continued straight and level. After about four minutes I caught them up closing very quickly. When about 400 yards away I pulled up to their level and as I did the starboard one did a gentle climbing turn to starboard. I gave him a burst from between 250–300 yards. He seemed to straighten out as though hit. I was still overtaking and closed to 150 yards giving him another burst before closing further to about 50 yards when I had to break up over him due to my extra speed. Just before I broke his engine and cockpit burst into flames and pieces flew past me. White smoke poured from him. I pulled out to one side and watched him turn slightly to starboard and crash into the middle of a wood. Flames and smoke leapt into the air.

Whilst watching this I looked round to see where the other 190 was and saw him on the other side of the wood about a mile away coming for me. I pushed everything forward and steered 320 degrees at zero feet. He chased me for about forty miles. My engine was very rough and occasionally puffs came from the port exhaust so I did not feel like playing with him. He was still a mile behind when I came to a round hill so I made a 360 degree turn round its base and found that I had lost him. I then throttled back and crossed the coast at a quiet spot.'

Chris Doll's record was closely matched by that of his squadron compatriot Warrant Officer R.A.B. 'Red' Blumer from New South Wales who shot down two Fw 190s, plus one shared, and a Bf 109G in a six week period commencing on 8 September 1943. This excellent run came to an end on 6 November 1943 when he in turn was shot down by flak during a 'Rhubarb' sortie near Evreux. With the help of the Resistance he was able to evade capture, his eventual return to the UK being made via Switzerland, Spain and Gibraltar. Blumer re-joined 91 Squadron in June 1944 in time to take part in the V-1 flying bomb campaign but he was killed on the 25th of that month when his Spitfire XIV (RM617) crashed prior to landing. His aircraft was seen to be flying normally but then dived straight into the ground.

The opportunities for pilots of the tactical reconnaissance squadrons to accumulate high scores in aerial combat were generally few and far between, however, the fact that Allied fighters could roam at will over German held territory towards the end of the war meant that the remaining elements of the *Luftwaffe* could be attacked when they were at their most vulnerable. The highest scoring Tac/R pilot was Flt Lt D.I. Hall of 414 Squadron who shot down four aircraft during a single sortie that took in the area around Neustadt on 2 May 1945

'I was on a Tac/R mission which I was unable to complete owing to weather. I lost my No.2 in the cloud and instructed him to return to base. I went below cloud and while flying west at zero feet at 1310 hrs I sighted one Fw 190 flying north at 50 ft at 100+ mph. I broke to starboard and rapidly closed on his tail. I opened fire at 250 yards using approximately 25 degrees port deflection and closed to 100 yards. I saw strikes on the fuselage and the enemy aircraft went straight in. Immediately in front of me I saw another Fw 190 which I overtook very rapidly and obtained only a short burst, opening fire at 50 yards. I saw strikes but was unable to observe the results due to the speed at which I passed him. A further Fw 190 was immediately ahead and I opened fire at 200 yards, closing to 50 yards. I saw strikes and flames and then observed the port wing falling off. Once again there was another Fw 190 immediately in line and I opened fire at 200 yards, closing to 100 yards. I saw strikes on the enemy aircraft which broke to port, began to pour black smoke and set on fire. I then broke to starboard and saw two Me 108s flying south in line abreast at approximately 50 ft. They broke in opposite directions and I closed on the one which had turned to starboard, opening

fire at 200 yards. I overshot but obtained strikes on the aircraft. He
continued to break to starboard so I turned to port and closed on
the other Me 108. I opened fire at 200 yards, closing to 50 yards. I
saw strikes and the aircraft went in, exploding on the ground.'

The end of the European and Pacific wars in 1945 unfortunately did not
mean a complete cessation of hostilities as trouble soon occurred in
several locations around the world, British forces having the difficult
task of policing Palestine until the creation of the state of Israel in 1948.
Part of the RAF's contribution to the area were the Spitfire FR.XVIIIs of
32 and 208 Squadron which saw action following raids on the airfield
of Ramat David by Spitfire IXs of the Egyptian Air Force on 22 May
1948. Three separate attacks were made during which five of the
Egyptian Spitfires were shot down including one which crashed after
being hit by ground fire. The most successful pilot was Flying Officer
Tim McElhaw of 208 Squadron who shot down two of the attackers in
quick succession.

# CHAPTER FIFTEEN

# Spitfires Post War

In the immediate post war years Griffon-Spitfires formed the equipment of a large number of Auxiliary Air Force squadrons which were reformed, initially on a one flight basis, in 1946. The aim of the AAF (it attained the 'Royal' prefix in 1947 in recognition of its wartime service) was to provide a reserve air force organised on a territorial basis. Having a vast pool of pilots with wartime experience, the AAF was able to draw on this valuable resource with the result that many former pilots who had taken up civilian posts gladly gave up much of their spare time to further their flying careers. The units that flew Griffon-powered Spitfires were as follows

| Squadron | Mark | Dates | Base | Remarks |
|---|---|---|---|---|
| 502 | F.22 | Sep 1948 – Mar 1951 | Aldergrove | To Vampire F.3 |
| 504 | F.22 | May 1948 – Mar 1950 | Hucknall/Wymeswold | To Meteor F.4 |
| 600 | XIV | Oct 1946 – Nov 1947 | Biggin Hill | To Meteor F.4 |
|  | F.21 | Apr 1947 – Nov 1950 |  |  |
|  | F.22 | Sep 1948 – Mar 1950 |  |  |
| 602 | XIV | Oct 1946 – Oct 1947 | Abbotsinch | To Vampire FB.5 |
|  | F.21 | Aug 1947 – Jan 1951 |  |  |
|  | F.22 | Oct 1948 – May 1951 |  |  |
| 603 | F.22 | Feb 1948 – July 1951 | Turnhouse | To Vampire FB.5 |
| 607 | FR.XIV | Nov 1946 – Mar 1948 | Ouston | To Vampire FB.5 |
|  | F.22 | Jan 1948 – Jun 1951 |  |  |
| 608 | F.22 | May 1948 – Jun 1951 | Thornaby | To Vampire F.3 |
| 610 | XIV | Nov 1946 – Apr 1949 | Hooton Park | To Meteor F.4 |
|  | F.22 | May 1949 – Aug 1951 |  |  |
| 611 | FR.XIV | Nov 1946 – Aug 1949 | Woodvale | To Meteor F.4 |
|  | F.22 | Feb 1949 – Nov 1951 |  |  |
| 612 | XIV | Nov 1946 – Oct 1949 | Dyce | To Vampire FB.5 |
| 613 | XIV | Dec 1946 – Dec 1948 | Ringway | To Vampire FB.5 |
|  | F.22 | Oct 1949 – Mar 1951 |  |  |

| Squadron | Mark | Dates | Base | Remarks |
|----------|------|-------|------|---------|
| 614 | F.22 | Jul 1948 – Apr 1951 | Llandow | To Vampire F.3 |
| 615 | XIV | Oct 1946 – Jan 1949 | Biggin Hill | To Meteor F.4 |
|  | F.21 | Jan 1947 – Jun 1950 |  |  |
|  | F.22 | Jul 1948 – Oct 1950 |  |  |

No.607 (County of Durham) Squadron was typical of the Auxiliary squadrons and was based at Ouston to the west of Newcastle upon Tyne. It had been formed at Usworth on 17 March 1930 as a light bomber unit and had flown Westland Wapitis until September 1936 when it converted to Hawker Demons and assumed a fighter role. Gloster Gladiators arrived in March 1939 and these were still being flown when the squadron was sent to France the following November as one of two Auxiliary units attached to the Air Component of the British Expeditionary Force (BEF). Hawker Hurricanes had been received by the time that the German *Blitzkrieg* was launched on 10 May 1940 and over the next eleven days the squadron claimed seventy-two German aircraft destroyed. After recuperating back at Usworth, 607 Squadron was heavily involved in the latter stages of the Battle of Britain and continued to fly Hurricanes throughout 1941, latterly in the fighter-bomber role. In 1942 the squadron moved to India where it was to remain until being disbanded at Mingaladon on 19 August 1946. During this period it flew Hurricanes, Spitfire VCs and VIIIs. No.607 Squadron was reformed at Ouston in June 1946, initially with Spitfire FR.XIVs, these being replaced by F.22s two years later.

By 1950 the squadron was under the command of Sqn Ldr Jim Bazin who was well acquainted with 607, having joined it as long ago as 1935. Bazin had fought in the Battle of France and had shot down several German aircraft, although the exact number cannot be confirmed as the squadron records were lost in the chaos that followed the German invasion. He later flew in the Battle of Britain and was awarded a DFC in October 1940, the citation stating that he had shot down ten enemy aircraft. Bazin's RAF career took an unusual turn in late 1943 when he converted to heavy bombers and he later commanded 9 Squadron flying twenty-five operational sorties in Lancasters, including one attack on the *Tirpitz*. After the war he returned to his pre-war occupation as an engineer and rejoined 607 Squadron in November 1946, eventually taking over as C.O. in 1949. He was assisted by Flt Lt A.B. Dunford as flight commander and Flt Lt Menzies who was in charge of operational training. No.607 Squadron's Spitfire F.22s were complemented by two Harvards which were mainly used for refresher and conversion training.

As part time fliers, Auxiliary squadrons could be badly affected by adverse weather, particularly during winter months, but in January 1950 No.607 Squadron fared reasonably well, achieving ninety-four hours in Spitfires and thirty-two hours in Harvards, with air-to-ground firing being carried out on Acklington's ranges at Druridge Bay on the 8th. On the first weekend in February seven Spitfires and one Harvard flew to Linton on Ouse to train with 92 Squadron (Meteor F.4). Each Auxiliary squadron was allocated a regular squadron for affiliation duties which helped the two air forces keep in close contact so that operating procedures and tactics were compatible. Interception practices were carried out on the Sunday morning involving three Auxiliary and four regular squadrons (two Meteor and two Hornet). The rest of the month was taken up with air-to-ground firing and interception exercises with the Fighter Control Unit at Patrington near Hull.

March saw the squadron make their monthly trip to Linton on Ouse, with the rest of their time being taken up with practice flying including 'snake' climbs, high level QGH descents in 'snake' and cine gun exercises. As the opportunities to fly were often restricted by bad weather, emphasis had been placed on acquiring the recently introduced White and Green instrument ratings which allowed pilots to fly more often in marginal weather. With suitably qualified pilots, snake climbs could be carried out in which a number of aircraft would follow each other at set intervals through cloud to (hopefully) emerge into clear air with the same spacings as they had started with, thereby allowing a quick form up into battle formation. A QGH procedure was a controlled descent through cloud using radio bearings and involved an outward track from a position overhead the airfield, followed by a 180 degree turn onto final approach.

By June, better weather allowed a total of 124 hours to be flown on Spitfires during the month commencing with fighter affiliation at Linton on Ouse on 3/4th. Four aircraft took part flown by Flt Lt Dunford, Flt Lt Menzies, Plt Off Hindson and P.II Percival with initial training comprising 'snake' climbs through cloud to operating altitude, tactical formation and a 'snake' QGH descent. In the afternoon 607 Squadron's Spitfires took part in an exercise with 92 Squadron involving visual intercepts and 'bouncing' by the Meteors at 20,000 ft. A busy weekend was completed with the elimination rounds to select the 12 Group competitors for the Cooper Trophy Air Race which was scheduled to take place during the RAF Display at Farnborough in July. P.II M.C. Butcher represented 607 Squadron and finished a very creditable second out of a field of twelve aircraft including Meteors and Vampires. All competitors were given a handicap time and Butcher completed the course (two laps of thirty-six miles) only two seconds behind the winning Vampire.

An unfortunate incident occurred on 24 June when a section of three

Spitfires were gaining altitude prior to carrying out a series of practice interceptions. The section was being led by Flt Lt Menzies with P.III Davison (No.2) and P.III J.A. Buglass (No.3). Having already climbed through 28,000 ft of cloud without breaking clear, Davison reported a lack of oxygen which prompted Menzies to order an immediate descent. During the let down the three aircraft became separated and only the section leader and his No.2 returned to base, contact having been lost with Buglass at some point after the formation had split up. It was later reported that his aircraft (PK394) had been seen to crash vertically out of cloud into the North Sea off Blyth.

The highlight of any Auxiliary squadron's year was the Summer Camp and in 1950 No.607 Squadron was required to fly down to Chivenor in Devon. The move was made on 8 July with nine Spitfires and four Harvards, the ground crews following behind in two Hastings and a Dakota. Normal training was carried out in the first week and it had been hoped to devote the second week to air-to-air firing, however, the Miles Martinets allotted for this task were four days late in arriving. When they eventually did turn up they were unfortunately all declared unserviceable. By the time that they had been fixed the weather was unsuitable with low cloud and bad visibility so that 607 had to be content with cine exercises and a few air-to-ground sorties on the ranges at St Merryn. A considerable amount of instrument flying training was achieved and although it was not possible to do any instrument rating tests during the camp, several were arranged to be completed after the squadron's return to its home base. Having averaged around thirty hours a day for the two week period of the camp, 607 flew back to Ouston on the 22nd to be stood down until the middle of August.

After its summer break, 607 Squadron began flying again on 16 August, however, the number of hours flown during the month amounted to only thirty-six, mainly as a result of the late start and the fact that a number of aircraft were in need of inspections after the trip to Chivenor. Two Spitfires were lost in accidents on the 20th, both aircraft running short of fuel in deteriorating weather. P.II Carter reported that he was baling out but was found dead near to his crashed aircraft (PK595) and Flg Off Curran was injured during a forced landing in PK393 near Boulmer. Sadly, another pilot was killed on 3 September when P.II Armstrong spun in on final approach to Ouston in PK498. The rest of the year was taken up with further training, although there was the inevitable decline in hours flown due to decreasing daylight and the onset of winter which meant that only thirty-seven hours were possible in December. The squadron continued to fly Spitfires into 1951 before re-equipping with Vampire FB.5s. These were flown for the next six years until No.607 was disbanded, along with the other Auxiliary squadrons, in 1957.

One of the most difficult jobs carried out by British forces after the end of the Second World War was the peacekeeping operation in Palestine. The new state of Israel was due to be formed on 15 May 1948 and in the run up to that date the situation between local Arabs and the Israelis deteriorated rapidly with the British caught between the opposing camps. Operating as part of the forces of occupation were the Spitfire XVIIIs of 32 and 208 Squadrons which were based at Ramat David, however, both Arab and Israeli fell victim to the somewhat preposterous idea that the RAF was dealing with the other side with a view to handing over its aircraft following the British withdrawal from the area, which was due to take place a week after the declaration of Independence. With tension running high, matters came to a head on the morning of 22 May 1948, the day the RAF was to pull out the area and fly to Cyprus. The sequence of events was recorded in the 32 Squadron Operations Record Book

'When the day finished yesterday the detachment was all ready for its move to Nicosia today, however, once more the unexpected took the field, this time in the form of the Egyptian Air Force. We were rudely awakened about 0600 hrs by two loud explosions. This unexpected commotion led everyone into the open and it became immediately obvious that a Spitfire aircraft which was still orbiting had dropped two bombs on the aircraft park whence everyone propelled themselves as rapidly as possible. On arrival at the park we found two of the 32 Squadron aircraft blazing fiercely and all the others in the line, except two, holed in many places by bomb splinters and bullets for the aircraft had strafed as it bombed. The aircraft then did two more half-hearted strafing runs which did no more damage and then went off. 208 Squadron were more fortunate than we and after a slight delay were able to scramble four aircraft in search of the intruder (nationality then unknown) as they had sustained little damage.

After the aircraft had scrambled, the remaining Spitfires were dispersed in the various blast bays but it was impossible to save the burning aircraft because of exploding ammunition. The scrambled aircraft returned without having been successful but from then on a standing patrol of two aircraft was maintained over the airfield. The next attack came about two hours later. This time three Spitfires came in from the north of the airfield and dropped six bombs. Three of them did no damage, but the others dropped beside the hangar on the aircraft park and did a fair amount of damage. Two airmen were killed beside the hangar and several were injured. These aircraft also strafed as they bombed and a Dakota which had just landed to collect stores was hit, two of the crew being killed and the other two badly wounded. Of the Egyptian Spitfires (as they were now recognised) one was shot down by an RAF Bren-gunner as he broke away from the attack and the other two were destroyed by the aircraft on patrol.

Shortly after this another two Egyptian Spitfires arrived but this time they only had time to drop one bomb before they were engaged by the patrol aircraft and destroyed. Unfortunately the one bomb they dropped fell beside a Dakota which had earlier been loaded with the personal kit of the groundcrews of the squadron and the whole lot was lost in the subsequent blaze. Later in the morning we were able to get three aircraft serviceable and these were put into the air to relieve 208 Squadron who until then had been supplying all the patrols. Shortly after this seven Spitfire XVIIIs arrived from Nicosia as reinforcements, of these three were from 32 Squadron so our rather dire position as regards serviceable aircraft was relieved somewhat and we were able to share the airfield patrols equally with 208 Squadron from then on. The patrols were continued till dusk but the Egyptians had learned of their mistake by this time and there were no more visitors.'

Thankfully 208 Squadron was not hit as badly as 32 Squadron and its ORB records the combats that took place that day

'As soon as the strafing had ceased four of our aircraft were scrambled. A pair went north and a pair went south but no contact was made. As soon as the four returned, a standing patrol of two aircraft was put up over the airfield with orders to shoot down any attacking aircraft. At 0830 hrs three more aircraft appeared over the airfield. They attacked immediately concentrating on the office hangar which they obviously thought was an aircraft hangar. They got one direct hit and three near misses, setting light to an unserviceable aircraft which was being stripped down just outside the hangar. They also strafed the airfield, hitting a Dakota which was one of three that had landed between the attacks. The enemy aircraft were then attacked by our patrol. F/O Cooper opened up on the first one, then F/O Bowie got a strike and it went straight down in flames west of the airfield. The second aircraft on being attacked dived away to the south followed by our section in close line astern. As soon as it was identified as hostile, F/O Cooper opened fire and scored hits on it. Pieces fell off and the aircraft dived to ground level where Cooper continued firing until it crashed into the ground at full speed. The third bandit strafed the airfield at low level and was hit by RAF Regiment Brens. It disappeared to the south losing height and glycol and was subse-

quently confirmed as destroyed. The third attack was just after
0900 hrs when two aircraft again attacked the airfield. The first
was chased to the south by F/O McElhaw and F/O Hully and was
shot down by McElhaw. The second aircraft was then bounced by
McElhaw who shot it down about two miles east of the airfield.'

The Egyptian authorities later blamed the attacks on a navigational
error and weather conditions which at the time were 0/10 cloud and a
visibility of at least 50 miles. The move to Nicosia by the RAF was finally
completed two days later.

Seven months later 208 Squadron found itself back in the firing line
once again as it was based at Fayid in the Suez Canal Zone. The Arab-
Israeli War of Independence was reaching its climax and Fayid was a
mere fifteen minutes flying time from the front line between Israeli and
Egyptian forces. On 7 January 1949 a section of four Spitfire FR.XVIIIs
of 208 Squadron comprising Flying Officers Geoff Cooper and Tim
McElhaw, with P II Sayers and P II Close as wingmen, took off to reconnoitre the front line. At the same time two Israeli Spitfire XVIs of 101
Squadron, flown by John McElroy from Ontario, Canada, and Chalmers
'Slick' Goodlin, an American, took off from their base at Questina. Both
were highly experienced pilots. McElroy was a 10-kill ace having flown
with 249 Squadron in Malta and later as C.O. of 416 Squadron, whilst
Goodlin had joined the RCAF in 1941 and had later become a test pilot
with the Bell Aircraft Corporation during which time he flew the rocket-
powered X-1. By an unfortunate twist of fate, the Spitfire FR.XVIIIs of
208 Squadron arrived over the front shortly after a strike by Egyptian
Spitfires and were immediately attacked by McElroy and Goodlin who,
not surprisingly, thought that the loitering aircraft were responsible for
the devastation on the ground. In a complete reversal of fortunes, the
RAF Spitfires were this time at the receiving end of a devastating attack
by the Israeli aircraft. Details of the combat were slow to emerge as is
evident from the following entry in the 208 Squadron ORB

'A bad day for the squadron. At 1115 hrs, a Tac/R team of four
aircraft led by Flg Off Cooper was despatched to cover the same
area as the day previous (the El Arish – Rafah road) and did not
return. When it became obvious that they had exceeded their
endurance, overdue action was taken and all aerodromes in the
Canal Zone contacted for news, but with negative results (it was
learnt afterwards that they had all been shot down by 'Jewish'
fighters). Four aircraft were brought to readiness for a search and
at 1500 hrs led by the C.O. [Sqn Ldr J.M. Morgan], and with fifteen
Tempests of 324 Wing as cover, a search was made over the recce
area. The high and medium cover was attacked by 'Jewish'

fighters, one Tempest being shot down. Considerable movement was observed on the El Arish – Rafah road and evidence of a battle south-west of Rafah, but none of the missing aircraft were found. In the evening news was received that Flg Off Cooper had been shot down and picked up by the Egyptian army and although wounded, was brought back from El Arish by train. From Flg Off Cooper's report it was established that his formation had been attacked by 'Jewish' Spitfire type aircraft and he assumed all four had been shot down. Cooper had in fact baled out, and been picked up by Bedouins and transported by camel to El Arish. He also stated that he saw one, and possibly two, of the other pilots go down successfully by parachute.'

Of the other three pilots, Flg Off McElhaw was taken prisoner by Israeli forces, as was P II Close who had suffered head injuries when he hit the tail of his Spitfire as he baled out. Sadly, P II Sayers was killed when his aircraft dived into the desert. The reaction of the RAF in the Canal Zone was one of stunned dismay and there was a desire to wipe out the fledgling Israeli Air Force, but despite the fact that Britain still did not recognise the state of Israel the units based in the region were told in the strongest terms that no direct action was to be undertaken. Israeli radio did not help the situation by claiming that the pilots had admitted receiving orders to photograph the position of Israeli troops in the Negev, a broadcast that the 208 Squadron ORB likened to German wartime propaganda. In the event the only action taken was a slight alteration to the colour scheme of 208 Squadron's Spitfires. As the Israeli machines had red spinners like the RAF aircraft, this colour was quickly changed to white, with white markings also being applied to the rudder for ease of identification in the air. With the passing of time, and the release of McElhaw and Close, the tension gradually eased and there were to be no further confrontations with the new power in the Middle East. By this time, however, trouble had flared up in Malaya and Spitfire FR.XVIIIs were heavily involved in the fight against Communist Terrorists. For a full account of the activities of 60 Squadron in this theatre see Chapter Sixteen.

Some of the most exacting flying carried out by Griffon-powered Spitfires in the post war period was that carried out by the THUM Flight based at Woodvale, situated on the coast between Liverpool and Southport. THUM was a convenient shortening of the words temperature and humidity, the work of the Flight involving the collation of weather data so that up-to-date information could be passed to weather stations throughout Europe. This type of activity had first been attempted during the First World War. Initial operations were on a fairly casual basis but the gathering of weather information became much more professional with the setting up of the RAF Meteorological Flight at Eastchurch in November 1924. This unit moved to Duxford soon after its formation where it subsequently flew Armstrong Whitworth Siskin fighters, one of its pilots being a very young Jeffrey Quill.

During the early years of the Second World War meteorological information had been derived from a number of special met flights operating under the control of Coastal Command and flying a variety of aircraft types ranging from Blenheims, Hampdens and Hudsons to B-17 Flying Fortresses. From 1943 specially adapted Halifax aircraft began to take on the role but with the cessation of hostilities the number of aircraft involved in the recording of weather data declined rapidly to the point where it was being carried out as a supplementary task by night-fighter Mosquitos. In early 1951 the Air Ministry awarded a contract to Short Brothers for the operation of a meteorological flight from Hooton Park in Cheshire. The aircraft to be flown on this type of work would have to have a good high altitude capability, long range and it would also need to be stable as the cockpit workload would be high throughout the flight as a result of the pilot having to monitor his recording instruments and note the results, together with other observations. The choice was quickly narrowed down to just one, the Spitfire PR.XIX which also had the advantage of being readily available as it was being phased out of the photo-reconnaissance role in favour of the Meteor PR.10. Although Hooton Park had initially been earmarked for the THUM Flight, the unit took up residence at Woodvale in July 1951.

The sorties flown by the THUM Flight followed a regular pattern and consisted of a low level transit from Woodvale to a point near Worcester, this being carried out every day at 0900 hrs. After measuring temperatures up to 1,500 ft above sea level, a climb was initiated to record the temperature at every 50 millibars down to 300 millibars pressure, which equated to an altitude of around 30,000 ft. A stepped climb was flown with the aircraft briefly levelled as each pressure setting was reached. In addition to recording temperatures, other features of the weather that had to be noted were cloud type and extent, visibility, turbulence, icing levels, precipitation, haze and the formation of condensation trails at altitude. The pilot also had the responsibility of ensuring that his aircraft was accurately positioned at all times during the climb which usually took around forty-five minutes. After all the readings had been taken the aircraft was flown to Liverpool Airport where the information was passed to the Met Office and it was here that the basic data was corrected for instrument, height and airspeed errors before being distributed throughout the weather network.

The Spitfire PR.XIXs delivered to the THUM Flight were PM549 'A', PM577 'B', PM652 'C' and PM631 'D', all of which had been retired from their former PR duties and modified by Short Brothers for meteorological work. Although all aircraft continued to carry full RAF markings and were painted PR blue, the pilots allocated to the Flight were civilians, however, all had previous service experience. The first C.O of the unit was Gordon Hargreaves who, sadly, was killed on 5 May 1952 when returning to Woodvale in PM549. His role was then taken over by John Formby who had considerable multi-engine experience having flown Short Stirlings with 299 Squadron and Oxfords with No.1513 Beam Approach Training (BAT) Flight. After the war he qualified as an instructor on Harvard and Prentice aircraft and was to remain with the THUM Flight during its remaining time on Spitfires.

The dangers of having to fly on a regular basis at all times of year and in all weather conditions, were highlighted on 4 March 1954 when Tommy Heyes, another ex-bomber pilot, was killed flying PM652. His aircraft came down over Shropshire on its way back to Liverpool Airport, apparently as a result of engine failure. The crash site was near the village of Church Pulverback and eye witness reports suggested that Heyes had manoeuvred his aircraft at low level to keep clear of the village, only to die in the resultant crash. With two of the original Spitfire PR.XIXs lost, PS853 'C' was delivered in March 1954, with PM651 arriving shortly after. The latter was involved in an accident that resulted in Cat 4 damage the following month, however, and it was replaced in August by PS915 'A'.

Not long after the loss of Tommy Heyes, another THUM pilot, John Wood suffered an engine failure in PS853 during a climb on 22 July 1954, although this time there was a happy ending. The engine began to run roughly at about 9,000 ft in cloud and then cut altogether. Knowing that the overcast extended down to low level, Wood released his straps and inverted his aircraft prior to baling out but on flying into slightly clearer weather, he decided to remain in the cockpit and assess his chances of carrying out a successful forced landing. As luck would have it he emerged from cloud within gliding distance of the disused airfield at Calveley where he performed a wheels-down, dead-stick landing. It transpired that the engine had failed due to a rich mixture cut caused by a fault in the carburettor.

The perils of operating piston-engined aircraft in a predominantly jet age were highlighted on 17 November 1954 when John Formby had to divert to Valley in PM577 due to bad weather at Woodvale. An improvement later in the day allowed him the opportunity to return to base, but when carrying out his pre-flight checks the Griffon appeared a little rougher than usual. This roughness increased considerably during the take off run, by which time Formby could smell the distinctive aroma of jet fuel, the ground crew having refuelled the aircraft with AVTUR instead of regular 100-octane fuel. Formby thus had a longer journey back to Woodvale than he had anticipated as PM577 was forced to remain for an engine change and for the fuel system to be flushed out.

The Spitfire PR.XIX proved to be ideally suited to its latter-day role and the occasions when meteorological readings could not be taken due to adverse weather conditions were few and far between. Servicing was carried out by Shorts at Woodvale, however, a shortage of spares eventually led to the decision being taken to retire the Spitfires in favour of the Mosquito T.35. Before this course of action had been finalised a trial was carried out using a Spitfire F.24 (VN315) to ascertain its suitability for the Met role but this variant proved to lack the stability of the PR.XIX and the idea went no further. The date set for the retirement of the Spitfires was June 1957 by which time over 2,800 weather sorties had been flown. The last flight was performed by John Formby in PS853 on 10 June, a date that marked the last ever sortie by an RAF Spitfire. The three remaining Spitfires were ferried to Duxford on 14 June and all remain airworthy today, PM631 and PS915 with the Battle of Britain Memorial Flight at Coningsby and PS853 with Rolls-Royce at Filton [PM577 was withdrawn from use in June 1956]. After disposing of its Spitfires, the THUM Flight did not survive much longer and was finally disbanded on 1 May 1959, its job then being performed by radar-tracked balloons.

# CHAPTER SIXTEEN

# Spitfires over Malaya

During the Second World War, Malaya came under the control of Japanese forces which had begun their devastating sweep through the Pacific and south-east Asia in late 1941. The only opposition to the occupiers came from local guerrilla forces, aided by the Allies, which fought a campaign of disruption. Known initially as Force 136 and later as the Malayan Peoples Anti-Japanese Army (MPAJA), this unit comprised several thousand Communist rebels, but as soon as the war ended their attention quickly turned to the overthrow of the British who had taken over control following the defeat of Japan. The rebel army, which was predominantly Chinese and was led by Chin Peng, who had been awarded an OBE for his resistance activities, changed its name to the Malayan Races Liberation Army (MRLA) and in June 1948 the first direct action was taken against Europeans in the area when three rubber plantation workers were murdered. Shortly after this atrocity the Government declared a state of emergency which was to last for the next twelve years, the British response being the implementation of Operation Firedog.

At the start of the insurrection RAF forces in Malaya were relatively thin on the ground, the main strike element being the Spitfire FR.XVIIIs of 28 and 60 Squadrons, detachments of which flew from Kuala Lumpur, the nearest suitable base for operations against the Communist Terrorist (CT) forces. These were soon aided by the Beaufighters of 45 and 84 Squadrons, with transport duties being undertaken by Dakotas of 110 Squadron. The Short Sunderland flying-boats of 209 Squadron were based at Seletar, Singapore and this airfield was also the home of 81 Squadron which performed photo-reconnaissance duties with Spitfire PR.XIXs and Mosquito PR.34s. Operations were far from straightforward as 90 per cent of the country was covered by thick jungle which allowed the rebels the luxury of being able to move without being spotted from the air. Air strikes thus had to be carried out

on the basis of advance information on the whereabouts of rebel strong-holds, a difficult task with a highly mobile force. The first air-to-ground mission of Operation Firedog (the codeword given to the RAF's response in Malaya) was carried out by two Spitfires of 60 Squadron on 6 July 1948 and this unit continued to use Spitfires operationally in this theatre for the next 2½ years.

Due to the increased terrorist activity throughout the Federation, the RAF task force was formed at Kuala Lumpur. On 2 July a detachment of three of 60 Squadron's Spitfire FR.XVIIIs (out of a total strength of eight) led by C.O. Sqn Ldr J.H.S. Broughton AFC took off from Sembawang to form part of this unit. All aircraft were fully armed with 60-lb rocket projectiles, in addition to their standard armament of two 20 mm Hispano cannons and two 0.50 in Browning machine-guns. Having had to abort a strike mission on the 5th due to low lying river mist, an attack was made on a jungle clearing the following day by Sqn Ldr Broughton and Flg Off T.W.F. De Salis, the former firing his six rockets in a salvo following a steep dive on to the target. After De Salis had fired his rockets the pair strafed the area around the edges. Information had been received that the insurgents had been using the clearing as a parade ground and had been using the surrounding jungle to sleep in. Later reports revealed that the attacks had been carried out accurately, but that the bandits had moved out several days before.

The next operation was carried out on the 15th and involved all three Spitfires in an attack on a target, said to be a Communist HQ, fifteen miles south of Bentung. Sqn Ldr Broughton went in first firing a pair of rockets, to be followed by Flg Off R.C. Bridges using his guns in case any bandits in the building were trying to get away, however, very little could be seen due to the thick jungle that surrounded the target. The other member of the section, Flg Off De Salis, fired a pair of rockets and the whole sequence was repeated without a single hit on the building, all of the eight rockets fired having overshot. Flg Off Bridges then went in and scored a direct hit with his first pair of rockets which succeeded in demolishing two-thirds of the building. A recce was then made of the area but nothing could be seen.

The first operations from Kuala Lumpur emphasized the importance of accurate map reading, especially when using the 1 inch variety, and whenever it was possible to obtain the authority to fly the aircraft on training sorties, the accent was put on low level navigation and pinpointing exercises. These were to prove invaluable on subsequent strike missions and piloting standards improved considerably in this respect. Back at Sembawang the remainder of the squadron carried out normal training duties, although their activities were curtailed con-siderably by the demands made on their aircraft by the Kuala Lumpur detachment. A continuous flow of serviceable aircraft was kept up between the two bases, the object being to maintain three fully operational Spitfires at the forward base. As it had been decided to do all weekly inspections at Sembawang, the remaining ground crews were kept extremely busy.

Operations began early on 21 July with Flg Off Bridges and Flg Off A.W. Paterson taking off at 0700 hrs for a strike mission just to the east of Telok Anson. On this occasion low cloud prevented positive identification of the target which meant a return to base, however, Paterson and Flg Off R.F. Adams tried again two hours later and had better luck. They were able to press home their attack and destroy one hut or 'basha' and put holes through several others, their handiwork being recorded by a 'cameraman', a 28 Squadron Spitfire FR.XVIII fitted with an oblique camera. By now the detachment at Kuala Lumpur had been increased in size to six aircraft, including two Spitfires from 28 Squadron. This tended to put further strain on the maintenance organisation although it was hoped that the situation could be managed satisfactorily. Sqn Ldr Broughton and Flg Off Adams set off in the evening to attack targets north west of Bentung and were able to fire off all their weaponry at a number of buildings and huts. After the strike Flg Off Adams returned to Sembawang where it was discovered that he had made a rather half-hearted attempt at shooting himself down by flying through his own rocket burst, a large piece of shrapnel having punctured his starboard radiator.

The target for the following day was the first for which photographs were available beforehand so that pilots could be briefed more fully. The day before a Spitfire of 28 Squadron had reconnoitred the area which was a few miles north east of Taiping and brought back clear images of a supposed insurgent camp on top of a small hill. Sqn Ldr Broughton and P.II J. Watson took off at first light and, after landing at Taiping, attacked the camp with rockets and guns, being assisted in the strafing by a third Spitfire from 28 Squadron. Although it was P.II Watson's first operational sortie since arriving at Kuala Lumpur, he scored a direct hit with a pair of rockets on one of the bashas. In the afternoon Flg Off Paterson and P.II Browne were ordered into the air on reports that some troops and the police were encountering opposition at Bertam, where the Kuala Lipis – Kota Bharu road crossed a tributary of the Pahang river. On reaching the area the troops signalled the aircraft to attack a group of huts which they did with their rockets, 20 mm cannon and 0.50 in machine-guns. The 60-lb rocket projectile was a notoriously inaccurate weapon and on this occasion no hits were obtained, although the area was liberally sprayed with gunfire.

The first sorties on the 25th were flown in the area of Seminyth, the target comprising a large tree with an observation post in it, a school building and several other structures nearby. The pilots involved were

Sqn Ldr Broughton (TP206), P.II Watson (TP225) and P.III Croudson from 28 Squadron. Broughton fired his rockets in a salvo of six and blew down one end of the school house, but Watson had two hang ups and a misfire. The rest of the target was strafed, a large explosion being seen behind the school house. In the afternoon, cover was provided to troops advancing along the Kuala Lipis road at Sungei Yu where an ambush had occurred a few days before.

During August anti-insurgent activity increased considerably at Kuala Lumpur and the detachment was given a regular supply of tasks to perform. No.60 Squadron's contribution was maintained at four aircraft and four pilots throughout the month, the most interesting and effective type of operation from the pilots' point of view being those flown in support of 'Shaw Force' which consisted of troops advancing down the valley from Gua Musang to Pulai. This unit had its own Air Liaison Officer or ALO (together with an Air Contact Team) who was able to brief the pilots in the air and direct them to any target that needed to be taken out. This was a much more flexible arrangement than the pre-arranged type of target that was usually laid on by the Army or the police, and was a lot more satisfying to fly as the assistance provided was much more immediate.

A major setback to offensive operations was experienced in early August when all of 60 Squadron's aircraft were declared unserviceable for rocket firing owing to two unfortunate cases of rockets being discharged while the aircraft were still on the ground due to faults in the electrical circuits. Both of these incidents were extremely regrettable as several civilian lives were lost as a result. The first occurred on 1 August when Flg Off Paterson landed back with his rockets still in place following an aborted strike. When the magnetos were switched off the starboard outer rocket fired and although it did not explode on landing, it hit a Chinese woman who was killed. On the 3rd six pilots were briefed for an attack on two separate targets ten miles north of Telok Anson, however, only the second section of three aircraft were able to get airborne. As the other Spitfires were taxying out and having their wheel well rocket plugs connected, the port inner rocket on Flg Off De Salis's aircraft fired and landed in the middle of a nearby town, exploding in a shop. One man was killed instantly and eleven other civilians were seriously injured, three of whom later died.

In the meantime, the other section led by Flg Off Bridges with P.III Browne and Flg Off Brie of 28 Squadron as Nos. 2 and 3, located their target which consisted of two separate groups of buildings. Bridges and Browne left one set of houses burning while Brie flattened the rest with a 500-lb bomb, the first time that bombs had been used by Spitfires in this particular conflict. The police and a detachment of Gurkhas went into the area after the strike and were able to capture thirty-four suspects, together with a considerable quantity of arms and ammunition. Following the incidents back at base, the use of rockets and bombs was prohibited pending an investigation into the cause and the two aircraft involved were grounded indefinitely for a complete electrical check.

The first operation after the 'runaway rocket' incidents occurred on 7 August and involved strafing a forested ridge about six miles east of Ipoh with cannon and machine-gun. The object of this exercise was to drive any insurgents who were in the area into the hands of the police who were positioned around the ridge. On the 13th the squadron flew on a co-ordinated strike with two Beaufighters of 84 Squadron in the Temerloh area. These aircraft were still cleared for rocket firing and the Spitfires followed up to strafe the target. A similar combined attack was carried out three days later in which the Spitfires used High Explosive-Incendiary (HEI) and ball ammunition for its 20 mm Hispano cannons. This was the first occasion that HEI and fully operational ammunition had been used and it was hoped that this would lower the gun stoppage rate which had been disconcertingly high up to that time.

During the month the squadron also flew a number of 'flag wags' which consisted of flying over areas where bandits had been active in order to boost the morale of the public and undermine that of the insurgents. This was regarded as a rather irksome task by the pilots, although word came back from planters to say that the sight of up to four Spitfires flying low over the jungle was very reassuring, especially as they were cut off from civilisation and possibly surrounded by bandits. Towards the end of August operations were started in the Johore area with sections of two aircraft giving offensive support to the forces on the ground.

September was a relatively quiet month with just three operations being flown from Kuala Lumpur. On the afternoon of the 16th the squadron took part in an experiment which it was hoped would become a regular event involving co-operation with the Army and the police. The ground forces, having chosen an area to raid, stood by in the vicinity while a Dakota dropped leaflets telling the inhabitants to stay where they were. The Spitfires then circled the area, making occasional dummy attacks to impress on the locals that they should do as they were told. In the meantime the ground forces moved in to try to root out any suspected terrorists. Radio contact was maintained with the Spitfires above which had sufficient fuel to remain in the area for around an hour. On the 17th two sections of three Spitfires assisted Beaufighters in a hill strike and a similar operation was laid on three days later. On this occasion, however, P.III Browne's Spitfire was assaulted on the ground by a fully armed Beau as he was taxying towards the runway prior to take off. The port outer wing of the Spitfire was completely destroyed and the Beaufighter damaged its own starboard propeller.

By early October 60 Squadron was cleared to begin dive bombing with 500-lb bombs and the first attack was flown on the 7th on two jungle clearings eight miles east of Raub. A 'maximum effort' saw four Beaufighters of 45 Squadron take the northerly target, with seven Spitfires (four from 60 Squadron and three from 28 Squadron) attacking the larger encampment to the south. All bombs fell within the target area which was then strafed with cannon and machine-gun. A repeat attack was carried out the following day, although on this occasion the Spitfires exchanged clearings with the Beaus. P.III Browne, who was flying TP225, was seen to drop his bomb successfully, but on pulling out of his dive his aircraft seemed to become uncontrollable and it eventually spun in, crashing into the side of a hill about two miles from the target. Search parties were sent to the area but were unable to reach the scene due to the extremely dense jungle and the nature of the local terrain. Further strikes were made near Raub in the next few days before a break from operations which lasted nearly a fortnight. On the 28 October bombing was carried out on two clearings north east of Kuala Lumpur and the month was rounded off on the 30th with a couple of 'flag wags'.

Having suffered its first loss of the campaign, RAF Kuala Lumpur had another difficult day on 12 November. A suspected bandit camp had been located on a ridge to the north east of Serendah, together with a lookout tree, and a strike was quickly put together. It was decided that two Spitfires would dive on the target from a height of 2,000 ft to deliver a strafing attack before clearing the area to allow three more Spitfires to come in and bomb from 8,000 ft. Afterwards all Spitfires would return to shoot up the entire area. The initial attack was by two Spitfires of 28 Squadron and they were followed by three aircraft from 60 Squadron flown by Flg Off De Salis, Flg Off Peter Sketch (28 Squadron) and Flg Off Paterson. De Salis started his dive and was closely followed by Sketch, with Paterson some distance behind. The first two dropped their bombs together, but as De Salis was climbing away he saw Sketch apparently unable to maintain lateral control of his Spitfire (TP231). Shortly afterwards the starboard wing seemed to blow up near the ammunition panel and the aircraft crashed. At midday a Dakota C.4 (KN633) of 110 Squadron set out to look for the crash site but in doing so it also came down in roughly the same area with the loss of five crew members. These included Flt Lt D.G. Ballard of 28 Squadron (and formerly of 60 Squadron) who had joined the flight to help with the search.

The total number of operational sorties flown in November amounted to a rather disappointing thirty-one, but as the squadron's pilot strength for most of the month averaged out at only three, this was, perhaps, not particularly surprising. Most operations involved strafing attacks, with several bombing missions, convoy covers and 'flag wags'. One of the latter was flown on the 23rd taking in Bentung, Mentakab, Maran, Kuantan and Sungei Lembing. As was usual for the time of year, the weather was poor over the swampy eastern side of Malaya with the cloud base continually below 1,000 ft. On the 30th a combined effort was laid on, the target being a tin mine and the surrounding area which it was thought was being used as a base by the terrorists. A hutted encampment was attacked by Flg Offs Adams, Paterson and De Salis with rocket-firing Beaufighters following up with a strike on the mine itself. The three Spitfires then flew back to Kuala Lumpur to refuel and re-arm before returning to the target to fly a patrol as troops moved into the area. Once again it transpired that the bandits had moved on, but at least from the air point of view the operation had been a success as the target had been severely damaged. This was in spite of the fact that 60 Squadron's redoubtable ALO had not been able to assist with the attack as he was bogged down in his contact car several miles away.

In December sixteen operational sorties were flown from Sembawang and eight from Kuala Lumpur. It had been hoped that the squadron detachment at Kuala Lumpur would be coming to an end, as the strains of operating what was effectively only half a squadron in two different locations was beginning to tell. This was due to the conflicting demands imposed by having to fulfil an operational commitment, together with training and servicing back at the home base. Despite earlier suggestions to the contrary, the detachment was officially re-formed on the 28th, the requirement being for four aircraft to be based at Kuala Lumpur once more, but, as only two Spitfires were serviceable at the time, two had to be borrowed from 28 Squadron. Sqn Ldr Broughton had another reason for wanting his squadron to operate from a single base as for the last six months he had not been able to form a football team composed entirely of his own men due to the fact that there had not been enough players in one place at one time. Reluctantly he had been forced to field several 'hybrid' teams with the assistance of other units, although he did concede that he had been able to form a 7-a-side hockey team with squadron members that had acquitted itself extremely well!

The New Year of 1949 brought much the same as before with the squadron being required to strafe or drop bombs in areas of the jungle as designated by the Army (rockets were still not being used). If this was becoming somewhat less than inspiring for the pilots involved it was at least better than their mission for the 10th which was to provide cover for an ammunition and troop train making extremely slow progress south from Penang. The most interesting operation carried out in

January was a strike on Batu Kuray in north Malaya on the 21st. Four Spitfires led by Flt Lt C. Griffiths took off from Kuala Lumpur at 0900 hrs to attack a bandit camp in the Sungei Pulau valley. This was hit with 500-lb bombs and strafed before the aircraft withdrew to Butterworth to refuel prior to returning to base.

The detachment from 60 Squadron remained at Kuala Lumpur until the middle of February when it handed over its operational duties to 28 Squadron before flying to No.27 Armament Practice Camp (APC) for several weeks of weapons training. All the pilots flew up to Butterworth except for Flg Off Bridges who missed out on the first week of the detachment as he was ill and 'confined to the closet'. During the month of March a total of 300 sorties were flown covering a wide range of exercises. Dive bombing was carried out using eight 11-lb practice bombs in steep and shallow dives from 8,000 ft against stationary and marine towed targets. Two 250-lb unfused bombs were also used; live bombs had been dropped at first but it was found that the fusing links were causing unsatisfactory release and some extremely large errors of over 100 yards had been experienced. Dropping the bombs unfused and without fusing links led to a big improvement. Rocket firing (concrete and 60-lb HE) took place in shallow, medium and steep (35 degree) dives against stationary and towed targets. Air-to-air firing and cine gun exercises were also completed satisfactorily.

A return was made to Kuala Lumpur on 2 April and the first operation to Sepang took place on the 4th, however, owing to a slight delay due to bomb circuit trouble the strike was postponed. Sepang was hit on several occasions in the next few days with 60 Squadron starting to use 16 x 20-lb fragmentation bombs instead of the regular 500-lb bombs. On the 11th an instruction was received that all squadron aircraft were henceforth to operate from Kuala Lumpur, but as before the prospect of a united unit soon wilted and Sembawang would continue to be used for the next four months. On 29 April an evening strike was made against a target near Bahau with 20-lb frag bombs and strafing. During the attack P.III Douglas had major problems with hang ups. He eventually operated the mechanism to jettison the wing racks, but one refused to budge. As was to be expected it fell off as he was coming in to land, luckily without causing any damage. Sqn Ldr Broughton had a similar problem in the morning when a single hung up bomb finally broke free when he was on the approach, again without hitting anything of note.

By June 1949 a shuttle striking system had been set up between Sembawang and Kuala Lumpur and the month saw the first operational use of rockets by 60 Squadron since the inadvertent firings of the previous year. At dawn on the 11th three Spitfires took off to intercept the cruiser HMS *Birmingham*. This was the last of a series of 'attacks' by a wide assortment of aircraft including Sunderlands, Mosquitos and Dakota 'heavy bombers'. After making a number of simulated rocket, bomb and strafe attacks, the pilots (Flg Off De Salis, Flg Off Paterson and P.II Forster) dropped practice bombs and fired their guns at a target towed by the ship. On the same day Flt Lt J.N. Yates had a major fright when his Griffon engine expired in spectacular fashion at 3,000 ft over Seletar. The big end failed and the pieces blew out through the crankcase, taking the engine bearers on both sides with them. He was heartily praised for the subsequent dead-stick landing which did not cause any further damage. As attacks could be called for at any time, it was no great surprise when a strike was requested on 12 June, a Sunday, on bandit positions near Mount Ophir. When the Spitfires were away, however, a heavy rain storm flooded the Pierced Steel Planking (PSP) airstrip and a diversion had to be made to Tengah.

Flt Lt Griffiths and Flg Off Bridges, two long standing members of the squadron departed on the 15th and to mark their leaving a four-ship formation aerobatic display was flown with Griffiths in the lead and Bridges in the box position. The Nos. 2 and 3 slots were filled by Sqn Ldr Broughton and Flg Off De Salis respectively. Afterwards Sqn Ldr Broughton put on a solo display which was noted for its high speed flypasts and upward rolls. Rocket attacks re-commenced on 24 June when Flg Off De Salis and Flg Off Paterson carried out a strike on Gunang Pulan and later in the day Flt Lt Yates, P.III F. Cordiner and P.IV Naish dropped 20-lb bombs and strafed near Mount Ophir again. A maximum effort was flown on 7 July with six Spitfires airborne at 0730 hrs, five at 1030 hrs and six at 1430 hrs attacking jungle areas east of the Yong Peng – Labis road. In between the Spitfire strikes the momentum was maintained by Beaufighters and Sunderlands, the latter taking all of 2½ hours to disgorge their load of 320 x 20-lb fragmentation bombs.

On 14 July Sqn Ldr Broughton also left the squadron at the end of his tour and was replaced by Sqn Ldr W.G.G. Duncan-Smith DSO DFC who had rejoined the RAF in 1948 following a wartime career which had seen him rise to the rank of Group Captain with command of 324 Wing in Italy. His overall total of seventeen enemy aircraft destroyed plus two shared marked him as one of the RAF's top scoring pilots. During his wartime career he was shot down by the rear gunner of a Do 17 during the Dieppe Raid on 19 August 1942, and on 2 September 1943 he spent five hours in the water after the engine of his Spitfire IX failed when he was engaged on an escort operation during the invasion of southern Italy. His first operational sortie after taking command of 60 Squadron occurred on 16 July when five Spitfires opened an offensive that was to be carried on throughout the following week against bandit hideouts on Mount Ophir. The last attack took place on the 22nd and afterwards the squadron was relieved for two days of rest and recuperation. Sadly, tragedy struck the squadron again on 27 July when P.IV Naish, who was returning from a strike in TP223, spun into the ground only a short distance from the runway at Sembawang.

Since the commencement of operations in Malaya No.60 Squadron had had a maximum of eight Spitfires at any one time with a fluctuating number of pilots available to fly them. In July 1949, however, it was decided to raise the squadron to full strength and in early August the aircraft carrier HMS *Ocean* arrived at Singapore with an additional batch of pilots and more aircraft. Eleven new pilots had joined the squadron by the second week in August and five Spitfire FR.XVIIIs had arrived by the 30th, with another three being made ready at Seletar. This meant that the squadron now had the resources to fly two flights of eight aircraft each. With such a large influx of pilots new to the theatre, the month of August was mainly devoted to training, in particular battle climbs and high altitude quarter attacks. The only operational sorties flown by 60 Squadron in August occurred on the 29th when four aircraft attacked a jungle clearing south west of Batang Malaka. The following day the squadron finally said goodbye to Sembawang and moved to Tengah, although operations would continue to be flown from the forward base at Kuala Lumpur.

September was a relatively quiet month with just five operations including one in co-operation with Beaufighters in the Tapah region on the 20th. On returning from this mission P.II Douglas had to make a wheels-up landing at Kuala Lumpur in TP221 when the undercarriage would not come down. He managed to put his aircraft down very gently and only superficial damage was caused. On 28 September three Spitfires exercised with the Royal Navy and made rocket attacks on a target towed by HMS *Constance*. October saw a similar level of activity with four offensive strikes, three from Kuala Lumpur and one from Tengah. During the month there were a number of accidents, including two avoidable wheels-up landings. In addition, P.III W.D. Dickinson had the misfortune to run into a ditch on landing at Kuala Lumpur, putting the aircraft onto its nose, and P.III W.D. Mellor had a starboard wheel come off his aircraft on landing. With so many new pilots the squadron departed to Butterworth on the 15th for another period of weapons training, eventually returning to Kuala Lumpur on 6 December. As well as the training commitment, six operations were carried out in November (two from Kuala Lumpur and four from Butterworth) and eight aircraft were provided to escort the Avro York that was carrying Air Chief Marshal Sir John Slessor who was visiting the command.

Towards the end of the year there was an increase in the number of operations flown and eventually a total of twenty-one anti-bandit strikes were carried out. The first after returning from Butterworth took place on 7 December when two strikes were made on the caves at Batu, with another attack in the Temerloh area. This region was hit again on the 10th and two persons seen in the target area were hurried on their way by cannon fire. In the morning of the 17th Flt Lt Cooke led an attack on a target near Mentakab. Another strike was laid on in the same area for the afternoon but bad weather forced an early return. When the Spitfires landed, however, it was discovered that P.III E.H. Loxton had not returned in TP195. It was later reported that he had been killed when his aircraft dived into the ground out of cloud eleven miles SSW of Kuala Lumpur. The Spitfire that Loxton had been flying had previously been noted as a 'rogue' aircraft and it had been dispatched to Seletar earlier in the year for major modifications to try to cure a high stalling speed. Whether this had any bearing on its loss will never be known.

The number of offensive sorties flown from Kuala Lumpur in January 1950 amounted to ninety although aircraft serviceability for the month was down as a high proportion of major services had become due and these could only be carried out at Tengah. The availability of aircraft was not helped when, from 18–23 January, all of the squadron's Spitfires were grounded following an instruction that the magnetos be checked for wear in the brushes. One of the recently arrived pilots, Plt Off W.G. Hestor, feared that he might have to walk home on the 6th when his engine began to run roughly following a strike in the Temerloh area but it kept going long enough for him to carry out an emergency landing back at base. On 10 January Flg Off Paterson led a strike on an area target at Kong Kai that had been marked by a Dakota dropping a parachute flare. By now some operations were being carried out by Harvards which had been converted to carry 8 x 20-lb bombs and on the 27th five strikes were flown, three by Spitfires and two by Harvards. During the month there were two serious accidents. P.III Hall crashed in TP219 when on a ferry trip from Tengah to Kuala Lumpur on the 20th and a Siamese pilot was killed when flying one of the squadron's aircraft after he crashed at Tengah following engine failure.

A so-called 'anti-bandit month' was launched on 1 February and the squadron was called upon twice to attack areas where the insurgents were thought to be operating. Sqn Ldr Duncan-Smith led the first formation, comprising P.II D.C. Evans, P.II Douglas and P.II T.J. Doe, to a target near Rawang. Bombs and rockets were used and the area thoroughly strafed. The second operation involved Flt Lt G.J. Smith, Flg Offs Paterson, P.I Kimmings and P.III Mellor flying to a target near Broga. On returning to Kuala Lumpur Mellor's Spitfire (TP234) suffered a collapsed undercarriage on landing and was a complete write off, the pilot escaping with minor cuts and bruises. On the 9th there was another incident of a rocket being fired inadvertently. This occurred when the armourers were loading an aircraft but on this occasion it fell harmlessly in a quarry, although one of the armourers did suffer slight burns as the rocket ignited. The total number of strikes flown from Kuala Lumpur in February was twenty-four, comprising eighty-five sorties, the only other accident being that to TP207 which hit a vehicle when on final approach to Tengah.

After a very quiet March in which only fifty operational sorties were flown, April was much busier and saw the squadron fly its greatest number of sorties (191) since the emergency began. Co-ordinated attacks by flights were carried out and proved to be very successful. One of the busiest days occurred on the 30th with three strikes during the course of the day, the first being against a target near Ipoh. Flt Lt Cooke led six aircraft and the bombing was carried out from 12,000 ft as the target was on a hillside at an elevation of 5,000 ft. At the briefing it had been stated that the troops who were waiting to enter the area after the bombing had been completed would not use smoke to indicate their positions, but after the first bomb landed smoke was seen to pour from several locations, showing a certain lack of confidence in 60 Squadron's accuracy. The Army need not have worried, however, as all bombs fell within the target area. The second strike of the day was by eight aircraft on Kluang and this was followed by the final raid on a target near Cheras. The only incident of the month befell Flt Lt Cooke who had a bomb hang up on this last mission. The jettison mechanism failed to work and the whole apparatus fell off as the Spitfire touched down, tearing several holes in the rear fuselage. The total amount of ordnance that the squadron expended in April amounted to 17 x 500-lb bombs, 564 x 20-lb bombs, 718 x 60-lb rockets, 23,900 rounds of 20 mm HEI/SAPI (Semi-Armour Piercing-Incendiary) and 46,740 rounds of 0.5 in ball ammunition.

On 4 May four aircraft took off from Kuala Lumpur to fly to Tengah as an exercise had been arranged with the American aircraft carrier USS *Boxer*. Unfortunately Flg Off Hestor, who was No.2 in the formation, experienced engine failure on take off in SM975 but he smartly selected undercarriage up before making a smooth belly landing between the runway and a nearby railway embankment. He emerged unscathed but unfortunately his Spitfire was a complete write off. The rest of the section (Flt Lt Cooke, P.II Cordiner and P.II Douglas) flew on to work with the carrier-borne aircraft, which consisted of Bearcats and Skyraiders, carrying out practice attacks on Changi, before returning to Kuala Lumpur in the evening As 60 Squadron was now fully established it was capable of deploying greater numbers of aircraft over any particular target than had previously been possible. In recent weeks sortie duration had also been extended so that in many cases operations were now lasting in excess of two hours. This meant that attacks could now be made north of Kuala Lumpur without having to land there to refuel before returning to Tengah. As a result Kuala Lumpur was not as important as it had once been and all aircraft still there were flown back to Tengah on 31 May from where most future operations would be carried out.

The celebration to mark the birthday of George VI took place on 8 June and after a prodigious effort by the ground crews, 100 per cent serviceability was attained which allowed a formation of fifteen Spitfires to be flown as part of the flypast. Other formations consisted of Sunderlands, Lincolns, Dakotas, Brigands, Mosquitos, Harvards, Austers and one Westland Dragonfly helicopter. A good show was marred by an unfortunate accident to TP230 flown by P.II Mellor who was No.11 in the landing sequence on return to Tengah. Having misjudged the final approach, Mellor's aircraft came down on the Angle of Glide indicators, bursting the starboard main wheel and the tail wheel. The resultant swing on touching down resulted in Cat 3 damage which was later deemed sufficient for the aircraft to be written off as being beyond economic repair.

On the following day Flt Lt Yates, Flt Lt Cooke and P.II Doe took part in a series of practice interceptions with 45 Squadron which had now converted to the Brigand B.1 ground attack bomber powered by two Bristol Centaurus 57 engines. This was a much more capable machine than the Beaufighter as it could carry an increased bomb load and was faster with a top speed of around 350 mph. Despite its improved performance it was still no match for a Spitfire FR.XVIII which could close on it without too much trouble. Violent evasive action by the Brigand could cause problems if a Spitfire pilot was less than determined with his attack, but it was found that if the full potential of the fighter was used it could be made to turn inside its adversary with relative ease during steep turns in either direction.

The difficulties of operating in Malaya were highlighted on the 16th when nine Spitfires armed with 20-lb fragmentation bombs and rockets took off for the Kluang area. The target consisted of two small hill tops surrounded by troops but on arrival it was found that the hills were almost completely covered in cloud with a base of 200 ft and most of the troop positions were also obscured. This called for very accurate positioning for blind bombing and rocketing and Sqn Ldr Duncan-Smith, together with his No.2, dived down below cloud to check the troop positions in relation to the target. Fortunately the troops had put up smoke indicators to mark their positions, but in some cases it was difficult to distinguish the smoke from the low cloud.

By mid 1950 the RAF forces in Malaya had the capability to hit terrorist targets with greatly increased firepower, including the Lincoln heavy-bombers of 57 Squadron which had flown out from their base at Waddington in March to be followed two months later by a detachment from 100 Squadron. On 23 June twelve Spitfires of 60 Squadron took part in a large strike in the Rawang area, following up pattern-bombing by Lincolns. The devastation on the ground was impressive and as the Spitfires commenced their attack the bomb craters left by the heavies were seen to be already filling with water and were practically touching, rim to rim. The trees that had been left standing were stripped of leaves and were black in colour.

Despite the use of such overwhelming force, the insurgents were still capable of launching attacks on isolated areas and on the 28th around eighty bandits struck at the police station at Kamsau. The station's radio aerial was knocked down in the early part of the battle, however, a very brave policeman climbed up and re-fixed it, whilst subject to heavy fire. This allowed a request for help to be made and 60 Squadron scrambled eight aircraft to give assistance. By the time the Spitfires arrived over-head the bandits had retreated to the jungle and the police were attempting to locate them. It was thought that they were likely to lay an ambush along the banks of a stream and so a strafing attack was made in this area in which seven of the bandits were killed.

July brought a total of nineteen strike missions in which 127 sorties were flown. The training commitment was not ignored and on the 5th P.II Mellor and P.III Randall took off from Tengah to carry out practice interceptions at 25,000 ft. Whilst they were airborne most of Malaya became 'clamped' as bad weather rolled in, requiring both pilots to make a controlled descent through cloud and land at Changi. This cloud was also made up of a well defined thunderstorm within which the conditions were very bumpy and both pilots were highly relieved to get back without having stripped their propellers.

The busiest day occurred on the 26th with three 'maximum effort' strikes. The first was to the Yong Peng region, the target being a large area with six selected pinpoint positions. The squadron flew eight aircraft in two finger four sections, led by Sqn Ldr Duncan-Smith and Flt Lt Cooke, which then divided into pairs when the target area was reached. Each pair then split up as individual aircraft had been allocated its own particular pinpoint. A second attack was made on the same area three hours later using the same technique. The final strike was against a large camp with accommodation for around 200 bandits (recently evacuated) at Kota Tinggi. Intelligence believed that the rebels were bottled up in an area of jungle nearby and so the Spitfires went in after an attack by Lincolns of No.1 Squadron, Royal Australian Air Force, flying their first mission since arriving in Malaya. Despite the fact that the camp was relatively large by Malayan standards, it proved to be a difficult one to find as the photo-reconnaissance for this area was not up to date and the surrounding rubber estates had been enlarged some-what since the pilots' maps had been produced.

August brought twenty-six operational strikes (160 sorties) with a high serviceability rate of 81.4 per cent. This was a particularly good effort considering the amount of flying carried out during the month which amounted to 181 hours on operations, with 198 hours non-operational. While most people were enjoying a Bank Holiday on the 7th, 60 Squadron, as often seemed to be the case, was called upon to carry out a mission, this time to the Kuala Pilah area. From the very start, however, everything appeared to go wrong. During his daily inspection, P.II Mellor was concerned that the starboard flap of his Spitfire ('A') seemed to be reluctant to retract, although he eventually decided to accept it. All eight aircraft got airborne successfully but fifteen minutes later P.III Buckle had to return to base due to excessive vibration. The remaining seven Spitfires carried out the strike although on the last bombing run P.II Tommy Mutch ('K') thought he had been hit, but the ensuing check found nothing amiss.

After 'flag waving' over Kuala Pilah and Tampin, all aircraft climbed up before setting course for base but it was not long until an ominous stream of white liquid began to trail behind NH852 ('B'), flown by P.II A.E. Cover, which proved to be glycol pouring out of the overflow as a result of a sheared pump in the cooling system. Cover broke away from the formation together with his wingman, P.II Mellor, his intention being to make a forced landing at Gementah, however, it soon became obvious that he would not be able to make it as his engine was becoming extremely hot and his vision was beginning to be impaired by smoke in the cockpit. Looking round for somewhere to put his aircraft down, the only possibility was a very small paddy field about seven miles east of Jasin which unfortunately had a fringe of rubber trees on the only side that offered a safe approach.

Circling overhead, P.II Mellor had a good view of Cover's forced landing which was made with far too much speed so that he touched down well over half way along the available space in a cloud of mud and water. Skating along the top surface of the paddy field he headed straight for some coconut trees lining a road and hit one of them with his port wing, completely uprooting it and flinging it into the air. This helped the aircraft avoid hitting some occupied huts, in front of which were standing some fear-stricken Malays, by spinning it round and causing it to hit several more trees, the Spitfire finally coming to rest right side up, with a broken back and one wing torn off. Miraculously, Cover was uninjured and was able to vacate the cockpit and walk along the remaining wing before waving his arms at Mellor to indicate that he was alright. Mellor then climbed to pass a report to Flt Lt Yates, his section leader, to the effect that the forced landing had been carried out successfully. This was greeted with a loud "What?" from Yates as it was the first that he had known of any drama below due to the fact that he had changed radio frequencies to talk to the Lincoln bombers that were due to continue the attack. Cover was later picked up by car and taken to Jasin where he had a few beers to celebrate his remarkable escape before being flown back to base in an Auster in the evening.

Throughout the rest of the year Spitfire operations continued although orders were received that the squadron would be converting to de Havilland Vampires the following January. In September command of the squadron was temporarily assumed by Flt Lt Yates as Sqn Ldr Duncan-Smith was recalled to the UK to attend a course at the Central Fighter Establishment (CFE) at West Raynham, eventually returning on 17 October. The following month he was checked out on a Meteor T.7 and by the end of November all squadron pilots had done likewise. On 2 December the first batch of six Spitfires departed to be replaced by Vampires, the arrival of which caused considerable comment in the local papers. As the squadron began its work up period with the Vampire, operations were continued with the remaining Spitfires, the last operation of the year involving four aircraft led by Sqn Ldr Duncan-Smith in a strike on Kota Tinggi. The very last operational sorties flown by 60 Squadron Spitfires took place on 1 January 1951 and involved an attack on the same objective. On this particular day six more Spitfires were flown from Tengah to Sembawang for disposal, the last two finally departing on the 11th. Having moved into the jet age 60 Squadron continued to fly Vampires until 1955 when these were replaced by Venoms. In 1959 the unit changed to the night/all-weather role and flew Meteor NF.14s and Javelin FAW.9s from Tengah until it was disbanded in April 1968.

The Malayan Emergency continued until 31 July 1960 by which time Chin Peng and the 400 or so remaining bandits were largely ineffective. Malaya had achieved its independence on 31 August 1957 and by that time the terrorists had been pushed back into two relatively small areas, Perak to the north-west and Johore in the south with the rest of the country largely free from their activities. Operation Firedog was officially ended by the RAF in October 1960. Of the other Spitfire squadrons that operated in the area, No.28 Squadron was withdrawn to Hong Kong in January 1949 with No.81 Squadron, a photo-reconnaissance unit, continuing to operate from Tengah and Seletar until 1954. The very last operational sortie flown by an RAF Spitfire was made by 81 Squadron's commanding officer, Sqn Ldr W.P. Swaby in PS888 on 1 April 1954.

# APPENDIX ONE

# Specifications

## SPITFIRE XII

| | |
|---|---|
| Dimensions | Span 32 ft 7 in; Length 31 ft 10 in |
| Wing Area | 231 sq.ft |
| Wing Loading | 32 lbs/sq.ft |
| Weights | Loaded Weight 7,400 lbs |
| Performance | Maximum speed 393 mph at 18,000 ft |
| Initial Rate of Climb | 4,960 ft/min |
| Service Ceiling | 40,000 ft |
| Normal Range | 329 miles (fuel capacity 85 gallons), 493 miles (112 gallons) |
| Armament | Two 20 mm Hispano cannon, four 0.303 in Browning machine-guns |
| Powerplant | Rolls-Royce Griffon III or IV of 1,735 hp |

## SPITFIRE XIV

| | |
|---|---|
| Dimensions | Span 36 ft 10 in (FR.XIV 32 ft 8 in); Length 32 ft 8 in |
| Wing Area | 242 sq.ft (FR.XIV 231 sq.ft) |
| Wing Loading | 34.7 lb/sq.ft |
| Weights | Loaded Weight 8,400 lbs |
| Performance | Maximum speed 448 mph at 26,000 ft |
| Initial Rate of Climb | 4,580 ft/min |
| Service Ceiling | 44,500 ft |
| Normal Range | 460 miles (fuel capacity 112 gallons), 850 miles (202 gallons) |
| Armament | Two 20 mm Hispano cannon, four 0.303in Browning machine-guns |
| Powerplant | Rolls-Royce Griffon 65 of 2,050 hp |

## SPITFIRE F.21

| | |
|---|---|
| Dimensions | Span 36 ft 11 in; Length 32 ft 8 in |
| Wing Area | 243.6 sq.ft |
| Wing Loading | 38 lbs/sq.ft |
| Weights | Loaded 9,182 lbs (9,411 lbs with contra-props) |
| Performance | Maximum speed 450 mph at 19,000 ft |
| Initial Rate of Climb | 4,900 ft/min |
| Service Ceiling | 43,000 ft |
| Normal Range | 580 miles |
| Armament | Four 20 mm Hispano cannon |
| Powerplant | Rolls-Royce Griffon 61 of 2,050 hp (Griffon 85 with contra-props) |

## SEAFIRE XVII

| | |
|---|---|
| Dimensions | Span 36 ft 10 in; Length 32 ft 3 in |
| Wing Area | 242 sq.ft |
| Wing Loading | 33 lbs/sq.in |
| Weights | Loaded 8,000 lbs |
| Performance | Maximum speed 387 mph at 13,500 ft |
| Initial Rate of Climb | 4,500 ft/min |
| Service Ceiling | 35,200 ft |
| Normal Range | 435 miles (740 miles with drop tanks) |
| Armament | Two 20 mm Hispano cannon, four 0.303 in Browning machine-guns |
| Powerplant | Rolls-Royce Griffon VI of 1,850 hp |

## SEAFIRE FR.47

| | |
|---|---|
| Dimensions | Span 36 ft 11 in; Length 34 ft 6 in |
| Wing Area | 243.6 sq.ft |
| Wing Loading | 42 lbs/sq.ft |
| Weights | Loaded 10,200 lbs (normal) 11,615 lbs (max) |
| Performance | Maximum speed 453 mph at 20,500 ft |
| Initial Rate of Climb | 4,800 ft/min |
| Service Ceiling | 43,100 ft |
| Normal Range | 400 miles (940 miles with drop tanks) |
| Armament | Four 20 mm Hispano cannon |
| Powerplant | Rolls-Royce Griffon 87/88 of 2,375 hp |

## SPITEFUL F.14

| | |
|---|---|
| Dimensions | Span 35 ft; Length 32 ft 11 in |
| Wing Area | 210 sq.ft |
| Wing Loading | 47 lbs/sq.ft |
| Weights | Loaded 9,950 lbs |
| Performance | Maximum speed 483 mph at 21,000 ft |
| Initial Rate of Climb | 4,890 ft/min |
| Service Ceiling | 42,000 ft |
| Normal Range | 564 miles |
| Armament | Four 20 mm Hispano cannon |
| Powerplant | Rolls-Royce Griffon 69 of 2,375 hp |

# APPENDIX TWO

# Top-Scoring Griffon Spitfire Pilots

| Pilot | Sqn/Wing | Mark | Destroyed | Probable | Damaged |
|---|---|---|---|---|---|
| Harries, R.H. W/C | 91 | XII | 10½ | I | – |
| Walmsley, H.E. S/L | 130/350 | XIV | 9¼ | – | – |
| Ponsford, I.R. F/L | 130 | XIV | 7 | I | 3 |
| Shepherd, J.B. S/L | 41 | XIV | 7 | – | – |
| Coleman, P.T. F/O | 41 | XII/XIV | 5¾ | – | – |
| Lord, G. F/O | 130 | XIV | 5½ | – | I |
| Gaze, F.A.O. S/L | 41 | XIV | 5 | – | – |
| Kynaston, N.A. S/L | 91 | XII | 4½ | I | I |
| Woodman, B.W. W/O | 130 | XIV | 4½ | – | 2 |
| Clay, P.H.T. W/O | 130 | XIV | 4 | – | 2 |
| Cowell, P. F/L | 41 | XIV | 4 | – | – |
| Doll, J.C.S. F/L | 91 | XII | 4 | – | I |
| Edwards, F.E.F. F/O | 130 | XIV | 4 | – | I |
| Hall, D.I. F/L | 414 | FR.XIV | 4 | – | 2 |
| Keefer, G.C. W/C | 125 Wing | XIV | 4 | – | I |
| Watkins, D.J. P/O | 350 | XIV | 4 | – | – |
| Woolley, F.G. W/C | 41/130/350 | XIV | 4 | I | – |
| Blumer, R.A.B. W/O | 91 | XII | 3½ | – | – |
| Stowe, W.N. F/L | 41/130 | XII/XIV | 3½ | I | I |
| Wilkinson, J.F. F/L | 41 | XIV | 3½ | – | – |
| Stenborg, G. F/L | 91 | XII | 3¼ | – | I |
| Andrieux, J. Capt | 91 | XII | 3 | 2 | – |
| Samouelle, C.J. F/L | 130 | XIV | 3 | – | 2 |
| Chalmers, J.A. P/O | 41 | XIV | 2¾ | – | – |

| Pilot | Sqn/Wing | Mark | Destroyed | Probable | Damaged |
|---|---|---|---|---|---|
| Gray E. F/O | 41 | XIV | 2¾ | – | 1 |
| Bangerter, P.M. F/O | 350 | XIV | 2½ | – | – |
| Gigot, G.F. F/O | 350 | XIV | 2½ | – | – |
| Knight, S.M. F/L | 402 | XIV | 2½ | – | – |
| Hegarty, F.M. F/O | 41 | XIV | 2¼ | – | – |
| Kicq, A. F/Sgt | 350 | XIV | 2¼ | 1 | – |
| Benham, D.I. W/C | 41 | XIV | 2 | – | – |
| Boels, H.A. P/O | 350 | XIV | 2 | – | – |
| Boulton, J.A. F/O | 130 | XIV | 2 | 2 | – |
| Glen, A.A. S/L | 41 | XII | 2 | – | – |
| Lambrechts, P/O | 350 | XIV | 2 | – | – |
| Lawson, R.W. F/O | 402 | XIV | 2 | – | – |
| Maridor, J–M. F/L | 91 | XII | 2 | – | 1 |
| McElhaw, T.J. F/O | 208 | XVIII | 2 | – | – |
| Muls, R. F/L | 350 | XIV | 2 | – | – |
| Nash, R.S. F/L | 91 | XII | 2 | – | 1 |
| Pauwels, E.G.R. P/O | 350 | XIV | 2 | – | 1 |
| Prendergast, J.B. S/L | 414 | XIV | 2 | – | – |
| Rake, D.V. F/L | 41 | XIV | 2 | – | – |
| Reid, D.J. F/L | 41 | XIV | 2 | – | – |
| Sibeth, P.E. F/L | 130 | XIV | 2 | – | 1 |
| Stevenson, I.T. W/O | 41 | XIV | 2 | 1 | 1 |
| Bruce, F/L | 130 | XIV | 1½ | – | – |
| Burrows, E.R. F/L | 402 | XIV | 1½ | – | 1 |
| Birbeck, C.R. F/L | 41 | XII | 1 | 2 | 2 |
| Bodtker C.S. Lt | 41 | XIV | 1 | – | – |
| Collis, R.T.H. F/L | 41 | XII | 1 | – | – |
| Doncq, M. F/O | 350 | XIV | 1 | – | – |
| Drummond, F/L | 402 | XIV | 1 | – | – |
| Dutton H.C. F/O | 402 | XIV | 1 | – | – |
| Earp, F/L | 130 | XIV | 1 | – | – |
| Fisher, R.R. F/L | 41 | XIV | 1 | – | – |
| Gordon, D.C. S/L | 402 | XIV | 1 | – | – |
| Groensteen, F/Sgt | 350 | XIV | 1 | – | – |
| Hanton, F.E.W. F/L | 402 | XIV | 1 | – | 1 |
| Hoornaert, F/L | 350 | XIV | 1 | – | – |

| Pilot | Sqn/Wing | Mark | Destroyed | Probable | Damaged |
|---|---|---|---|---|---|
| Howarth, D. F/L | 350 | XIV | I | – | – |
| Hudson, G.W. F/Sgt | 130 | XIV | I | – | – |
| Hume, M.R.D. S/L | 130 | XIV | I | – | – |
| Innes, B.E. F/L | 402 | XIV | I | – | – |
| Lavigne, F/L | 350 | XIV | I | – | – |
| Lawrence, J.B. F/L | 402 | XIV | I | – | – |
| Lee, T.B. F/O | 402 | XIV | I | – | – |
| Leva, P/O | 350 | XIV | I | – | – |
| MacConnell, C.B. F/O | 402 | XIV | I | – | – |
| MacElwain, J.R. F/L | 2 | XIV | I | – | – |
| Matthew, I.G.S. S/L | 91 | XII | I | – | I |
| Middleton, W.M. F/L | 430 | XIV | I | – | – |
| Moyle, F/Sgt | 41 | XIV | I | – | – |
| Plisnier, A.M. F/L | 350 | XIV | I | – | – |
| Rossow, V.J. W/O | 41 | XIV | I | – | – |
| Sherk, D. F/L | 402 | XIV | I | – | – |
| Sleep, K.S. F/L | 402 | XIV | I | – | – |
| Smith, D.H. W/C | 41 | XII | I | – | I |
| Smith, R.D.A. F/O | 41 | XIV | I | – | – |
| Speare, A.R. F/L | 402 | XIV | I | – | – |
| Spencer, T. S/L | 41 | XII | I | – | – |
| Taggart, R.J. F/L | 402 | XIV | I | – | – |
| Trevorrow, F/O | 130 | XIV | I | – | – |
| Van Wersch, F/O | 350 | XIV | I | – | – |
| Warren, Sgt | 130 | XIV | I | – | – |
| Whittaker, D.W. F/O | 402 | XIV | I | – | – |
| Young, W.O. F/O | 402 | XIV | I | – | – |

# V-1 Aces

| Pilot | Sqn | Mark | Destroyed | Shared |
|-------|-----|------|-----------|--------|
| Kynaston, N.A. S/L | 91 | XIV | 21 | – |
| Burgwal, R.F. F/O | 322 | XIV | 19 | 5 |
| Nash, R.S. F/L | 91 | XIV | 17 | 3 |
| Johnson, H.D. F/L | 91 | XIV | 13 | 1 |
| Plesman, J.L. F/L | 322 | XIV | 11 | – |
| Cruikshank, A.R. F/O | 91 | XIV | 10 | 1 |
| De Bordas, H.F. Capt | 91 | XIV | 9 | 1 |
| Topham, E. F/O | 91 | XIV | 9 | 1 |
| Jongbloed, G.F.J. F/L | 322 | XIV | 8 | 2 |
| Newbery, R.A. S/L | 610 | XIV | 8 | 2 |
| Moffett, H.B. F/L | 91 | XIV | 8 | – |
| Bond, P.M. S/L | 91 | XIV | 7 | 3 |
| Elcock, A.R. F/L | 91 | XIV | 7 | 1 |
| Collier, K.R. F/O | 91 | XIV | 7 | – |
| Marshall, W.C. F/L | 91 | XIV | 7 | – |
| Spencer, T. S/L | 41 | XII | 7 | – |
| Van Eedenborg, C.M. S/L | 322 | XIV | 7 | – |
| Balasse, M.A.L. F/O | 41 | XII | 6 | 2 |
| Janssen, M.J. F/Sgt | 322 | XIV | 6 | 2 |
| Van Arkel, J. F/O | 322 | XIV | 6 | 1 |
| Draper, J.W.P. F/L | 91 | XIV | 6 | – |
| McPhie, R.A. F/O | 91 | XIV | 5 | 3 |
| Maridor, J–M. Capt | 91 | XIV | 5 | 2 |
| Shepherd, J.B. S/L | 610 | XIV | 5 | 2 |
| Jonker, J. F/O | 322 | XIV | 5 | 1 |
| Cramm, H.C. F/Sgt | 322 | XIV | 5 | – |
| Neil, H.M. F/O | 91 | XIV | 5 | – |

| Pilot | Sqn | Mark | Destroyed | Shared |
|---|---|---|---|---|
| Van Beers, R.L. F/Sgt | 322 | XIV | 5 | – |
| Faulkner, J.A. F/O | 91 | XIV | 4 | 2 |
| Bangerter, B.M. F/L | 610 | XIV | 4 | 1 |
| McKinley, G.M. F/O | 610 | XIV | 4 | 1 |

# Griffon Spitfire Losses – WWII

| Date | Serial | Mark | Sqn | Pilot |
|------|--------|------|-----|-------|
| Remarks | | | | |
| 23/04/43 | EN601 | XII | 41 | F/L T.R. Poynton (k) |
| Shot down by JG 26 near Dieppe | | | | |
| 03/05/43 | EN612 | XII | 41 | Sgt W.R. East (k) |
| Shot down by JG 2 in the Channel | | | | |
| 16/06/43 | EN627 | XII | 91 | F/O Seydel (wnd) |
| Shot down SE of Dover during ASR sortie | | | | |
| 16/06/43 | MB835 | XII | 91 | Sgt W. Mitchell (k) |
| Shot down SE of Dover during ASR sortie | | | | |
| 18/07/43 | EN233 | XII | 41 | F/O T.A.H. Slack (ev) |
| Shot down by JG 2 | | | | |
| 18/07/43 | EN235 | XII | 41 | F/O R.H.W. Hogarth (k) |
| Shot down by JG 2 | | | | |
| 27/08/43 | EN611 | XII | 41 | F/O D. Heywood (PoW) |
| Shot down by JG 26 near St Pol | | | | |
| 27/08/43 | EN236 | XII | 41 | P/O L.A Prickett (PoW) |
| Shot down by JG 26 near St Pol | | | | |
| 01/09/43 | EN230 | XII | 91 | W/O Bishop (Inj) |
| Hit by flak during convoy patrol and ditched in the Channel | | | | |
| 06/09/43 | MB796 | XII | 41 | F/O R.J. Boyd (k) |
| Shot down by flak near Rouen | | | | |
| 08/09/43 | MB852 | XII | 91 | P/O C.R. Fraser (PoW) |
| Shot down by fighters near Vitry | | | | |
| 16/09/43 | EN617 | XII | 91 | F/Sgt B.G. Mulcahy (PoW) |
| Shot down by fighters near Beaumont le Roger | | | | |
| 19/09/43 | MB799 | XII | 91 | F/O G.W. Bond (k) |
| Shot down by JG 26 during escort operation to Lille | | | | |

| Date | Serial | Mark | Sqn | Pilot |
|------|--------|------|-----|-------|
| Remarks | | | | |
| 19/09/43 | MB800 | XII | 41 | F/Sgt S.H. May (ev) |
| Shot down by JG 26 south of Dunkirk | | | | |
| 22/09/43 | EN608 | XII | 41 | F/O C.R. Birbeck (safe) |
| Baled out over the Channel after combat with fighters | | | | |
| 24/09/43 | MB802 | XII | 41 | F/L H.L. Parry (PoW) |
| Shot down by fighters near Poix | | | | |
| 24/09/43 | MB805 | XII | 91 | F/L G. Stenborg (k) |
| Shot down by an Fw 190 in a head-on attack near Poix | | | | |
| 03/10/43 | MB834 | XII | 41 | F/Sgt J.A.B. Gray (k) |
| Shot down by Fw 190s over the Somme area | | | | |
| 06/11/43 | EN626 | XII | 91 | W/O R.A.B. Blumer (ev) |
| Shot down by flak in the vicinity of Evreux | | | | |
| 06/01/44 | EN223 | XII | 91 | F/O H.F. Heninger (k) |
| Baled out over France after engine cut due to fuel problem | | | | |
| 20/01/44 | EN606 | XII | 91 | Sgt A.H. Exelby (Inj) |
| Hit by two other aircraft on landing after ASR sortie | | | | |
| 23/01/44 | MB832 | XII | 91 | Sgt J.H. Hymas (PoW) |
| Shot down by fighters over France | | | | |
| 31/01/44 | EN618 | XII | 91 | F/Sgt R.K.Y. Fairbairn (k) |
| Collided with EN613 during operation to Dieppe | | | | |
| 31/01/44 | EN613 | XII | 91 | F/O D.R. Inskip (k) |
| Collided with EN618 during operation to Dieppe | | | | |
| 12/03/44 | RB172 | XIV | 91 | F/Sgt C.E. Sayer (k) |
| Crashed near Turnhouse following scramble | | | | |
| 29/04/44 | RB187 | XIV | 91 | F/O J.A. Collis (k) |
| FTR patrol of Thames Estuary | | | | |
| 02/05/44 | RB141 | XIV | 322 | Sgt H.C.A.J. Roovers (k) |
| FTR patrol over the Channel | | | | |
| 22/05/44 | RB162 | XIV | 610 | F/O. H.H. Percy (k) |
| Shot down by flak – Guernsey | | | | |
| 28/05/44 | RB175 | XIV | 610 | F/O B.T. Colgan (PoW) |
| Force landed after being hit by flak near Lamballe | | | | |
| 02/06/44 | MB832 | XII | 41 | F/O H.A. Wagner (PoW) |
| Shot down by flak – Guernsey | | | | |
| 07/06/44 | MB881 | XII | 41 | F/O K.B. Robinson (k) |
| Shot down by flak over the Channel | | | | |
| 09/06/44 | MB794 | XII | 41 | F/O J.G.H. Refshauge (wnd) |
| Shot down by flak near Carentan | | | | |
| 12/06/44 | MB842 | XII | 41 | F/O M.A. Balasse (safe) |
| Baled out over the Channel | | | | |

| Date | Serial | Mark | Sqn | Pilot |
|------|--------|------|-----|-------|
| Remarks | | | | |

**18/06/44  MB876  XII  41  F/L T.A.H. Slack (safe)**
Shot down by flak over the Channel

**18/06/44  EN231  XII  41  Sgt J.P. Ware (safe)**
Baled out over the Channel after running out of fuel

**29/06/44  –  XIV  322  F/Sgt W. De Vries (safe)**
Crash landed at Kingsnorth after being hit by AA fire

**09/07/44  RB153  XIV  610  F/Sgt I.F. Hakanssen (k)**
Baled out after engine cut in attack on V-1 near Dungeness

**12/07/44  RM678  XIV  322  W/O J.A. Maier (k)**
Crashed near Lympne after V-1 blew up at close range

**12/07/44  RB142  XIV  610  F/O G.M. McKinley (k)**
As above, crashed near Newhaven

**26/07/44  RM743  XIV  91  F/L E.G.A. Seghers (k)**
Anti-Diver patrol, hit V-1 near Dungeness

**31/07/44  RM654  XIV  91  F/O P.A. Schade (k)**
Collided with Tempest near Bexhill during Diver patrol

**03/08/44  RM656  XIV  91  F/L/ J.P. Maridor (k)**
Crashed near Benenden after attack on V-1

**17/08/44  MB880  XII  41  F/O R. van Goens (k)**
Ditched in the Channel after running out of fuel

**23/08/44  EN226  XII  41  F/L T.A.H. Slack (PoW)**
Force landed near Hesdin

**30/08/44  RB150  XIV  610  W/O J.J.D. Bonfield (k)**
FTR patrol of Boulogne area

**01/09/44  MB831  XII  41  F/O P.B. Graham (PoW)**
Shot down by flak near Ghent

**01/09/44  RM695  XIV  130  –**
DBR during armed recce to area around St Omer

**03/09/44  EN622  XII  41  W/O P.W. Chattin (k)**
Shot down by fighters

**18/09/44  –  XIV  610  F/Sgt W. Shaw (safe)**
Hit by ground fire near Schouwen Island

**05/10/44  RM763  XIV  130  W/C A.G. Page (Inj)**
Hit by flak and force landed near Apeldoorn

**04/11/44  NH716  XIV  350  S/L L. Collignon (safe)**
Force landed near Aachen

**14/11/44  RM671  XIV  350  –**
DBR landing at Amiens

**08/12/44  RM749  XIV  130  F/L/ D.J. Wilson (k)**
Shot down by fighters during armed recce of Munster area

| Date | Serial | Mark | Sqn | Pilot |
|------|--------|------|-----|-------|
| Remarks | | | | |
| 10/12/44 | NH719 | XIV | 610 | F/O W.A. Nicholls (PoW) |
| Engine cut during armed recce near Munster, baled out | | | | |
| 15/12/44 | RB149 | XIV | 610 | F/O E.G. Hill (k) |
| Hit by flak near Munster | | | | |
| 18/12/44 | RM699 | XIV | 41 | W/O A.S. Appleton (PoW) |
| Hit by flak near Munster | | | | |
| 18/12/44 | RM746 | XIV | 610 | F/L B.M. Madden (k) |
| Shot down by fighters over northern Germany | | | | |
| 18/12/44 | RM736 | XIV | 610 | W/O T. Higgs (k) |
| Flew into high ground during armed recce | | | | |
| 22/12/44 | RM811 | XIV | 2 | F/L D.S Buckie (k) |
| Broke up in the air near Oosterbeek | | | | |
| 22/12/44 | – | XIV | 130 | F/L H. Walmsley (safe) |
| Hit by friendly fire near Liege | | | | |
| 24/12/44 | RM690 | XIV | 350 | S/L L. Collignon (Inj) |
| Shot down by flak – Malmedy | | | | |
| 25/12/44 | RM673 | XIV | 350 | F/O J.M.F. Vanderperren (k) |
| Shot down by flak – Malmedy | | | | |
| 31/12/44 | RM818 | XIV | 430 | F/O J.N. McLeod (k) |
| Baled out after engine began to overheat due to glycol leak | | | | |
| 01/01/45 | RM803 | XIV | 2 | F/L P.J. Garland (k) |
| Crashed on landing at Gilze-Rijen | | | | |
| 01/01/45 | RM760 | XIV | 130 | F/O C.A. Joseph (k) |
| Hit by friendly fire, spun in near Malmedy | | | | |
| 01/01/45 | – | XIV | 430 | F/O W.P. Golden (Wnd) |
| Shot up by fighters prior to taking off at Eindhoven | | | | |
| 01/01/45 | – | XIV | 430 | F/L R.F. Gill |
| As above | | | | |
| 16/01/45 | RM767 | XIV | 41 | F/O N.P. Gibbs (safe) |
| Hit by flak near Vogelsang | | | | |
| 16/01/45 | RM762 | XIV | 130 | S/L P.V.K. Tripe (safe) |
| Baled out after being hit by ground fire near Malmedy | | | | |
| 16/01/45 | RM815 | XIV | 130 | F/O K.M. Lowe (Inj) |
| Force landed after being hit by flak near Malmedy | | | | |
| 16/01/45 | RM655 | XIV | 130 | F/O G. Jones (safe) |
| As above | | | | |
| 16/01/45 | RM619 | XIV | 350 | F/L H.J. Smets (PoW) |
| Baled out near Aachen after being hit by flak | | | | |
| 23/01/45 | RM765 | XIV | 41 | F/L M.A. Balasse (k) |
| Shot down by Fw 190D of JG 26 near Munster | | | | |

| Date | Serial | Mark | Sqn | Pilot |
|------|--------|------|-----|-------|
| Remarks | | | | |

23/01/45    RM756    XIV    130    F/O W. Dobbs (safe)
Declared Cat E on return to base due to flak damage

23/01/45    NH711    XIV    350    F/Sgt R. Huens (k)
Shot down by flak near St VIth

23/01/45    RM731    XIV    610    W/O G. Tate (k)
Baled out on being hit by flak

26/01/45    RB167    XIV    610    F/O W.H. Wilson (safe)
Shot down by flak during armed recce near Munster

08/02/45    RM805    XIV    2    F/L G.K. Malcolmson (k)
Crashed during dead stick landing – out of fuel

09/02/45    –    XIV    610    F/L J. Lee (safe)
Shot down during armed recce

10/02/45    RM842    XIV    41    F/L D.J.V. Henry (PoW)
Force landed after being hit by flak

11/02/45    NH685    XIV    350    W/O J.W.L. Laloux (safe)
Shot down by flak

11/02/45    –    XIV    402    F/L W.G. Hodges (k)
Crashed on return to base

11/02/45    RM846    XIV    402    F/O W.D. Whittaker (safe)
DBR after hitting HT cables during armed recce

11/02/45    RN120    XIV    610    W/O M.F. Harding (k)
Shot down near Paderborn

13/02/45    RM819    XIV    412    F/L R.P. Harding (PoW)
Shot down attacking Bf 110

14/02/45    RM677    XIV    610    F/L W.M. Lightbody (k)
Shot down by flak near Boxmeer

21/02/45    RM839    XIV    402    F/L L.G. Barnes (safe)
Hit by flak near Hamm

21/02/45    RM758    XIV    402    F/O J.C. McAllister (DoW)
Crashed on return as a result of flak damage

22/02/45    RM789    XIV    41    F/O D.F. Tebbitt (PoW)
Force landed with flak damage

24/02/45    RM790    XIV    41    F/L T.R. Burns (wnd)
Hit by flak attacking train

25/02/45    RM906    XIV    402    F/L W.S. Harvey (PoW)
Shot down by flak near Enschede

26/02/45    RM739    XIV    350    S/L T Spencer (PoW/Esc)
Baled out after being hit by flak near Rhode

27/02/45    RM708    XIV    2    F/L L. Woodbridge (safe)
Baled out near Venlo when aircraft developed glycol leak

| Date | Serial | Mark | Sqn | Pilot |
|------|--------|------|-----|-------|
| Remarks | | | | |
| 27/02/45 | RM865 | XIV | 130 | F/O W Dobbs (Inj) |
| Hit by flak near Dulmen | | | | |
| 02/03/45 | RN123 | XIV | 41 | F/O C.H. Mottershead (k) |
| FTR ops to Nijmegen | | | | |
| 02/03/45 | RM750 | XIV | 130 | F/L G.G. Earp (PoW) |
| Shot down by JG 26 | | | | |
| 02/03/45 | RM914 | XIV | 130 | F/O N.W. Heale (PoW) |
| As above | | | | |
| 18/03/45 | RM812 | XIV | 2 | S/L C.E. Maitland (k) |
| Hit by flak near Emmerich | | | | |
| 25/03/45 | MV258 | XIV | 402 | S/L L.A. Moore (k) |
| Shot down by flak attacking train | | | | |
| 26/03/45 | RN125 | XIV | 2 | F/L A. Krakowski (safe) |
| Baled out after engine caught fire | | | | |
| 26/03/45 | MV255 | XIV | 41 | 2/Lt C.S. Bodtker (Inj) |
| Force landed at Volkel following engine failure | | | | |
| 30/03/45 | RM713 | XIV | 130 | F/L T.L. Trevorrow (safe) |
| Baled out after hitting a tree during an armed recce | | | | |
| 01/04/45 | RM871 | XIV | 2 | F/L C.J. Blundell-Hill (k) |
| FTR from ops to Zwolle | | | | |
| 01/04/45 | RN196 | XIV | 130 | W/O A.D. Miller (Ev) |
| Force landed after engine failure | | | | |
| 04/04/45 | RB183 | XIV | 350 | F/O R.C. Hoornaert (safe) |
| Hit by flak, force landed Lingen | | | | |
| 05/04/45 | SM818 | XIV | 130 | F/O H.C. Finbow (wnd) |
| Hit by flak, force landed Ahaus | | | | |
| 05/04/45 | RB185 | XIV | 350 | F/O A. Cresswell-Turner (wnd) |
| Shot down by JG 26 near Cloppenberg | | | | |
| 08/04/45 | RM808 | XIV | 130 | Sgt G. Warren (safe) |
| Hit by flak, force landed near Verden | | | | |
| 10/04/45 | LA203 | F.21 | 91 | F/L A.R. Cruikshank (safe) |
| Baled out off the Dutch coast after being hit by flak | | | | |
| 10/04/45 | LA229 | F.21 | 91 | F/O J.A. Faulkner (safe) |
| As above | | | | |
| 11/04/45 | RN212 | XIV | 130 | F/L P.E. Sibeth (safe) |
| Baled out after aircraft suffered damage during ground attack | | | | |
| 11/04/45 | RM904 | XIV | 402 | P/O G.F. Peterson (k) |
| Shot down by flak near Arnhem | | | | |
| 14/04/45 | RM932 | XIV | 402 | S/L D.C. Laubman (PoW) |
| Baled out after being hit by flak near Saltan | | | | |

| Date | Serial | Mark | Sqn | Pilot |
|------|--------|------|-----|-------|
| Remarks | | | | |

16/04/45   RN208   XIV   41   W/O J.A. Chalmers (safe)
Crash landed after running out of fuel

16/04/45   RM843   XIV   402   F/L J.E. Maurice (safe)
FTR ops to Salzwedel

19/04/45   SM827   XIV   130   F/O W.H. Carter (Inj)
Crash landed – engine failure

19/04/45   RN203   XIV   130   F/O V. Murphy (PoW)
Shot down by fighters

19/04/45   RM766   XIV   130   W/O P.H.J. Clay (PoW)
As above

19/04/45   –   XIV   130   S/L F.G. Woolley (safe)
Baled out after being hit during shipping strike – Bay of Wismar

19/04/45   SM814   XIV   350   S/L T. Spencer (PoW)
Shot down during shipping strike – Bay of Wismar

19/04/45   RM727   XIV   402   –
Hit by flak near Parchim

19/04/45   RN204   XIV   402   F/L H.A. Cowan (k)
As above

20/04/45   NH313   XIV   268   F/L B. Thistle (safe)
Baled out after being hit by flak

20/04/45   RM744   XIV   350   F/L K. Smith (PoW/Esc)
Hit by flak, force landed near Schwerin

20/04/45   NH686   XIV   350   W/O J. Groensteen (k)
Shot down by fighters over Berlin

20/04/45   RM875   XIV   402   W/O V.E. Barber (ev)
Shot down by flak

24/04/45   RM696   XIV   41   F/Sgt L.H. Smart (safe)
Collided with another Spitfire on landing ex ops

24/04/45   RM618   XIV   350   F/L G.R.J De Patoul (safe)
Shot down by fighters near Wismar

24/04/45   NH813   XIV   414   F/O F.R. Loveless (safe)
Baled out following engine failure near Hamburg

26/04/45   RM821   XIV   430   F/O L.P. Hedley (k)
Baled out following engine failure near Verden

27/04/45   NH691   XIV   130   W/O A.D. Miller (k)
Shot down by Ju 88 – Wismar

01/05/45   RM850   XIV   430   F/O G.W. Bouck (k)
FTR ops near Hamburg

02/05/45   SM833   XIV   130   F/L W.N. Stowe (safe)
Damaged by bomb blast and force landed near Schwerin

| Date | Serial | Mark | Sqn | Pilot |
|------|--------|------|-----|-------|
| | Remarks | | | |
| 03/05/45 | – | XIV | 268 | F/O R.B. Mumford (safe) |
| | Baled out after being hit by flak | | | |
| 03/05/45 | NH835 | XIV | 402 | F/L J.A. O'Brien (safe) |
| | Baled out after aircraft suffered damage during ground attack near Hamburg | | | |

# Index